Materials for Conservation

Organic consolidants, adhesives and coatings

C. V. Horie

Keeper of Conservation
The Manchester Museum

Butterworth-Heinemann
Linacre House, Jordan Hill, Oxford OX2 8DP
225 Wildwood Avenue, Woburn, MA 01801-2041
A division of Reed Educational and Professional Publishing Ltd

A member of the Reed Elsevier plc group

OXFORD AUCKLAND BOSTON
JOHANNESBURG MELBOURNE NEW DELHI

First published 1987
Reprinted 1990, 1992, 1994, 1995, 1996, 1997, 1998, 1999

British Library Cataloguing in Publication Data
Horie, C. V.
Materials for conservation: organic consolidants, adhesives and coatings
(Butterworth-Heinemann series in conservation and museology)
1. Art objects – Conservation and restoration
2. Museum conservation methods
I. Title
069.5'3 N8560

ISBN 0 7506 0881 1

Library of Congress Cataloguing in Publication Data
Horie, C. V. (Charles Velson)
Materials for conservation
Bibliography: p.
Includes index
ISBN 0 7506 0881 1
1. Coatings 2. Adhesives 3. Art-conservation and restoration
I. Title II. Series
TP156.C57H67 1987 667'.9 87–13830

Printed and bound in Great Britain by MPG Books Ltd, Bodmin, Cornwall

Materials for Conservation

Conservation and Museology Series

Series Editors: *Arts and Archaeology*

Stephen G Rees-Jones
Courtauld Institute of Art, University of London

Architecture

Derek Linstrum
Institute of Advanced Architectural Studies, University of York

US Executive Editor: **Norbert S Baer,**
New York University, Conservation Center of the Institute of Fine Arts

Consultants: **Sir Bernard Feilden**

David Bomford
National Gallery, London

C V Horie
Manchester Museum, University of Manchester

Published titles:
Artists' Pigments *c.* 1600–1835, 2nd Edition (Harley)
Conservation and Exhibitions (Stolow)
Conservation and Restoration of Works of Art and Antiquities (Kühn)
Conservation of Building and Decorative Stone (Ashurst, Dimes)
Conservation of Glass (Newton, Davison)
Conservation of Historic Buildings (Feilden)
Conservation of Library and Archive Materials and the Graphic Arts (Petherbridge)
Conservation of Manuscripts and Paintings of South-East Asia (Agrawal)
Conservation of Marine Archaeological Objects (Pearson)
Conservation of Wall Paintings (Mora, Mora, Philippot)
The Museum Environment, 2nd Edition (Thomson)
The Organic Chemistry of Museum Objects (Mills, White)
The Textile Conservator's Manual (Landi)

Related titles:
Manual of Curatorship
Materials for Conservation
Museum Documentation Systems

Preface

The conservation of historic materials requires the application of a wide range of knowledge and skills. The aim of this book is to provide background information on one aspect of conservation treatments: the properties of organic consolidants, adhesives and coatings as they affect the treatment of objects. The variety of film-forming and binding materials, together with associated materials such as oils, is not covered by a single descriptive term. The inadequate word 'polymer' or 'resin' will often be used to encompass these materials. The vast number of commercial polymers and formulations creates considerable scope for harmful as well as beneficial changes in the practice and philosophy of conservation. Polymer science has increased our insight into polymer properties, offering the potential for valuable improvements in treatments and the materials used. It is my hope that the reader will assess the use of both new and old materials on objects more rigorously.

This review comes at the end of an era in conservation practice. In the past, materials were applied in a traditional manner, frequently with no evaluation of the merits or consequences of the addition. When new, synthetic materials were introduced commercially, these were used in the same role, often without much evaluation because they appeared to be better. Testing of the industrial products was later carried out, sometimes thoroughly, in order to rank them in suitability for particular roles. This is the phase of development which I hope is passing. In its place, treatments are being developed, incorporating materials with appropriately specified properties, designed to fulfil a defined conservation need.

Conservators must know about the added material and its effects on objects before making a decision on whether, and how best, to incorporate a material into a treatment for the object. Part I outlines the properties of polymers that are important in the interaction of polymers with objects. Chapters 1 and 5 provide a qualitative introduction and summary of the scientific basis for defining and assessing those properties which are covered in the intervening chapters. Part II provides a detailed consideration of individual polymers, their properties and uses in conservation. Most polymer types that have been used in the conservation of objects are included. At the end of the book are appendices which summarize data referred to in the text.

There are various introductory texts in this field for conservators (Crafts Council, 1983; Feller *et al.*, 1971; Anon, 1968). Many books are available for schools and the general public which outline the concepts and properties of polymers. More detailed reference books which assume some knowledge of chemistry include Brydson (1982), Roff and Scott (1971) and Mark *et al.* (1964ff). The reader is assumed to have access to publications of the International Institute for Conservation. Polymers that have been adequately described in those publications have been given a slighter treatment here to avoid duplication.

Conclusions

1. The interactions between objects and polymers, etc. are ill-understood. Assuming that the object is the primary concern of the conservator, consolidants, adhesives and coatings should be applied only when necessary to the survival of the object. They should not be used as an alternative to proper packaging, environmental control, etc. Given the difficulties of removing polymers, they should be applied sparingly.
2. One of the most difficult tasks of a conservator is reversing the conservation treatment of an object before starting new stabilization treatments, etc. Publication of past treatments, assessments of their effects and reversal methods is rare but most welcome to the conservator who must treat objects with comparable problems. Conservation is dependent on the material history that survives. The history of conservation, which is rarely written, is an integral part of conservation studies.
3. Most commercial polymers are produced for industrial applications that are ephemeral by conservation standards. Conservators both past and present have used products whose suitability is untested. A few new products specified and tested for conservation are coming on to the market, but their composition remains proprietary. These must be viewed with the suspicion held for any commercial material. There is

sufficient information available to enable formulations to be developed to conservation standards and revealed in the public domain. These recipes would reduce the need for commercial products of unknown composition and variability.

Acknowledgements

The impetus for the writing of this book was given to me by Professor R. G. Newton and I wish to thank him and Mrs J. Newton for their support in the early stages of its formation. The need for a conservation text on polymers, etc. has been made clear to me by students of conservation at various institutions who, by their interest and questions during lecture courses, have prompted me to look more closely at the problems of objects and the treatment of them. Miss L. Bacon, Professor S. Rees-Jones, my wife (Dr D. Kenyon) and Professor W. J. Feast have kindly read through portions of the text and suggested valuable improvements both in style and content.

The data on individual products has been collated from information supplied by their manufacturers. The ready supply of data sheets and samples of the products from all the manufacturers listed in Appendix 5 enabled the compilation of the tables and, in some cases, the evaluation of properties important for conservation. I was pleasantly surprised by how many manufacturers provided advice and unpublished data on their products, so increasing insight into their application for conservation.

I wish to thank the following for advice and data which helped to clarify specific points or wider issues: Dr R. L. Feller, Dr S. G. Croll, Mr G. Berger, Dr E. P. Mel'nikova, Professor Dr K. Ueberreiter, Dr J. Winter, Professor W. C. Wake, Professor J. D. Ferry and Dr N. Tennent.

Contents

Appendices 181

To my father

Many of the materials mentioned in this book are hazardous to the operator or other people and property. Although some hazard information has been provided, the responsibility for ensuring the completeness or accuracy of the appropriate hazard information is the responsibility of the person undertaking the process.

The mention of a material or process does not constitute a recommendation for its use on objects – usually the reverse.

The author and publisher accept no responsibility for the consequences of the application of information or opinion expressed in this book.

Part I
Background Information

1 Introduction

1.1 Use of resins in conservation

Resins are used for many purposes in the conservation of objects:

Consolidants
Adhesives
Coatings
Moulding
Casting
Support stands
Display and storage materials.

This list is ranked according to the intimacy of contact with the object. The closer the contact, the more likely the object is to be affected by the polymer properties. In the first four categories the resin is applied to the object rather than the other way around. These are therefore of greater concern.

In conservation it is an important discipline to study an object before one works on it. One should:

(a) Find out what is wrong with the object.
(b) Discover the cause of the defect.
(c) Decide on the type of action.
(d) Choose the appropriate method and materials.

Neither (a) nor (b) are discussed in this work, but both (c) and (d) are determined by the potential and limitations of the available materials. The possible roles that the resin will play in the conserved object must be examined closely. Resins frequently serve two purposes at once. When sticking friable pottery, the adhesive may also consolidate and strengthen the edges. When coating loose paint, the varnish will both cover the paint flakes and stick them to the substrate. These dual roles may be of great importance when the time comes to reverse the treatment.

Now the role(s) of the material have been stated, the required properties may be specified. In the real world one can never satisfy all the ideal specifications, and value judgements must therefore be made about the relative importance of the various properties required. Normally the choice is restricted to the products commercially available. These can present a bewildering range of different materials which claim to do the same job, and one must choose between them in an educated way.

The detailed specifications will vary from one application to another but some general guidelines can be given.

1. On setting, the product must not change the object physically or chemically.
2. The product should remain totally removable at any time in the future without harm to the object.
3. The product must not alter so as to affect the object physically or chemically.
4. The product should have a long service life.
5. The product should be easily worked or removed without harm to the operator.

The general term 'product' has been used rather than a specific description such as polymer, as it is rare for a pure polymer to be applied. Much more frequently the product is applied as a mixture, e.g. in a solvent, or as a precursor to the polymer.

The last three requirements are largely determined by the exact details of the product. However, the first two merit a separate discussion.

1.2 Setting processes

In all the cases where a product is applied to an object, it must be applied in a fluid state in order to achieve a coverage of the interstices of the object. One cannot achieve a good coating by applying beads of solid polymer. This basic requirement usually restricts the range of materials to those that can be put into liquid form in conditions that do not harm the object. In any application of a coating, adhesive or consolidant, adhesion between the polymer and the object must be ensured. Lack of adhesion can lead to the separation of parts of an object or to the penetration of water and pollutants along the object's surface. These requirements for good adhesion are of course reversed when using moulding materials or temporary supports for the object. To be in a liquid form when applied, the polymer or its precursor may be in a mobile carrier or itself be liquid.

Methods of applying the polymer are various:

1. One can use a liquid as a non-setting adhesive. Some adhesives remain as liquids. These are the contact adhesives used in pressure-sensitive tapes and labels.
2. A product can be applied as a molten liquid which cools, so forming a solid. Heat-activated adhesives in laminating systems are of this type.
3. Some materials such as oil paint and epoxy resin are applied as liquid prepolymers which set by chemical reaction to form a polymer.
4. A solution of polymer sets by evaporation of the solvents. This is the most common method of applying polymers in conservation, but it is of declining importance in industry. An example of a conservation use is picture varnish.
5. The polymer can be applied in a hot solution which sets by cooling. The swollen solid will then lose its solvent by evaporation, e.g. bone glue.
6. Some polymers are applied in emulsions or dispersions. An emulsion sets to a film, first by loss of the dispersant, usually water, and then by coalescence of the small polymer particles. In order for this to happen the particles must be soft enough to flow into one another. Poly(vinyl acetate) emulsion 'white glues' and wax polishes are examples of this type.
7. Prepolymers may be applied in gaseous form and reacted directly in contact with the object.

Similar polymers can be prepared and applied in different forms. Acrylic polymers can be applied in solution, as emulsions, as pressure-sensitive adhesives or as prepolymers. The method of application depends on the role of the polymer and on the circumstances of application. A polymer can be applied using a combination of these methods. For example, a polyurethane lacquer used on stained glass (Bettembourg, 1976) is made from two components, mixed and applied in solution. The solvent evaporates and the two components react to form the polymer.

In passing from a liquid to a solid, shrinkage occurs. This can be large (a 20% solution of a polymer must reduce to one fifth of its volume on setting) or small (less than 0.5% for some silicone rubbers).

1.3 Reversibility (Horie, 1983a; Hellwig, 1981)

The decision to add or remove later materials when working with inadequate original objects has had a long and controversial history. Thorensen's proposed restoration of the Parthenon sculpture and the Cleaned Pictures Exhibition (Hendy, 1947) were highly publicized examples of alterations normally carried out routinely by conservators. These changes must of course be recorded in a detailed way to help future conservators decide what may be removed. Equally the changes must not cause harm to the original, however this is defined. Harm can be assessed in many ways. Aesthetic alterations were the first to receive condemnation. With increasing and changing awareness of the significance of alterations to the materials of the object, 'harm' has been extended to include physical deterioration of the object. The use of salt-contaminated mortars for mounting porous stone has been shown, many years after use, to cause damage to the original object. Techniques of examination have now progressed sufficiently that contamination with materials added by conservators may invalidate analytical investigations. An obvious example is the use of carbon-14 dating: a sample contaminated with paraffin wax (derived from oil) will appear millions of years old, whereas a sample contaminated with modern beeswax will appear recent.

Ideally a treatment used on an object should not cause any changes following the complete cycle of application, ageing and removal. Changes to an object can result from chemical or physical effects of the added material. The liquid product which is applied may have solvent effects on the object. These may be immediate as in the cockling of paper by water-based adhesives. Alternatively the object may dissolve slowly in the polymer – some inks on maps migrate slowly into laminating adhesives (Baynes-Cope, 1975). The product itself may react with the object, thus ensuring the impossibility of removal without disruption of the object's surface. For example, poly(vinyl alcohol), PVAL, is sufficiently stable, when considered by itself, to be used in some fields of conservation (De Witte, 1976) but it will permanently fix to textiles and paper immediately on application (Thomson, 1963). During setting, the product may shrink, causing physical damage to the object which may not be revealed until the supporting polymer is removed – many pieces of friable pottery have been damaged in this way by glue. Resins used for consolidating paint films can change the optical environment of the particle, and this usually results in a severely altered appearance of the object.

Changes also occur as the polymer ages under the influence of time, air, light and heat. Cross-linking or oxidation of the chains may cause a polymer to become insoluble in solvents that can be safely used on an object (Feller, 1971c). The polymer may also cause the object to degrade more rapidly than it otherwise would have done (Berger and Zelinger, 1975; Baer *et al.*, 1976). The cause of these deleterious effects is probably a combination of chemical reactions induced by the polymer and the physical restraint imposed by the polymer on a very different type of material.

Removal of a polymer usually involves the use of solvents, all of which cause swelling of the polymers and perhaps the object. This is likely to cause disruption of those parts of the object which are embedded in the polymer. Solvents necessary to remove polymers frequently threaten or cause damage to an object. This continues to be a cause of concern in the conservation of paintings (Stolow, 1971) and in many other fields.

The reversibility of a treatment is thus determined by the properties of the polymer, those of the object and how they interact. A polymer may be applied to one object and be completely removable, e.g. a lacquer on metal. However, when it is applied to a porous material or one with which the polymer reacts, it may be impossible to remove more than a small proportion of the same polymer. New techniques, such as plasma cleaning (Daniels *et al.*, 1978), may enable the removal of otherwise intractable polymers.

Four categories of reversibility may be defined.

1. Many treatments have no known method of reversal. There is no method of removing a cross-linked polymer from a porous object, e.g. silanes in stone.

2. A treatment which allows an object to be taken back to a state that approximates to the pretreatment state is the most basic level of reversibility. An example is the dismantling of a restored pot into its component sherds.

3. A higher standard of reversibility was that demanded by picture restorers in Berlin in the 1840s; that the treatment when reversed should not affect subsequent treatments (House of Commons, 1852–53). This is one of the necessary requirements for a facing technique on paintings.

4. Techniques for examination are increasingly sensitive and require uncontaminated samples. It is unlikely that many treatments can be reversed to remove every trace of the polymer applied yet make no alteration to the object.

The extent of reversal of many treatments has not been tested. From the limited evidence available there appears to be little hope of complete reversibility being achieved. It has been shown that only 50% of soluble consolidants applied in solution to porous objects such as stone and pottery (Horie, 1983a) can be removed by extracting with solvents. In most cases where a consolidant is necessary, the object will be too weak to withstand the processes of removal. However, even in the case of an acrylic lacquer on new glass, complete removal is not certain. With more delicate surfaces, such as paintings or friable wood, a choice has frequently to be made between leaving some of the unwanted material, such as a varnish, and removing some of the original object with the coating.

Most objects that have been in care for a length of time have undergone repeated preservation treatments. Frequently one of the more difficult tasks for a conservator is reversing past treatments to allow better techniques to be applied. Embedding friable pottery sherds in cement or repairing paper with rubber-based self-adhesive tape can prove difficult to reverse without damaging the object. For this reason a treatment must always be designed as a complete cycle of application, ageing and removal. The extent of reversibility of the proposed treatment must be assessed against other possibilities and their relative merits.

The responsibility for choosing the correct materials and methods of application lies with the conservator carrying out the treatment. There are few bad materials as such but there are many examples of inappropriate applications. The conservator must have sufficient understanding of the processes involved to enable evaluation of the possible irreversible effects on a particular object. Limits of knowledge and the risks involved can be made explicit in justifying the chosen treatment method.

1.4 History

Objects are made for use, however that use is defined, and must undergo repair and maintenance to retain their usefulness. The methods used for repair of objects were usually similar to those used originally to make them. Objects were often more or less re-made without much regard for the original state. This is exemplified by the treatment of Egyptian mummies by their contemporaries (Harris and Wente, 1980) and the mediaeval re-working of wall paintings (Marijnissen, 1967) when they became damaged. Where an object was not amenable to re-working, familiar methods and materials were adapted to restore its usefulness. Repair of materials such as pottery might have been achieved by riveting (Williams, 1983). The concept of conservation, that the original object is intrinsically interesting and worth preserving, has been widespread only in the past few hundred years. Some examples from the more distant past include the consolidation of St Cuthbert's coffin in 1104 (Cronyn and Horie, 1985) and the restoration of historic ceramics by the Japanese.

The techniques that could be applied were limited by the materials available. The basic range which most societies possessed included starch pastes, plant gums and resins, protein binders of glue or albumin, beeswax and fats. As technology and trade developed, a wider range of resins became available and drying oils were introduced. These natural products were the only materials available for the repair of objects until the late 19th century (Masschelein-Kleiner, 1978). They were, and still are, widely used.

None of these natural products lend themselves to easy analysis, especially after ageing. It may thus be difficult to distinguish materials of the original object from the later additions. This may account for the fact that there are few studies detailing the conservation history of individual objects.

From the point of view of Europe, the available resins included colophony, mastic and sandarac, depending on the area (Gettens and Stout, 1965). These would originally have been applied in liquid form, perhaps as heated balsam or dissolved in drying oils. Trade in other resins later enlarged the range available. Only from the 17th century were solvents (spirits of turpentine and spirits of wine) used for dissolving and applying resins. Dammar was first recommended as a picture varnish in the early 19th century (Feller, 1966). Paraffin wax (Salzer, 1887) and natural rubber (Rathgen, 1905) were applied in the late 19th century.

During this period, when the wealth of natural products was being introduced, the first synthetic polymer, cellulose nitrate, was being developed for conservation (Posse, 1899). By the early 1920s other cellulose derivatives (Scott, 1923; Jenkinson, 1924) and silicone compounds (Grissom and Weiss, 1981) had been introduced. There is hardly a polymer which has not been suggested and used for a conservation application. The unrecorded work of an adventurous conservator in the past may cause complications during the inevitable re-treatment of the object.

The materials used in the past may be significantly different from modern materials of nominally the same composition. In reviewing the solubility of dammar, Mantell *et al.* (1942) found that the solubility range they determined was very different from that found by previous workers who had studied dammar. An early study of poly(vinyl acetate), PVAC, in 1929 obviously used a material that was less pure and less stable to light ageing than the modern products (Gamble and Stutz, 1929). This is a good reason for retaining in the conservation record samples of polymers that come from the same batch as was used on an object.

2 Polymer science

2.1 Film-forming materials

The guidelines in Chapter 1 are very general and do not help much when materials must be chosen from the many available products. The products can be described by many properties, such as clarity, strength and stability, which will be determined by the chemical structure, the physical state of the material and how it is applied. (For general references see Preface.) Many materials form films when spread out properly. In general, the longer the molecule, the stronger the material. Where great strength is required, long molecules are used: cellulose for wood, collagen for sinew, and polyethylene for plastic bags. When wood and sinew are converted into cellophane and glue, the long molecules are released from their fibrous state and reduced in size. Films prepared from these derived materials have less strength than the original source materials but more than films prepared from small molecules.

Most natural film-forming materials – resins, gums and waxes – are made up of molecules which are large by comparison with solvent molecules but small by comparison with synthetic polymers. Because of this, only those natural materials that are composed of very large molecules, such as natural rubber or cellulose, find a continuing industrial demand. Natural materials are also being replaced in conservation by the more versatile synthetic alternatives. Increased size and strength are frequently only a minor part of their advantages over the natural predecessors.

Film-forming materials which are useful as coatings, consolidants or adhesives all have large molecular size as a common factor. Most film-forming materials, both natural and synthetic, are based on polymers. A polymer is a large molecule built up from many small identical units, called monomers. In order for a polymer to be formed from monomer molecules, each monomer molecule must be able to join up with two other molecules. Continued reaction of these difunctional monomers produces a straight-chain

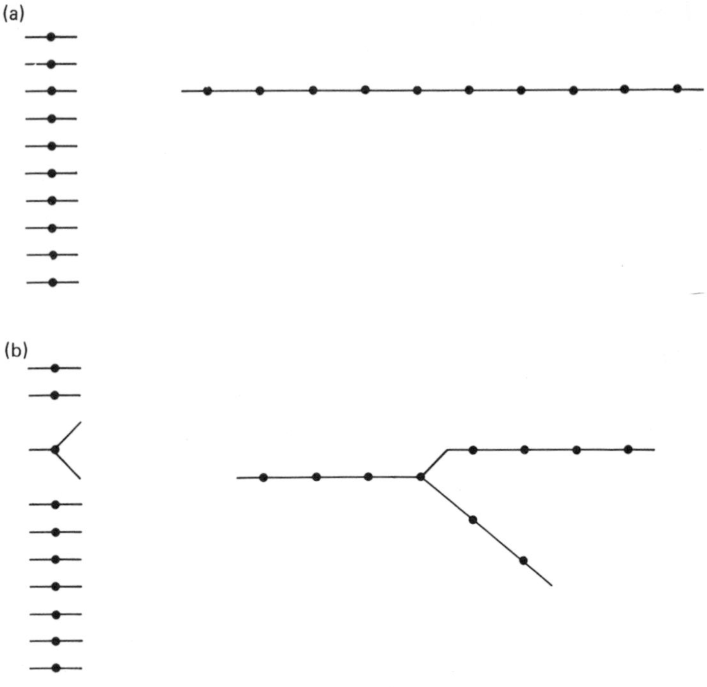

Figure 2.1 (a) Straight-chain polymers are formed from difunctional monomers. (b) Branched polymers are formed from difunctional and trifunctional monomers

polymer (*Figure 2.1(a)*). If some of the monomers can react with three others, a branched chain results (*Figure 2.1(b)*).

At this stage each of these polymers is composed of discrete molecules that can be separated from one another. As there are no formal chemical bonds attaching one polymer molecule to another, the molecules can flow past one another. They can be dissolved in solvents, and will melt when heated; because of this latter property they are called thermoplastics. If there are sufficient trifunctional monomers, the chains join up to one another, as shown in *Figure 2.2*. It will then be impossible to separate one chain from another without breaking a chemical bond. The many molecules are joined up into a cross-linked immobile mass. This will not melt with heating, but will only soften; nor will it dissolve in solvents, but will only swell, although it may be broken down by some solvents.

The change in properties with increasing size of the molecules is best illustrated by the alkanes. This family of materials is

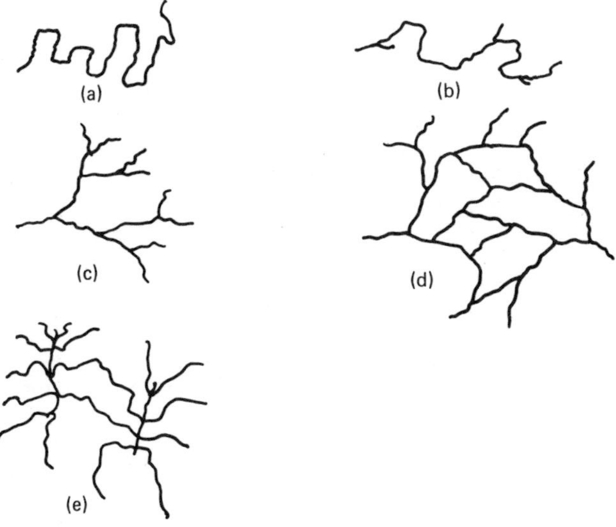

Figure 2.2 Monomers can form different shapes of polymer (from Brydson, 1982). (a) Randomly coiled linear thermoplastics, e.g. PMMA. (b) Slightly branched thermoplastics, e.g. PVAC. (c) Highly branched thermoplastics, e.g. polyurethane foam prepolymer. (d) Cross-linked polymers with trifunctional junctions, perhaps formed by reaction of (c), e.g. epoxy resin. (e) Cross-linked polymer with tetrafunctional junctions, e.g. polyester casting resin

composed only of carbon and hydrogen, and makes up the bulk of petroleum. The first member of the series is methane, with one carbon atom and four hydrogen atoms. It is a gas at room temperature. The formula for a molecule of methane is CH_4:

$$\begin{array}{ccccc} & & H & & \\ & & | & & \\ H & - & C & - & H \\ & & | & & \\ & & H & & \end{array}$$

Methane

Other members of the series are ethane, with two carbon atoms, and pentane with five:

$$\begin{array}{ccccccc} & & H & & H & & \\ & & | & & | & & \\ H & - & C & - & C & - & H \\ & & | & & | & & \\ & & H & & H & & \end{array}$$

Ethane

$$\begin{array}{c} H \\ | \\ H\!-\!\!\left(\!C\!\right)_5\!\!-\!H \\ | \\ H \end{array} \quad \text{or} \quad \begin{array}{ccccccccccccc} & & H & & H & & H & & H & & H & & \\ & & | & & | & & | & & | & & | & & \\ H & - & C & - & C & - & C & - & C & - & C & - & H \\ & & | & & | & & | & & | & & | & & \\ & & H & & H & & H & & H & & H & & \end{array}$$

Pentane

As the number of carbon atoms in the chain increases, the molecules become progressively larger and their boiling and melting points rise (Table 2.1). All these materials have similar

Table 2.1 Properties of hydrocarbons (with the composition C_nH_{2n+2}) as they vary in molecular weight

Number of carbon atoms	*Name of compound*	*m.p.* (°C)	*b.p.* (°C)	*Form usually encountered*
1	Methane		−162	Fuel gas
2	Ethane		−88	Fuel gas
4	Butane		0	Fuel gas
5	Pentane		36	Liquid fuel (gasoline)
16	Hexadecane	18	292	Liquid fuel (kerosene)
20	Eicosane	36		Grease (weak solid)
16–30	Paraffin wax	45–60		Wax (weak solid)
350–1500	Low molecular weight polyethylene	80–100		Tough solid
>30 000	High molecular weight polyethylene	c.130		Stiff strong solid

chemical properties. The larger members of the homologous series can be considered to be successive members formed from the methylene unit, i.e.

$$\left(-\underset{\displaystyle H}{\overset{\displaystyle H}{\underset{|}{\overset{|}{C}}}}- \right)_n$$

In practice, ethylene is used to make the polymer. A commercial polymer is commonly named after the monomer from which it is made, so the polymer is called polyethylene in this instance. An alternative method of nomenclature is based on the chemical structure of the polymer; under this system the above polymer would be called polymethylene, following IUPAC (International Union of Pure and Applied Chemistry) rules (IUPAC, 1976). The use of IUPAC rules implies that the structure of the polymer is known in detail. However, the structure of commercial polymers are frequently not well defined. For this reason the internationally recognized trivial names and abbreviations (ISO R1043, 1975; IUPAC, 1974; Elias, 1977) will be used here, with the IUPAC names being listed in Appendix 1.

Polymers are distinguished by two properties that set them apart from materials made up of smaller molecules – the variability of molecular weight and the glass transition temperature.

2.2 Molecular weight and size (Billmeyer, 1971)

A molecule is a chemical combination of atoms. For many molecules, this grouping of atoms can be expressed as a chemical formula, e.g. $C_6H_{12}O_6$ (glucose) (*Figure 2.3*). The molecular

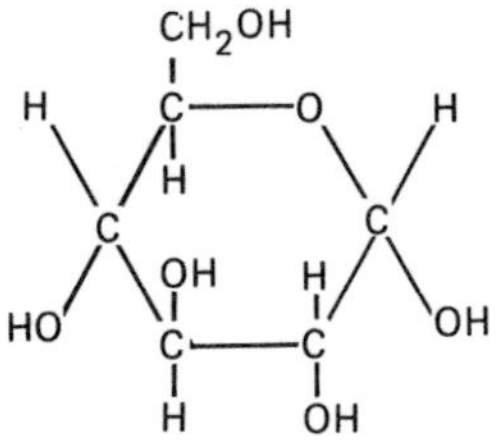

Figure 2.3 A glucose molecule, $C_6H_{12}O_6$, exists normally as a ring (glucopyranose) shown here or as a straight chain

weight (M_r) can be found by adding up all the component atomic weights:

12 (atomic weight of carbon) × 6	=	72
1 (atomic weight of hydrogen) × 12	=	12
16 (atomic weight of oxygen) × 6	=	96
molecular weight of glucose		180

The natural resins used for picture varnishes are made up of larger molecules, some of which have been separated and identified. The molecular formula of one of these molecules (dipterocarpol (Cheung, 1968)) is $C_{30}H_{50}O_2$, M_r 442, a typical value for the constituents of dammar resin.

The molecular weight of a polymer molecule is obtained in a similar manner to that of a smaller molecule. The molecular weight of a single molecule can be determined by multiplying the weight of the repeating unit by the degree of polymerization (DP). For instance, with a DP of 1150, polyethylene has a molecular weight of 1150 × 28 (the weight of the monomer unit) = 32 200, neglecting the very small contribution that the end groups make. However, in any sample of polymer one has a mixture of molecules with different molecular formulae. The molecules are very similar as they differ only in the number of monomer units incorporated. When DP is small, less than about 10, the polymer molecules are sufficiently different to be separated. These molecules are called oligomers. For many polymers the degree of polymerization can be thousands or even millions. It is then impossible to separate molecules into their different sizes.

What is the molecular weight of a mixture of molecules?

Different molecular weights can be calculated for the same sample to give emphasis to different ways of considering the molecules. Two averages, number average molecular weight (M_n) and weight average molecular weight (M_w) are commonly used. M_n is used when the number of molecules in a sample is being considered, e.g. chemical reactivity of end groups in epoxy resins. M_w is important when contributions of the weight of each molecule determine the property, e.g. strength. The molecular weight of different polymer samples can be determined by a relatively simple viscosity measurement (ISO R1628, 1970). This is

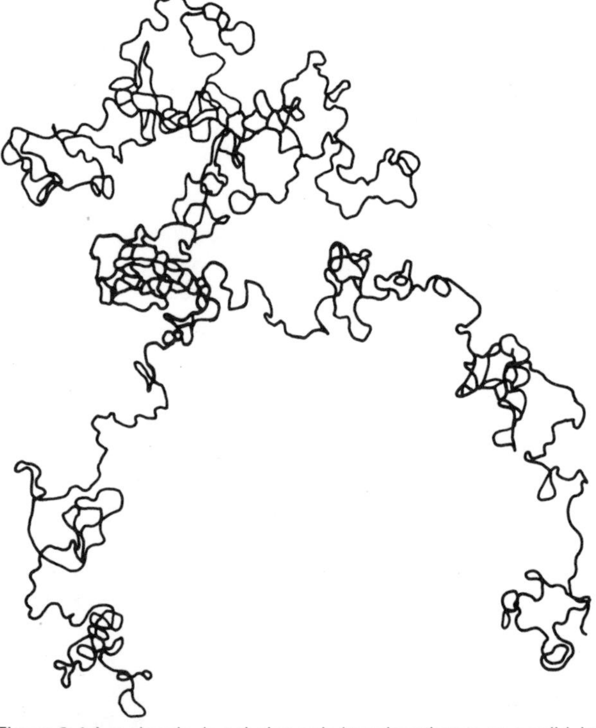

Figure 2.4 A molecule, in solution or in its relaxed state as a solid, is coiled and contorted in three dimensions. This diagram is a theoretical model of a polyethylene chain with 500 monomer units (Treolar, 1975). Reproduced with the permission of Clarendon Press

the standard method for checking batches or for following the changes of a polymer with ageing. Polymers increase the viscosity of a solution because the large molecules create a resistance to flow. A typical molecule in solution might look like *Figure 2.4*, if captured in a snapshot. In a good solvent the molecule is more spread out, and in a poor solvent it contracts, with corresponding changes in viscosity. There is no hard edge between a polymer molecule and the solvent as there is for a droplet of oil in water. A better analogy is strands of spaghetti floating in a pan of water.

2.3 Glass transition temperature (Ferry, 1982)

The glass transition temperature (T_g) of a polymer is important in choosing a consolidant, adhesive or coating, and is an accurate

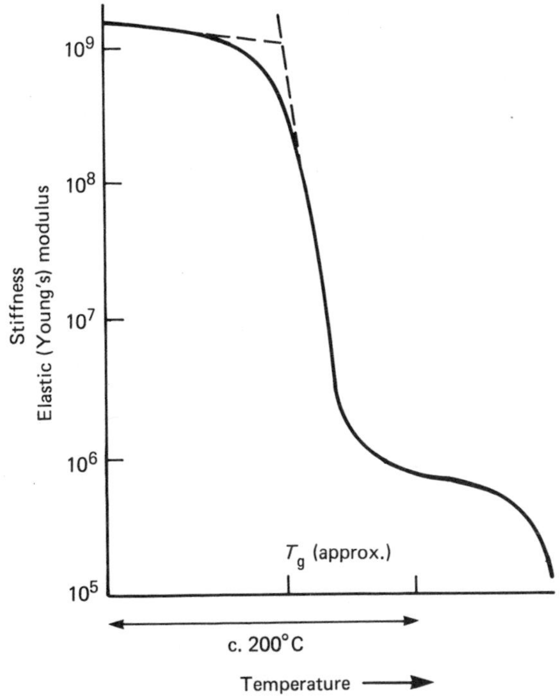

Figure 2.5 The glass transition temperature (T_g) indicates the temperature at which a glassy material starts to change to a flaccid material. The shape of the curve is similar for most thermoplastics, although the value of T_g can range from −123 to 250°C (for polymers). Redrawn from Nielsen (1974)

indication of the softness of the polymer. This has two aspects. A polymer which is too soft will lead to cold flow in an adhesive or dirt pick-up in a coating. A polymer which is too stiff may crack when stressed or may not be able to respond to movements in the object. Most polymers applied to objects have T_g around room temperature.

Polymers go through various stages as they are heated from a very low temperature. All polymers can be cooled to form brittle solids; rubber, for example, can be broken like glass when cooled in liquid nitrogen. As the temperature is raised, the polymer changes from a glassy state to a rubbery one. This change is not sharp but occurs over a small range of temperatures. The temperature of this transition is called the glass transition temperature (*Figure 2.5*). Specifying T_g is a matter of judgement, or preferably, of extrapolation. T_g is conventionally defined as the (extrapolated) inflection point in the specific gravity/temperature curve. It determines many of the mechanical and some of the chemical properties of a polymer (Appendix 1). Below T_g, the material will not flow but will stretch only slightly before breaking. Thermoplastics and cross-linked materials both undergo changes when heated through T_g. Thermoplastics above T_g can be considered as liquids and will therefore flow, however slowly, when forces are exerted on them. They thus become plastic and can be shaped by heating. Cross-linked materials cannot flow but may become rubbery above T_g. Mechanical properties of a polymer therefore change around T_g. This is indicated by the change in stiffness (modulus of elasticity) on raising the temperature of a polymer. Similar examples of change around T_g are apparent in many different types of property: refractive index, specific gravity, impact resistance, etc.

Above T_g large sections of the polymer chains are able to move cooperatively in adjusting to stresses. Below T_g the chain segments are frozen into place. Three effects can act against the internal movements: the stiffness of the polymer chain, intermolecular forces such as hydrogen bonds, and the interlocking of bulky side groups. For instance, poly(ethylene oxide) (PEO) has low stiffness of the chain, no side groups to interlock and therefore a low T_g, −55°C. Polystyrene chains are stiffened by the presence of the phenyl groups on the chain and T_g is correspondingly higher, 95°C.

The ability of the polymer chains to move past one another and adjust to a changed situation depends not only on how mobile the chains are, i.e. how much above T_g the polymer is, but also on how fast the change is made. The value of T_g can be lowered by increasing the time scale of the force. When an object is stuck together for display, the time scale is long – perhaps many decades. There is an approximate relationship between T_g and the time of measurement. Most T_g measurements are made over time scales of around one minute. If the measurement time is increased to 10 minutes, T_g will drop by 3 °C. If the time is decreased to six seconds, T_g will rise by about 3°C. This change of T_g for every 10-fold change in time has important implications for polymers with T_g around room temperature. A material with T_g of 30°C (measured over one minute) will have an effective T_g of 12°C when used on an object for 1.2 years. It is obvious that the T_g of a polymer is lowered considerably over time, with unfortunate results for the attached object (*Figure 2.6*). This flow occurs not only with adhesives but also with coatings. When a dust particle

Figure 2.6 The slumping, after 30 years, of a piece of wood stuck in place with poly(vinyl acetate) (Cronyn and Horie, 1985)

lands on a soft surface, the polymer will gradually flow around it. This results in dirt pick-up where the dirt has become part of the polymer film. The dirt cannot be removed without removing the polymer film. If an adhesive is used to attach a book binding, the stresses of opening or closing a book will be applied in a fraction of a second. An effective adhesive must be able to adjust within this time span, e.g. wax/polyethylene mixtures. The effective T_g of a polymer used in this situation will be considerably higher than that used for sticking an object.

The T_g of a polymer increases slightly with increased molecular weight because the chains have less freedom of movement. Their freedom of movement can be increased by separating the chains. Low molecular weight additives will lower the effective T_g. Non-volatile liquids, plasticizers, are commonly added to stiff plastics in order to make them flexible. Poly(vinyl chloride), PVC, is frequently modified in this way. The same effect occurs with solvents (*Figure 2.7*). A film of poly(methyl methacrylate), PMMA, is above its T_g at room temperature if it holds less than 20% toluene. As the film dries it will therefore cease to flow while

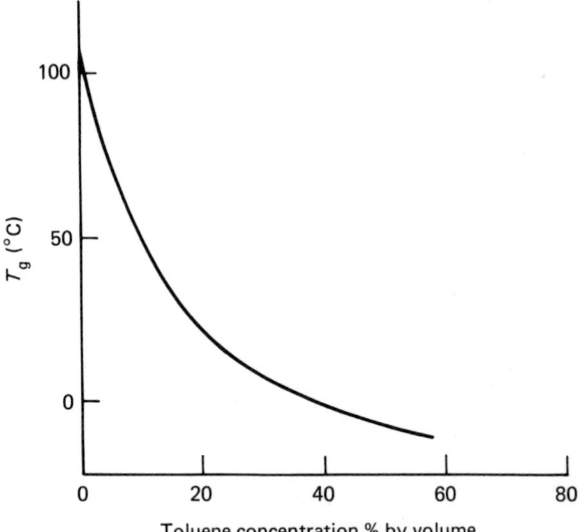

Figure 2.7 Depression of the glass transition temperature (T_g) of poly(methyl methacrylate), T_g = 105 °C, by the incorporation of toluene. The T_g of a film formed from a solution of PMMA in toluene will gradually rise during the evaporation of the solvent (Croll, 1979). T_g is reduced by a fall in molecular weight (M_n) and is therefore greatly affected by addition of low molecular weight material such as solvents

still containing up to a fifth of its volume as solvent. As this solvent evaporates, the polymer film will shrink. A good solvent for the polymer has a greater effect in reducing T_g than a poor solvent. There will thus be less volatile material remaining when flow in the polymer film stops, and less consequent shrinkage will occur. This has important implications for both reversibility and adhesion.

The T_g of a cross-linked polymer is complicated by the inability of the molecules to flow past one another (*Figure 2.8*). These materials change at T_g from a glass to a rubber which can be stretched by force but which will revert back to the original shape when the force is removed. Cross-linked resins will reduce to a limiting stiffness, which is not much reduced by increasing temperature. As the density of the cross-links rises, T_g also rises. When the chain length between the cross-links drops below a

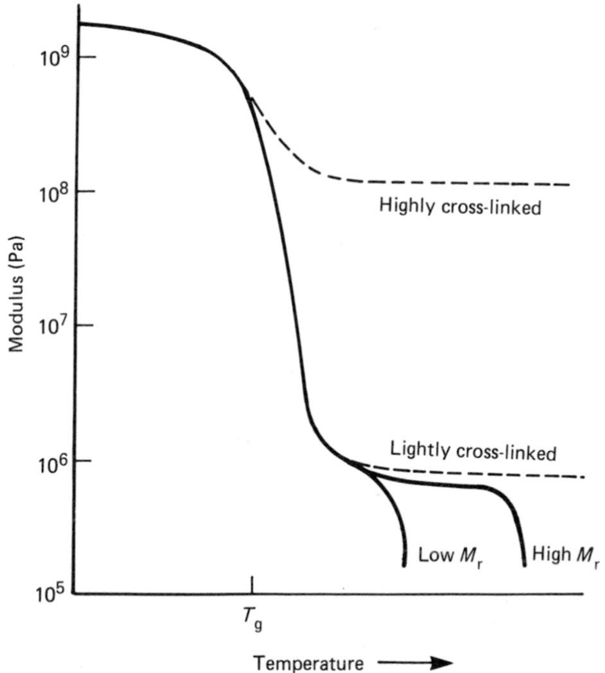

Figure 2.8 Effect on its stiffness (elastic modulus) of heating a polymer. Although T_g is only slightly affected by the molecular weight of the polymer, physical properties above T_g are more affected. A low molecular weight polymer will quickly become fluid, whereas a high molecular weight polymer will require a higher temperature. Cross-linking prevents flow and thus imparts a stiffness which is increased as the cross-linking density increases

critical length, the lack of freedom of movement eliminates the T_g phenomenon, e.g. with formaldehyde resins.

T_g is not the only transition that occurs on changing the temperature of a solid polymer. Other minor transitions contribute to the toughness of the polymer by absorbing energy on impact. The effect of heating a polymer above T_g is determined by the structure of the polymer. Most of the polymers used on objects are amorphous thermoplastics, and only show T_g before liquefying. Some polymers (polyethylene and wax are the best examples) are partly made up of crystals. The crystals melt at a higher temperature (T_m) than T_g, causing a second transition in properties on heating or cooling.

2.4 Mechanical properties (Brown, 1981; Nielsen, 1974)

Resins vary from extremely flexible but strong rubbers to brittle weak materials such as the natural resins (*Figure 2.9*). Contrasts can be made in the ability to be stretched without permanent distortion (elasticity of rubber), in the distortion caused by

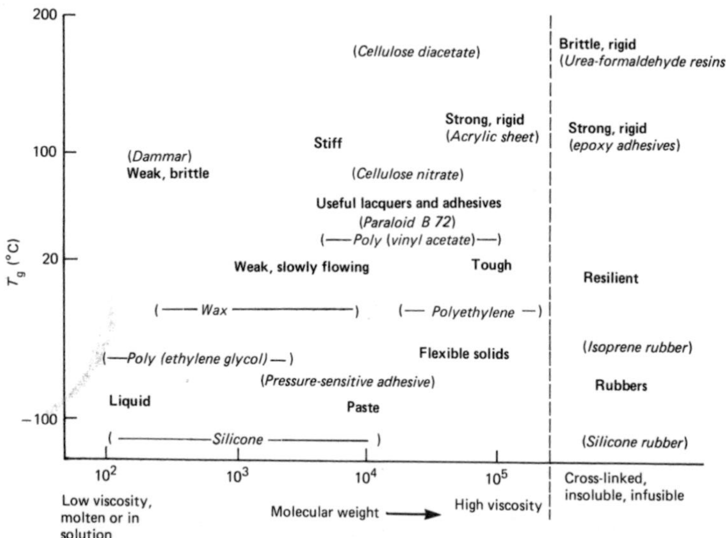

Figure 2.9 Physical properties of polymers related to their molecular weight (M_r) and glass transition temperature (T_g). Polymers which can form crystals, e.g. wax and polyethylene (Chapter 6) are more rigid than the molecular weight and T_g would suggest

stretching (polyethylene distorts if stretched too much), or in the force required to cause fracturing (dammar films break if little force is applied).

The mechanical properties of a polymer sample are determined by many factors. Those mentioned above include the molecular weight (with distribution of molecular weights) and the glass transition temperature, allied with the speed and temperature of testing. In addition, the way in which a sample is prepared is important. For example, a polymer film cast from solution will be weaker than a heat-moulded film. Also, polymers change on ageing as internal stresses relax or chemical reactions take place.

The mechanical properties are usually important in choosing a polymer. Highly specified standard tests, e.g. ISO/R527, are widely used for commercial evaluation, but these are rarely of direct relevance to conservation applications (Berger and Zelinger, 1984). A polymer responds to a pulling force (tensile stress)

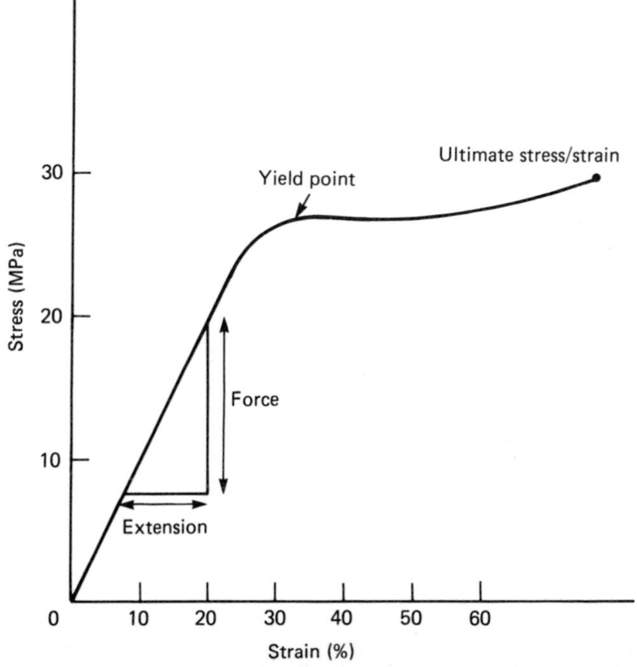

Figure 2.10 Generalized tensile stress/strain curve of a polymer (Winding and Hiatt, 1961)

$$\text{Elastic (Young's) modulus} = \frac{\text{Stress}}{\text{Strain}} = \frac{\text{Force (per unit area of sample cross-section)}}{\text{Extension (per unit length of original sample)}}$$

by being stretched (tensile strain). The mechanical properties of a polymer can be described partly by the values derived from the tensile stress/strain curve (*Figures 2.10, 2.11*). As a polymer is stretched the sample goes through various stages. The first part of the curve describes the elastic properties of the polymer, when the sample can be stretched without permanent distortion. This elastic region is described by the modulus of elasticity (Young's modulus). If a rubber band is pulled or an acrylic sheet is bent, they will snap back into their original shapes when the force is released. Stiffer materials have high values of Young's modulus, i.e. more force is required to stretch them. They are usually well below their glass transition temperatures. Some thermoplastics above their glass transition temperatures will start flowing immediately force is applied. They will therefore have no elastic properties. As the stretching is continued, many polymers will suddenly distort irreversibly at the yield point; polyethylene is a

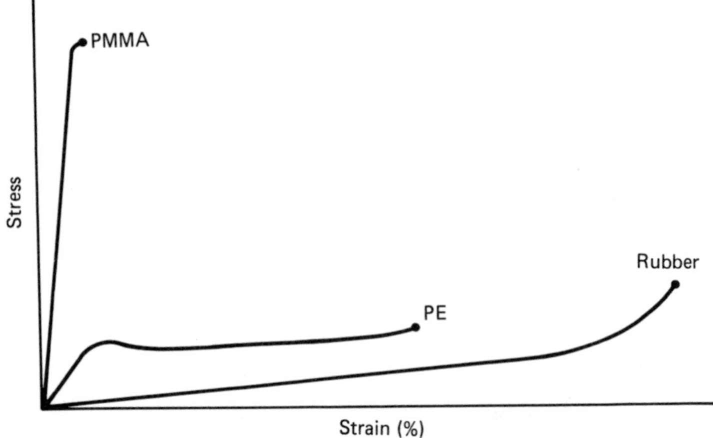

Figure 2.11 Different types of stress/strain properties (Winding and Hiatt, 1961) of poly(methyl methacrylate) (PMMA), polyethylene (PE), and natural rubber (approximate values)

	Young's modulus (MPa)	*Ultimate stress* (MPa)	*Ultimate strain* (%)	*Comment*
PMMA	3200	7	4	Strong but brittle
PE	200	1	500	Less strong but tough
Rubber	1	2	800	Weak but can be stretched

good example. The distortion will continue with further stretching until the material finally breaks, at the ultimate strength. Little distortion will take place if the polymer is well below its glass transition temperature or if it is highly cross-linked. The ultimate strength is reduced if the molecular weight is reduced.

These polymer properties have considerable effects on the object. A polymer with a high Young's modulus requires a high force to achieve small stretching. If it is applied to wood which then expands with rising humidity, a tension is set up between the object and polymer. The strong polymer will resist stretching and will tend to pull off, probably with part of the wood surface attached. If the polymer is relatively weak, i.e. it has low ultimate strength, movement in the wood will cause the polymer to crack. Craquelure of paint varnishes is probably caused by this effect. If the polymer stretches irreversibly with the expansion, subsequent contraction of the wood will lead to bubbling or wrinkling of the film (Berger and Russell, 1986).

The tensile test is useful for polymers applied as films. Other applications require the assessment of different properties. Values analogous to tensile elasticity, yield and ultimate stress/strain can be obtained from bending and compression tests, used for evaluating mounting and reinforcement methods (Bradley, 1984). Other types of mechanical test can also provide valuable information, e.g. tearing strengths (for silicone rubbers) and resistance to peeling (for textile and paper adhesion techniques). For most conservation purposes, the strength of applied polymers is greater than needed, sometimes dangerously so.

2.4.1 Hardness

The term 'hardness' encompasses a range of properties. Four main measures of hardness are widespread; resistance to indentation, scratch resistance, damping of a pendulum, and flexibility.

Indentation hardness is commonly used to indicate the hardness of rubbers. A soft, flabby, silicone rubber would have a Shore A hardness of 20, and a hard, stiff, rubber a hardness of 70.

Scratch resistance, or resistance to physical marring, is frequently measured by rubbing abrasives over a surface and assessing the damage at the end of the test. Pencil hardness is used to assess the hardness of a coating, though it may not be reliable. A pencil is sharpened to a point and drawn at 45° across the polymer surface (Corcoran, 1972). The hardness of the hardest pencil that does not mar the surface is assigned to the polymer.

The hardness or resilience of a coating may be described by the

Sward rocker hardness (ASTM D2134-66). Plate glass has a hardness of 100, and a thin film of poly(vinyl acetate) has a hardness of 63 (Feller, 1971a). Sward hardness is partly determined by the glass transition temperature, but it cannot be used reliably to compare coatings of widely differing types (Sato, 1984).

A common method of measuring the flexibility of a polymer coating is to take a film of standard thickness and bend it around a series of cylinders, or a conical mandrel (Schurr, 1972). The diameter of the smallest mandrel that the film can be bent around without cracking demonstrates the flexibility of the polymer.

2.5 Optical properties (Judd and Wyszecki, 1975)

2.5.1 Refractive index

The refractive index (n_D) determines properties such as reflection and transmission when the polymer is in combination with other substances, e.g. pigments, the object or air (*Figure 2.12*). These

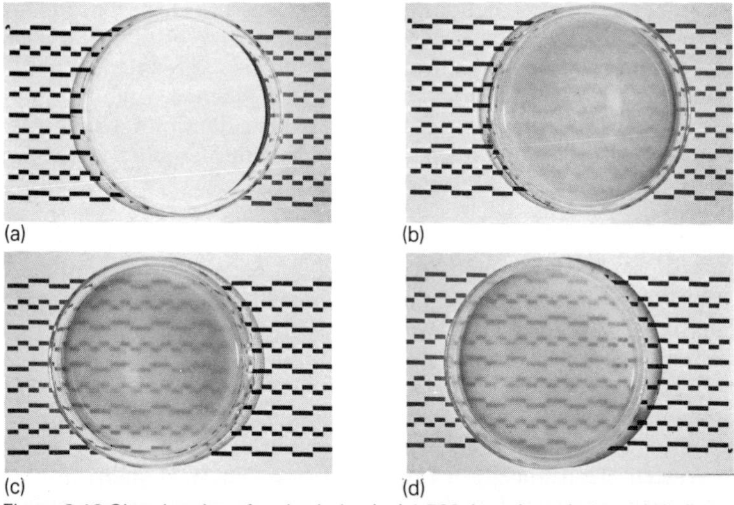

Figure 2.12 Glass beads, refractive index (n_D) 1.529, have been immersed in fluids (media) of different n_D. When the difference is great, e.g. air ($n_D = 1$) (a), most of the incident light is reflected from the bead's surfaces. As the match between the medium and substrate improves, the reflection from the interface decreases, so improving the transparency of the mixture – pyridine ($n_D = 1.507$) (b) and carbon disulphide ($n_D = 1.628$) (c). A good match of refractive indices allows the light to penetrate through deep layers of the mixture and enables the inherent colour of the beads (grey) to be seen – mixture of solvents ($n_D = 1.529$) (d)

reflections can prove important, for example when choosing an adhesive for glass (Tennent and Townsend, 1984a) or a varnish for oil paintings (De Witte *et al.,* 1981). Reflections occur on the microscopic scale when pigments are surrounded by medium. As linseed oil ages, the refractive index of the linoxyn rises, from c. 1.48 (Roff and Scott, 1971) to 1.57 (Feller, 1957), approaching the values of mineral pigments. Oil paint therefore becomes more transparent with time. A polymer applied from solution retains solvent for a considerable time and can take years to reach its final value (Tennent and Townsend, 1984a). Loss of plasticizer or variation of moisture content with humidity changes will have an effect on the refractive index.

2.5.2 Colour (Billmeyer and Salzman, 1981; Thomson, 1978)

The colour of most polymers is restricted to a yellow tinge. This is usually reported in terms of the yellowness index (ASTM D1925-70) which is calculated from reflection or transmission measurements. In comparing two materials, a difference of about two points in the index is just visible under good conditions of viewing (Tennent and Townsend, 1984b).

2.5.3 Gloss (Hunter, 1975; Easthaugh, 1984)

Gloss is the description of a shiny surface, opposite to matte. Various methods are available for measuring different types of gloss. The gloss of varnishes is usually assessed by measuring the specular reflection using 60 incident and 60 reflected light (ASTM D523-80; ISO 2813-78). The degree of gloss can prove useful in reporting the changes in the properties of coatings (De Witte, 1975b) and to assess the type and level of gloss of acceptable treatments.

2.6 Polymerization (Billmeyer, 1971)

Polymers are built up by reacting monomers together, each monomer molecule being able to react with at least two other molecules. Two main mechanisms are used commercially, vinyl polymerization and condensation polymerization, with addition polymerization normally being used for cross-linking resins. Other mechanisms are employed which are frequently specific to the polymer being formed. Polymers may be applied as finished molecules or as prepolymers which are reacted *in situ.*

Vinyl polymerization is used to produce poly(vinyl acetate) and to cure polyester casting resins. Vinyl polymerization results from the ability of a carbon–carbon double bond to open (*Figure 2.13*). This occurs under the influence of an initiator. Free radicals are the usual and most convenient initiators. The radical is not destroyed in the process but is transferred on to the end of the chain, creating a chain reaction. Free radicals are extremely reactive and may incorporate impurities into the chain, e.g. oxygen. Free radicals are generated from unstable chemicals, e.g. benzoyl peroxide, by heat, for instance during the laboratory or commercial preparation of polymers, or by catalysts, as during the curing of polyester casting resins. Alternatively, high-energy radiation, ultraviolet or γ rays, may be used. The length of the polymer chains can be controlled by adding chain transfer agents. Where a single monomer has been used, a homopolymer is produced. Copolymers can be made in a similar fashion by mixing two or more monomers. Four conditions of polymerization are used (Table 2.2).

Dispersion polymers (Feast, 1982) (incorrectly but commonly termed emulsions) are heavily contaminated, when dried, by the

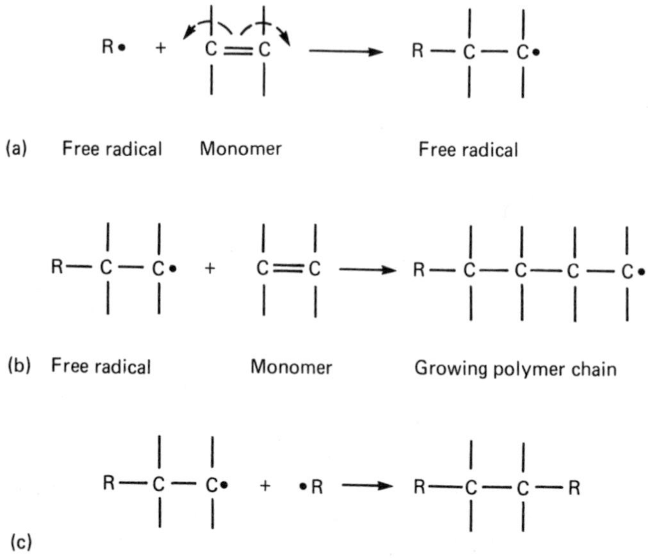

$$R\bullet + C{=}C \longrightarrow R{-}C{-}C\bullet$$

(a) Free radical Monomer Free radical

$$R{-}C{-}C\bullet + C{=}C \longrightarrow R{-}C{-}C{-}C{-}C\bullet$$

(b) Free radical Monomer Growing polymer chain

$$R{-}C{-}C\bullet + \bullet R \longrightarrow R{-}C{-}C{-}R$$

(c)

Figure 2.13 Vinyl free-radical polymerization process. (a) First stage of polymerization. (b) The chain grows step by step without interruption by the addition of monomer molecules. (b) Combination of two growing chains, which stops the polymerization process for these chains

Table 2.2 Vinyl polymerization methods

Method	*Ingredients used (relative parts)*	*Form of polymer produced*	*Relative advantages*
Bulk	Monomer (100) Initiator (0.5)	Solidified melt, in lumps	Purest chemically but may contain chain irregularities, e.g. branching
Suspension	Water (350) Monomer (100) Initiator (0.5) Suspending agent (1)	Small beads	Slightly contaminated with suspending agent, e.g. gelatine/talc. Convenient for handling and dissolving
Solution	Solvent (100) Monomer (100) Initiator (0.5)	Solution	Solvent may be incorporated into polymer. Can be used directly as solution
Emulsion	Water (180) Monomer (100) Emulsifying agent (5) Initiator (1)	Dispersion (emulsion)	Emulsifying agents are incorporated into solid polymer, leading to reduction in properties, e.g. clarity, stability to yellowing. Can be used directly as dispersion

emulsifiers. The polymer, frequently a copolymer, is usually of high molecular weight or may be cross-linked. The polymeric emulsifiers used may be neutral, e.g. poly(vinyl alcohol) and cellulose ethers, or ionic, e.g. sodium carboxymethyl cellulose or poly(acrylic acid). Sensitive materials can be damaged by these dispersions, which may have an inappropriate pH (acidity/alkalinity), corrosive salts, or volatile additives, e.g. ammonia. The viscosity of a dispersion is completely independent of the molecular weight of polymer in the droplets. High percentages of polymer, up to 70% can be held in a stable dispersion at very low viscosities compared with equivalent polymer solutions. The viscosity can be increased by adding water-soluble polymers, which increase the viscosity of the medium, or by adding solvents which swell the particles. Polymers in dispersion have many advantages during handling and application. However, since they are complex mixtures, the effects on objects are more difficult to predict. When a dispersion dries, the particles are forced together. In order for these particles to coalesce into a coherent film, the polymer particles must flow into one another. The polymer must therefore be soft enough to flow, i.e. be above its glass transition temperature. The polymer itself may have a low glass transition temperature. Alternatively, the glass transition temperature may be lowered by additives. Plasticizers soften the polymer but would not be used in a polymer for conservation. Solvents are used widely to permit film formation at low temperature, and the formation of an ultimately hard film as the solvent evaporates. Only small amounts of solvent are tolerated before the dispersion is destabilized. The lowest temperature at which a coherent film is created is called the minimum film-formation temperature (MFFT) (*Figure 2.14*). Both the MFFT of the dispersion and the

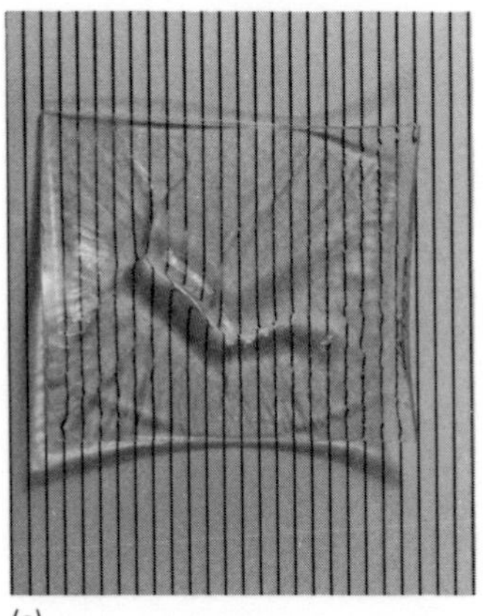

(a)

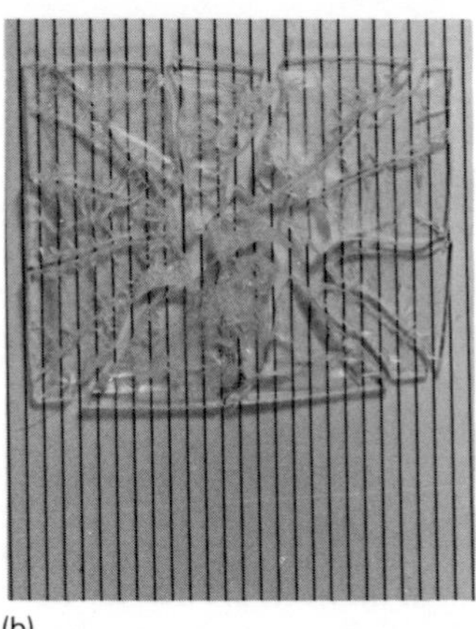

(b)

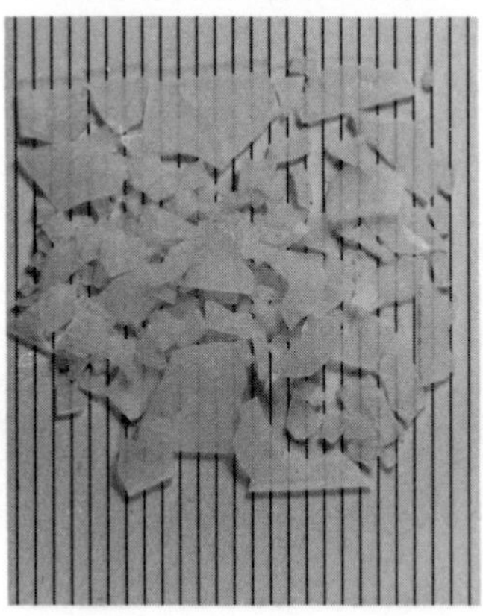

(c)

Figure 2.14 The effect of minimum film-formation temperature (MFFT) of a dispersion on its drying behaviour. Primal (Rohm & Hass) dispersions were allowed to dry at room temperature, c. 21 °C, in a silicone rubber mould. An MFFT above room temperature results in incomplete coalescence of particles and poor film formation. The cracks and distortion which occur in the films result from the movement of water and shrinkage during drying. (a) AC-34 MFFT 12 °C. (b) AC-73 MFFT 37 °C. (c) B-85 MFFT 90 °C

glass transition temperature of the final film are important properties.

Condensation polymers are used, both as thermoplastics, e.g. nylon, and cross-linking resins, e.g. phenol–formaldehyde resins. Condensation polymerization proceeds differently from vinyl polymerization. Two molecules react together to eliminate a small molecule, usually water; hence the name condensation. Chains are built up by isolated reactions to form the polymers. Copolymers can be produced by a variety of compatible monomers.

Many other reactions are used for preparing synthetic polymers, both by modification of existing polymers and by the cross-linking of existing prepolymers. These methods are discussed under the entries for individual polymers.

2.7 Deterioration of polymers

Polymers used in conservation must not change and cause harm to the objects. Most polymers are applied to objects in the hope, if not the expectation, that the process need not be repeated for 20 years as a minimum and 100 years in most circumstances. However, this lifetime is long by comparison with commercial uses: "... copolymers [of polyacetals] have lasted in a creep test for up to two years, a longer period than the operational life of a typical car" (Barker and Price, 1970).

The useful life of a polymer has to be defined for conservation. Feller has provided a rule of thumb for classifying materials (Feller, 1978). Class A1 should last for more than 500 years; class A2 should last for more than 100 years; class B should last 20 to 100 years; class C would last less than 20 years; and Class T is suggested for a temporary use of less than six months. It is likely that a material used for temporary fixing can never be entirely removed (Section 1.3). It is therefore necessary that even these have long-term stability.

Deterioration is any change in the polymer which makes it unfit for use in its context. Many changes may be undergone by polymer films; they can yellow, become brittle, weaker or insoluble, shrink, flow, become dirty, and, when applied to objects, react with them over short or long periods.

The primary causes for these changes are usually chemical reactions in the film, though physical properties control dirt pick-up and flow. The agents of deterioration – light, heat and oxygen – act on the weaknesses inherent in the polymer film. All these influences interact in a complex and often uncertain manner.

2.7.1 Degradation studies (Grassie and Scott, 1985)

Vinyl polymers are the most intensively studied group because of their nominal uniformity of structure. The less uniform thermoplastic and cross-linking resins have not been investigated in such detail and have only recently attracted concerted efforts at understanding their degradation. A chain is only as strong as its weakest link – in no field is this more true than in polymer chemistry. The study of polymer deterioration is largely the location and study of these weak links. Parallel to the deterioration studies are efforts put into the industrial development of stabilizers to prevent the deterioration. The major chemical changes which can occur are: cross-linking between chains; chain scissioning; and oxidation of the main chains or side groups. These chemical changes in the polymer structure may reveal themselves as increasing insolubility, reduction in strength, increasing polarity and change in colour.

Thermal deterioration

Purely thermal degradation is probably unknown at room temperature or even in direct sunlight, though it will occur during the processing of polymers. However, thermal degradation studies reveal the forms of degradation that occur in more complex situations. They also provide a quick test for the effects on degradation of minor modifications to the polymer or its formulation.

Poly(vinyl chloride) (PVC) undergoes reaction along the main chain. Theoretically the structure should not break down below c.300°C (David, 1975) but even good grades of PVC degrade below 100°C, producing HCl:

$$-\underset{H}{\overset{H}{C}}-\underset{Cl}{\overset{H}{C}}-\underset{H}{\overset{H}{C}}-\underset{Cl}{\overset{H}{C}}- \rightarrow -\overset{H}{C}=\overset{H}{C}-\underset{H}{\overset{H}{C}}-\underset{Cl}{\overset{H}{C}}- + HCl \rightarrow -\overset{H}{C}=\overset{H}{C}-\overset{H}{C}=\overset{H}{C}- + 2HCl$$

Long sequences of conjugated double bonds are created, leading to light absorption and a yellow discoloration of the polymer. The process is prompted by imperfections in the chain and by impurities such as solvents or metal ions. Discoloration can occur early in the life of a polymer, long before physical properties are affected.

Pendant groups on a polymer chain can react without affecting the main chain structure. For example, poly(vinyl alcohol) can dehydrate to form ether cross-links:

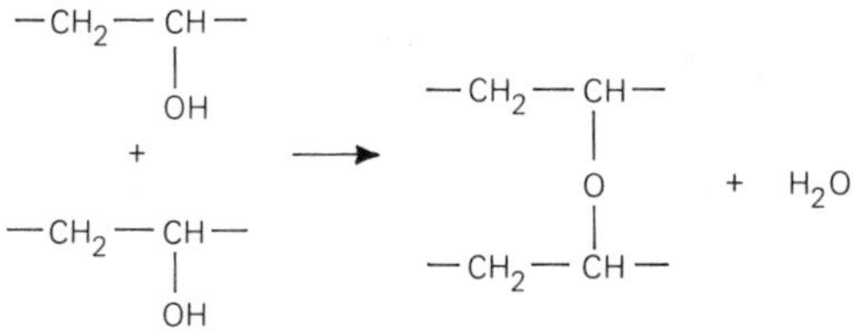

$$-CH_2-CH(OH)- \;+\; -CH_2-CH(OH)- \longrightarrow -CH_2-CH(-O-CH(-CH_2-)-)- \;+\; H_2O$$

Various structures in a polymer molecule cause it to become more reactive and thus unstable (*Figure 2.15*). When they form part of the main chain of the molecule, they cause particular instability. Many natural resins contain these groups and are thus less stable.

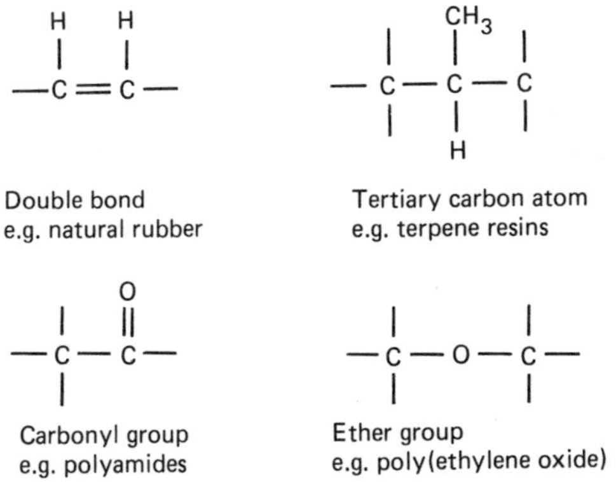

$-C(H)=C(H)-$

Double bond
e.g. natural rubber

$-C-C(CH_3)(H)-C-$

Tertiary carbon atom
e.g. terpene resins

$-C-C(=O)-$

Carbonyl group
e.g. polyamides

$-C-O-C-$

Ether group
e.g. poly(ethylene oxide)

Figure 2.15 Destabilizing groups in a polymer molecule. These may be part of the structure of the polymer, or may have been introduced during polymerization, processing or ageing

Photolytic deterioration (Ranby and Rabek, 1975)

Many polymers used in conservation are exposed to light. Light can be visualized as being a stream of small packets of energy, quanta. No material is totally transparent. Absorbed energy will cause heating but a small proportion may initiate chemical change. Light of different colours is composed of quanta of different energies, red being least energetic and blue most energetic. Ultraviolet radiation is yet more energetic.

Each chemical reaction requires a minimum amount of energy to activate the breaking of the first chemical bond. The energy of a quantum of ultraviolet radiation is sufficient to break many of the chemical bonds in polymers. Impurities, e.g. metal ions, and imperfections, e.g. oxygen incorporated into the polymer, are affected by visible light. Visible light causes slow changes in polymer properties (Feller *et al.*, 1981). Ultraviolet absorbers and stabilizers are used to increase the life of the unstable polymers such as PVC and PE. Although polymers used in conservation are more stable than these, the proposed lifetime is also much greater. Efforts have therefore been made towards incorporating ultraviolet stabilizers into coatings (Feller, 1976a; Lafontaine, 1981). Most conservators would be suspicious of a material that might migrate into the object. Covalently bound stabilizers, incorporated during polymerization, are much more attractive (Nelson and Wicks, 1983). Stabilizers of all sorts must be chosen with care and tailored to individual polymers. The wrong stabilizer may increase the rate of oxidation or discoloration.

Oxidation (Rabek, 1975; Feller *et al.*, 1981)

Although heat and light provide the activation energy, reactions with oxygen usually cause the greatest damage. Oxidation occurs with all organic materials but the resistance of different materials varies greatly. Polyethylene oxidizes at an appreciable rate in the dark at 60°C, whereas poly(methyl methacrylate) is stable at 170°C (Hawkins and Winslow, 1964). Polymers that contain oxygen in their backbone, such as cellulose derivatives, are far less stable.

Oxidation is essentially the reaction of oxygen with radicals formed in the polymer. The first process is initiation, the production of free radicals at imperfections and reactive points in the molecules. Once the radical has been created, it can react with oxygen to form peroxides and hydroperoxides, –OOH. Hydroperoxides are moderately stable but can be broken down under the influence of light, heat or catalysts to continue a self-initiating process of oxidation. The radicals and peroxides formed can cause oxidation of the main or side chains – chain-scission or cross-linking respectively. The chain reaction will be terminated by reactions of the radicals with molecules which lead to stable, non-reactive products. Many other reactions occur during the oxidation which result in the production of small, volatile fragments. The oxidation process may therefore result in an increase in weight by incorporation of oxygen, e.g. during the oxidative cross-linking of drying oils, or a loss in weight by degradation of polymers, e.g. during the photo-oxidation of poly(vinyl butyral) (Ciabach, 1983).

Four stages of oxidation can be identified (Feller, 1977): inception (adjustment of the polymer to the conditions of exposure); induction (build-up of peroxide groups in the polymer); steady oxidation (reaction of the reactive groups in the polymer); and finally decline (the reactive groups used up). For many purposes the induction period is the maximum usable life of a polymer. This may be extended by adding antioxidants or ultraviolet absorbers. It can be shortened by exposure to ultraviolet radiation or catalysts.

This outline has followed changes in the oxygen adsorption of the polymer. However, other changes result from the oxidation. The polymer may become unacceptably deteriorated at relatively early stages in the oxidation process. Yellowing, chain scission or cross-linking are all effects which occur after low levels of reaction. Unfortunately these subtle effects, together with increase in polarity, may remain undetected until the conservator comes to remove the polymer. All polymers must be expected to oxidize, either quickly or slowly, with time. The photo-oxidation of natural varnish resins results in increased polarity and in increased weight as oxygen is absorbed (Feller, 1976b). This is also observable with Paraloid B-72, an extremely stable polymer. Many polymers applied to objects are mixtures, e.g. dispersions, wax/resins. The deterioration of each component may take place separately or synergistically.

Pigments

The influence of pigments on the ageing of synthetic resins has been studied for commercial reasons. The choice of pigments is unexpectedly important (Hoffman and Saracz, 1972; Irick, 1972). For example, the oxidation of propan-2-ol in the presence of various white pigments showed a wide range of reaction rates with different pigments. The relative rates were titanium dioxide (anatase) 10, zinc oxide 4, titanium dioxide (nutile) 4, barium sulphate 2, and barium tungstenate 0.3. Because of the other useful properties of titanium dioxide, pigments are now surface-treated to reduce the catalytic activity. Many pigments, organic and inorganic, can increase the oxidation of polymers. One should choose pigments for conservation purposes that will have the least harmful effects on the polymeric medium.

Substrate

Polymers have been shown to affect the deterioration of objects where they have been studied, e.g. paper (Baer *et al.*, 1976) and canvas (Berger and Zelinger, 1975). The object can in principle make an enormous difference to the ageing behaviour of the applied polymer. However, this seems to have been noticed in only a few cases. Most objects in conservation are old ones and have themselves started to degrade to some extent. Cellulose rapidly oxidizes, forming peroxide complexes (Daniels, 1984) which will start the main process of oxidation immediately.

Other effects are possible. Poly(vinyl alcohol) becomes insoluble and fixed to textiles on drying at room temperature (Thomson, 1963). The reason is uncertain, but is probably a combination of oxidation and reaction between the alcohol groups on the polymer and the acid oxidation fragments on the object (Dunn *et al.*, 1968). Decaying glass has an alkaline surface which can cause hydrolytic degradation of adhesives and lacquers. Degradation and other reactions can occur rapidly along a metal/polymer interface (Chan and Allara, 1972). It may be possible to pretreat the object or include stabilizers in the polymer to reduce the extent of reaction. Some polymers react together to form insoluble products. This happens particularly with water-soluble polymers (Table 3.2).

Gaseous pollution

Pollutants affect polymers to varying extents, though they are usually of less importance than oxygen or water (Kamal and Saxon, 1967). Both sulphur dioxide and nitrogen oxides (Jellinek and Flajsman, 1969) increase the rates of oxidation under ultraviolet, causing chain scissioning. It has been known for many years that ozone reacts with double bonds, a particular problem of rubber, causing chain scission (Murray and Storey, 1964). Double bonds occur as impurities in many commercial polymers. The effects are similar to, and contribute to, oxidation processes.

Hydrolysis

Those polymers that were originally prepared by condensation reactions may undergo hydrolysis. Polyamides and cellulose derivatives are at risk of chain breaking at the susceptible points. This has led to severe degradation of polyurethane foams, prepared from polyester prepolymers, used in wet storage of objects. Cured polyester resins can be broken down by hydrolysis, leading to leaching and cracking (Abeysinghe *et al.*, 1982).

Cross-linking and chain scissioning (Charlesby, 1960; Feller and Bailie, 1966)

The thermoplastic resins are commonly used in the expectation that, in theory, they can be removed by solvents. It is therefore important that they do not become insoluble for any reason. One reason for insolubility in a solvent is cross-linking between the polymer chains to form an intractable three-dimensional network. This is the same process, but occurring over a longer period, as a resin being deliberately cross-linked. A considerable effort by the conservation world has been put into the search for thermoplastic polymers resistant to cross-linking (Feller, 1976a). The alternative reaction to cross-linking is chain scissioning. The molecular weight is halved for each break and the polymer is considerably weakened. This can happen to both thermoplastic and thermosetting resins, whose strength and ability to be stretched without breaking are reduced.

In industry the effects of cross-linking are viewed in two ways. If a thermoplastic cross-links slightly after processing, it will acquire thermal and mechanical stability. Polyethylene has been extensively modified in this way to improve stability. Cross-linking and scissioning reactions during ageing obviously affect the usable life of a polymer. Too much, especially of scissioning, can make the polymer rapidly useless. Cross-linked polymers also undergo further cross-linking and chain scissioning reactions, resulting in changes in properties.

Relationship between cross-linking and chain scissioning

Of considerable importance to conservators is the distinction between those thermoplastics which remain permanently soluble and those that become more or less insoluble with age. The two reactions of cross-linking and scissioning occur relatively independently and their rates respond differently to changes in the deteriorating environment. When a polymer only reacts by chain scissioning it will remain permanently soluble, become weaker and may eventually liquefy. The opposite to a scissioning polymer is a purely cross-linking polymer. Each time a cross-link occurs a molecule increases in size. Only the most inappropriate polymers for conservation, e.g. poly(butyl methacrylate), undergo cross-linking alone (Feller, 1977). For most polymers the effect of both reactions occurring simultaneously must be considered.

By following the changes in molecular weight of a polymer, it is possible to determine the rates of cross-linking (p) and chain scissioning (q). The ratio of cross-linking to chain scission (p/q) defines the character of the polymer. If $p/q = 2$ (two cross-link units are needed to form one cross-link), the average size of the molecules will not change. If $p/q < 2$, the polymer will form an insoluble portion. If $p/q > 2$, the polymer will gradually degrade and will not cross-link, even in part. These figures apply only to the original polymer under study. The continual breakage and formation of new bonds will change the physical and chemical properties of the polymer, particularly if oxygen is incorporated into the chain during the process. A polymer might become so changed that the cross-linking or scissioning behaviour is also changed. The ratios are altered considerably by changing the test temperature, particularly around the glass transition temperature. Cross-linking reactions are not so likely to occur below the glass transition temperature when the chains cannot move towards each other. These methods and results have proved a powerful tool in preparing a polymer to order (Maxim *et al.*, 1968).

A conservator might therefore include in his specification of a thermoplastic for use on objects the limits of acceptability of p, q and their ratio p/q. From these values a prediction may be made about the useful life of the polymer *in situ*.

Physical deterioration

A polymer can deteriorate physically in various ways: it may shrink, expand, flow, crack or absorb dirt. These changes may result from the inherent properties of the polymer, from a change in these properties or from outside influences. Polymers applied to objects are normally around their glass transition temperatures. They can thus adjust, by flowing, to the movements in the object. A polymer that is well below its glass transition temperature and is weak may crack if the object moves. If the polymer is above its glass transition temperature it will tend to flow, particularly when placed under stress. Liquid adhesives in self-adhesive tapes can be sucked by capillary action into porous substrates. Traces of low-T_g polymer left on the surface after incomplete removal may hold dirt, causing disfigurement of the surface.

There is always some shrinkage of a polymer in going from the liquid state to the solid state. Shrinkage of polymers after they have set is usually due to loss of some of the film-forming material. Plasticizers are frequently added to glassy polymers to reduce their rigidity, e.g. flexible PVC coatings and celluloid. Over time, the additive can diffuse out of the film. This process of removal is helped by washing or by absorption into an adjacent porous material. The shrinkage which results can cause damage if it distorts the attached object. Other results are brittleness and cracking of the polymer. For these reasons the use of plasticized polymers should be avoided. Small molecules formed as fragments during oxidation may be lost by evaporation, washing or absorption. An example is the shrinkage and cracking of linseed oil putty, which degrades severely towards the end of its life.

2.8 Testing of polymers

The ideal way to test a polymer for conservation purposes is to apply the polymer to a likely range of objects, of little value, using various application methods, leave them for a time, say 100 years, then reverse the treatment and assess the results. This is, in practice, how many conservation treatments have been traditionally developed and assessed. However, it is not a realistic way to discover slightly or even grossly unsuitable methods that are newly proposed.

The first part of any test procedure is to decide on the role of the polymer and the general characteristics it must have. Many requirements are specific to the task in hand and may not be discovered until full-scale experiments are attempted. Usually a small range of polymers will then be shown to be apparently suitable. The reversibility of the treatments must also be tested before continuing to the next stage of accelerated ageing.

2.8.1 Assessment of the polymer before and after ageing

Evaluation methods for polymer properties may be divided into two groups. First are those designed by researchers into polymer properties. Few conservation institutions, even the biggest, have routine access to these techniques. International standard tests and scientific investigations are usually carried out by people and for reasons unconnected with conservation. All require the outlay of considerable expense and time before consistent results are achieved. Ideally, of course, polymers used on objects should be subjected to the same rigorous specification and routine scrutiny demanded for industrial materials.

The second group of tests are those that can be efficiently carried out by the working conservator; these are necessarily simpler and less rigorous. They can, however, be equally or more informative concerning conservation. The conservator should if possible carry out simple investigations on every batch of material to be used on objects. If the samples and results of tests are retained on file, they will become a valuable resource (by natural ageing) when the treatment must later be assessed or reversed. The samples and tests are more valuable if they are prepared in the same way over many years. During ageing tests on polymers, sufficient samples should be prepared to answer all the likely questions that might be asked of the polymer. Tests should be carried out on both newly acquired products and products that have been stored. Many products such as dispersions and epoxy resins deteriorate while in the liquid form (Christensen and Pedersen, 1982).

2.8.2 Setting properties

It is enlightening to be able to handle a sample of the solid polymer. A useful method for forming a sheet of polymer is to cast the liquid into a silicone rubber mould, c. 75 × 75 × 1 mm deep. A silicone mould can only be used with materials that do not seriously swell the rubber, e.g. emulsions, epoxies and wax. Preparing a hand sample for a liquid that reacts with the mould material, e.g. solutions in organic solvents, is more difficult. One can allow a puddle on a polyethylene or waxed glass sheet to dry, but it is difficult to achieve uniformity between samples in this way. Equipment is commercially available for the purpose (Sheen).

The shrinkage of a setting polymer occurs in two stages – while it is still mobile and later when the chains can no longer flow past one another – the gel state. The gel can be caused by chemical cross-linking or by increasing entanglement of the chains, preventing movement. Shrinkage before the gel point is only of concern if one has to fill a volume completely, e.g. taking a cast from a mould or ensuring that an object is completely consolidated. Shrinkage after the gel point can be more serious. Damaging shrinkage is a combination of two properties, the post-gel shrinkage and the elastic modulus (the force necessary to stretch the set polymer). Total shrinkage must be measured by taking a known volume of liquid polymer and measuring the volume after setting.

Post-gel shrinkage of a thermosetting resin is relatively easy to assess. A simple method is to take an impression from a steel rule, using a release agent if necessary. Gross changes in length can be measured in the mould of the engraved scale, using the rule itself or a travelling microscope. An alternative method is to cast a cylinder of the polymer in a steel mould (*Figure 2.16*). Shrinkage occurs mostly during the initial setting but can continue for a

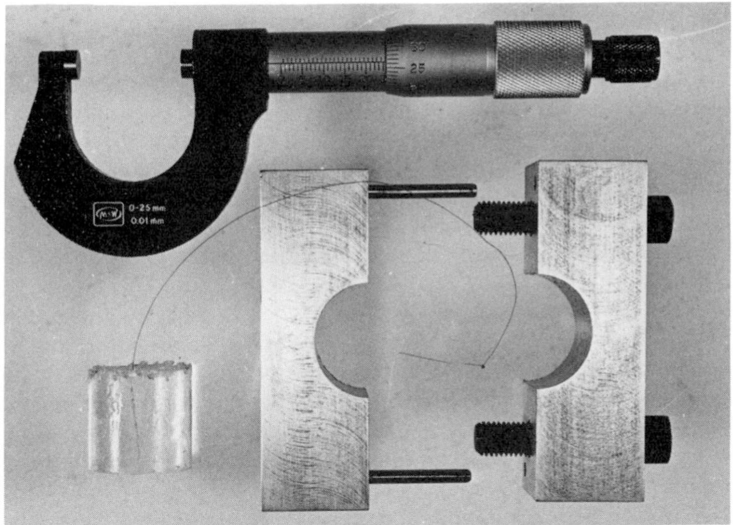

Figure 2.16 A stainless-steel cylindrical mould (internal diameter 25 mm × 25 mm high) with a micrometer for measuring the diameter. A sample of polyester has a piece of thread cast in to aid specific-gravity measurement

considerable time afterwards. Samples must therefore be measured initially and at increasing intervals until a stable value is achieved. Thermoplastics cast from emulsions or solutions also reduce in volume during drying but the post-gel shrinkage is not measured easily (Blackshaw and Ward, 1983). The method introduced by Werner (1962) of casting a film into plywood (or cardboard) frames appears inconsistent (De Witte, 1975a). A method of measurement has been developed (Croll, 1979) but is not suitable for the conservation laboratory.

2.8.3 Solubility

There are three aspects to solubility that are important: what liquids dissolve the material, what is the viscosity of the solution formed, and to what extent does the material dissolve? For cross-linked polymers the swelling effect of solvents is also important. The viscosity of polymers either in solution or as prepolymers is usually derived from manufacturers' data.

Manufacturers' information for polymer/liquid combinations is often insufficient for conservation purposes and tests must therefore be carried out. A known weight of the solid polymer is placed in the test liquid to form a 20–40% solution which only half fills the container; 10 ml is adequate. The closed container is agitated for 24 hours. At the end of the 24 hours, the container is inspected and the liquid placed in one of three classes: solvent, borderline and non-solvent. A totally clear solution implies that the liquid is a solvent. A turbid liquid implies that the liquid is borderline. If the liquid is in two phases, e.g. has solid particles apparent or has separated into two layers, the liquid is classed as a non-solvent. Only liquids of interest need be tested, though two comprehensive sets are suggested in the standard test (ASTM D3132-72).

If the polymer is only partly soluble, the degree of solubility can be assessed. The liquid is decanted or filtered off after the 24 hours' mixing. Both the soluble and insoluble portions can be dried in pre-weighed containers to constant weight in a vacuum desiccator or by gently warming (40°C) in the oven. The percentage solubility can be established from either or both of the determinations.

The swelling behaviour of a cross-linked resin is usually determined on a volume basis. A known weight of polymer, whose density has been determined, is placed in a pre-weighed container. The solvent is added. After swelling has stopped, usually within 48 hours, the polymer is quickly freed of liquid and weighed in its container to prevent premature evaporation of the liquid. The volume increase of the polymer is derived from the following:

$$\text{volume increase} = \frac{(W_s - W_p)D_p}{D_s \times W_p} \times 100\%$$

where W_s = weight of swollen polymer (g)
W_p = original weight of polymer (g)
D_p = density of polymer (g/cm^3)
D_s = density of solvent (g/cm^3)

The effects of chain scissioning or cross-linking can be assessed by the solubility measurements or by chromatographic techniques. Ideally, gel-permeation chromatography can be used to follow the changes in molecular weight (Nelson and Wicks, 1983). Simpler paper chromatographic techniques were originally used to follow these changes (Feller, 1971b).

Feller has proposed a series of solvent mixtures which may be used to assess the removability of a picture varnish (Feller, 1976b, 1978) (Table 2.3; *Figure 2.17*). These have proved useful in following changes in solubility and swelling of low-polarity

Table 2.3 Feller's series of solvents having a steadily increasing polarity

Solvent number	*Volume % of*			*Teas parameters*		
	Cyclohexane	*Toluene*	*Acetone*	f_d	f_p	f_h
1	100	0		94	2	4
2	75	25		91	3	6
3	50	50		87	5	8
4	25	75		83	6	11
5		100		80	7	13
6		87.5	12.5	76	10	14
7		75	25	72	13	15
8		62.5	37.5	68	16	16
9		50	50	63	20	17
10		25	75	55	26	19
11			100	47	32	21

Solvent mixtures for testing varnishes

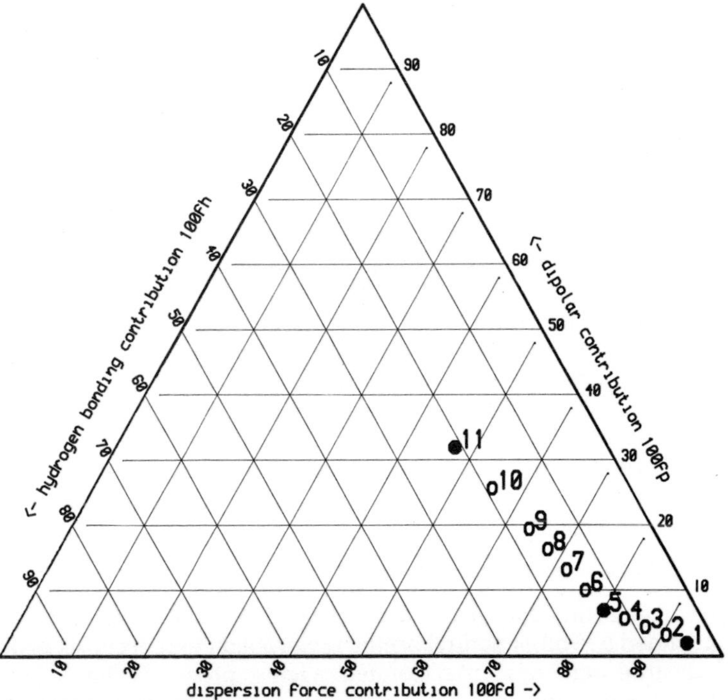

Figure 2.17 Teas plot of solvent mixtures of cyclohexane (1), toluene (5) and acetone (11) for assessing the solubility of picture varnishes (Feller,. 1976b, 1978) (see Table 2.3 and section 3.2)

coatings that have been aged, both artificially and naturally. The mixtures can be used in two ways. A simple test of the proportion of an ageing polymer that dissolves in each solvent mixture may indicate that the polymer requires increasingly polar solvents for dissolution, or that the polymer becomes insoluble in any solvent, or possibly both effects. Picture varnishes are normally removed by rolling solvent-laden swabs over the surface. The use of these solvent mixtures may indicate the least polar solvent required to remove the coating in a reasonable time. For a more accurate estimate of solution properties over a critical solvent range, the composition of the mixtures used can be adjusted in smaller steps.

2.8.4 Dirt pick-up

A film may be applied to a white tile or a glass sheet and placed in a suitably dusty environment. Two effects can be noted – the amount of dust adhering to the surface and the amount of dirt held by the polymer after washing. The attraction exerted by a polymer on dust particles depends partly on the static charges that build up on the surface. In many cases the likelihood of incorporation of dirt into a polymer will be apparent from the glass transition temperature of the polymer.

2.8.5 Adhesion

The adhesion of a polymer film to a substrate (Corcoran, 1972) is frequently assessed by pulling at a scored polymer film with self-adhesive tape (ISO 2409-1972). The polymer is coated on to the relevant substrate. After thorough drying, the film is scored with a knife or special cutter with two sets of 11 lines at right angles, normally at 1 mm spacing, to form 100 squares. Self-adhesive tape is rubbed down over the scored area then pulled off. The proportion of squares of film that are removed either before or after the removal of the tape is a measure of the lack of adhesion.

2.8.6 Accelerated ageing

Predicting the changes in properties that will occur over an extended period of natural ageing is a problem that occupies many industrial scientists. Accelerated ageing processes have been shown to be only crude approximations to the natural situation. As they are usually the only experimental tools available they must be used, but with care and understanding of their defects.

There are two main methods of accelerating the ageing process: (1) by concentrating on the effects of only one environmental influence, e.g. light, while keeping other influences constant; or (2) by subjecting the sample to extremes of all the influences expected, e.g. in weatherometers. The former method is a sharp tool to clarify and study single effects which are combined in the latter experiments. If one is studying beefsteak and using a scalpel to divide it up, one may never discover how tough it is.

The usual technique is to choose the apparently important influences and subject the material to extreme conditions of these. It is important that the extreme conditions employed are the same conditions, but magnified, as will be experienced in normal existence. The following paragraphs indicate the methods by which ageing might be accelerated. Relevant properties of the polymer and polymer/substrate may then be reassessed to follow the changes.

Light

Changes induced in a polymer depend on two principal factors: the quality and quantity of radiation. An alteration in the quality of the light, e.g. by changing the higher energy ultraviolet content, can change the type of reaction (Kinmonth and Norton, 1977). In most cases radiation will produce the same effect whether provided at a high intensity for a short time or at a low intensity for a longer time. This is the basis of accelerated ageing but there are exceptions, e.g. some oil paints are bleached by strong light. High-intensity light will cause heating which may lead to drying of the specimen or raising of the temperature above the glass transition temperature of the polymer. Specialist light-ageing apparatus is available, though a somewhat slower but more easily managed light source is a bank of fluorescent lamps. These radiate little heat, have closely controlled and specified spectral output, can conform closely to gallery conditions and, as important, are relatively inexpensive to instal. Running 24 hours a day, they cause ageing more than eight times faster than would be experienced on a moderately lit gallery (Blackshaw and Ward, 1983).

The monitoring of total exposure to radiation is a necessary part of testing. A widely used method of monitoring light exposure is the use of blue wool fading standards (ISO 105-1978). The eight standards have been chosen to fade at different rates. Standard 1 is very fugitive, fading visibly in an hour of sunlight. Standard 8 is so light-fast that the wool disintegrates when fading occurs.

Unfortunately the assessment and interpretation of the results requires care. It is important that the spectral output of the source and relative humidity during exposure be determined if realistic comparisons are to be made between different experimental conditions.

If the material becomes unserviceable before blue wool Standard 3 starts to fade visibly, it is placed in Feller's class C (Section 2.7) (Feller, 1978). If the material is more stable than Standard 3 but deteriorates before Standard 6 starts to fade, it is placed in class B. Those materials that survive as well or better than Standard 6 are placed in class A. Feller has suggested some standard polymer materials which can be compared to the material under test when light-ageing; these are Paraloid B-72 (*Rohm & Hass* for class A and poly(*n*-butyl methacrylate (Elvacite 2044) (*Du Pont*) for class B.

Heat

At absolute zero (−273°C, 0 K), there is no movement or reaction. In order to increase the temperature one has to supply energy. This energy goes into making the atoms move and collide violently. A small proportion of the collisions will result in chemical reactions. The higher the temperature, the more energy is available and the more likely are the chemical reactions to occur. Reactions that require a low energy to activate them will occur at low temperatures. The rate of a chemical reaction is thus determined by the activation energy of the reaction and the temperature. This relationship is shown mathematically by the Arrhenius equation (see Thomson (1978) for further discussion):

$$k = Ae^{-E_a/RT}$$

where k = rate constant for the reaction
A = a constant
E_a = activation energy
R = gas constant
T = temperature in Kelvins

According to this equation, increasing the temperature increases the reaction rate. However, reactions with different activation energies are affected to different extents. On increasing the temperature, all the reactions will speed up but the relative importance of the reactions will change as well. The rate of a reaction can be assessed from simple observations of a change in the property of the material, e.g. yellowing, or by more complex analyses of the reaction processes (Gabbay and Stivala, 1976). *Figure 2.18* shows two possible results. The solid straight line demonstrates the normal situation – a single reaction with an activation energy of 100 kJ/mol. From a knowledge of this straight line, the change occurring at any given combination of temperature and time can be confidently predicted. However, the curved line is an example of a more complex situation, two reactions occurring together. One has an activation energy of 100 kJ/mol, the other an activation energy of 250 kJ/mol. Without some knowledge of the shape and slope of the curve, predicting properties from single measurements can be misleading.

One would not expect a conservation material to have a degradation reaction with an activation energy below that of

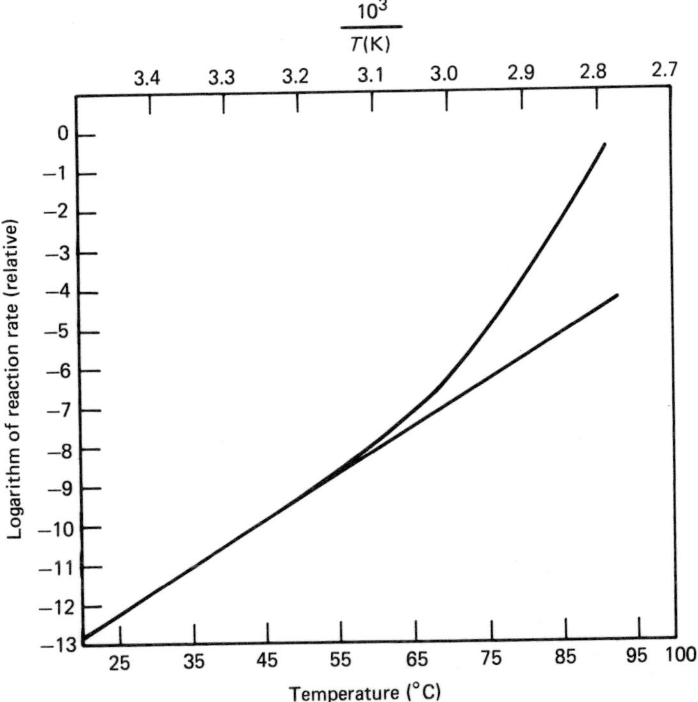

Figure 2.18 Comparison between the rates of deterioration at different temperatures of two different (hypothetical) materials. The straight line is for a material with a single deterioration reaction with an activation energy of 100 kJ/mol. The curved line is for a material with two simultaneous reactions with activation energies 100 and 250 kJ/mol. The reaction rate is on a logarithmic scale

good-quality paper, about 95 kJ/mol (Barrow, 1964) or indeed cellulose (E_a = 124 kJ/mol) (Browning and Wink, 1968). Cellulose seems to deteriorate in an uncomplicated way, and heating of samples is a standard method of predicting the lifetime of paper (Gray, 1969).

The situation is more complicated with synthetic polymers. On raising the temperature above the glass transition temperature, many properties change, including the rates of the deterioration reactions. One must ensure that raising the temperature of the test does not change the polymer from its glassy to the plastic state (*Figure 2.19*). Where a polymer is to be applied or used at high temperatures, e.g. poly(ethylene oxide) and wax, it should also be tested in that condition.

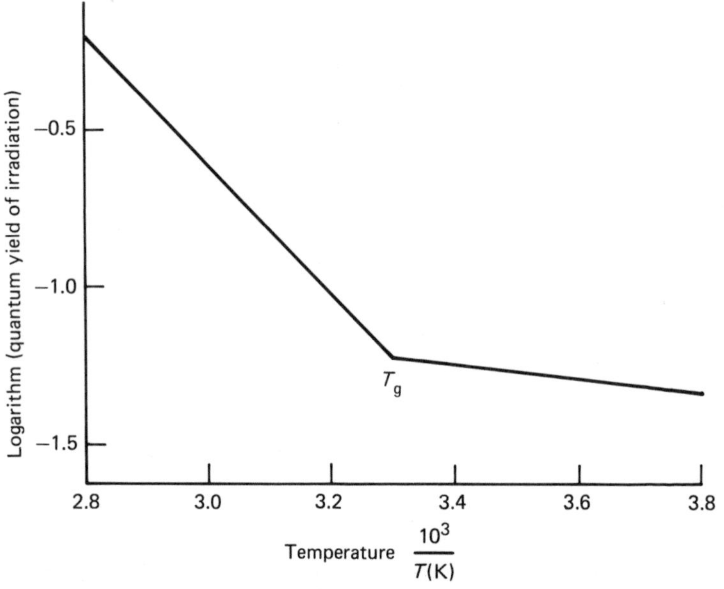

Figure 2.19 The rate of chain scissioning of poly(vinyl acetate) (Mowilith 70) (Hoechst) under the influence of ultraviolet light (253 nm) at different temperatures. This Arrhenius plot has been drawn conventionally with temperature increasing to the left. The rate of reaction increases markedly around the T_g (30 °C) on increasing the temperature (Geuskins *et al.*, 1972)

Water

Many polymers are used in contact with water. The conditions may be made more extreme by heating the water (but see above), by changing the pH or dissolved salts, or by using alternating wet/dry periods. Polymers which react with water, often by hydrolysis, will be sensitive to changes in pH. A notable example reported in conservation is the cross-linking of soluble nylon in even mildly acidic conditions (Bockoff *et al.*, 1984).

Impurities

Reactions between the added material and the materials of the object can cause changes in both the polymer and object. It would be useful for screening tests to be carried out using model objects. This procedure is routinely used in paper conservation research, where the chemical variation between objects is relatively minor. Unfortunately, it is carried out infrequently.

2.9 Identification of polymers

Many different polymers have been used on objects. The choice of treatment or reversal methods frequently depends on knowledge of the polymers used in the past on the object. The unambiguous identification of a polymer requires the sacrifice of large samples or the use of high technology (Hummel Scholl, 1978–82). Differentiating between similar copolymers may require the synthesis of samples of known composition to enable detailed comparison with the unknown (De Witte *et al.*, 1978). The use of simpler methods (see, e.g., Braun, 1982) is a compromise between ease of use and rigorous identification.

In some fields of conservation, relatively few polymers have been used. Identification is then simplified to distinguishing between a handful of alternatives. Unfortunately, most polymers have been altered by natural ageing and may give different results from those found with modern equivalents. In addition, mixtures of polymers or additives can complicate the identification process by giving positive results in a confusing manner. The first stage is to remove the polymer (safely) from the object, by scraping some off or by dissolving it. Frequently the physical properties provide valuable pointers to the likely polymer. A preliminary evaluation of a polymer can be made by the solubility, first in water (Table 2.4), and then in organic solvents (Table 2.5). Reaction with iodine solutions can provide additional clues for water-soluble materials (Table 2.5), and water-insoluble materials (Howie, 1984). Further investigations need resources beyond those found in most conservation laboratories.

Table 2.4 Polymers affected by water

Polymer	*Effect of cold water*	*Effect of hot water after soaking in cold*	*Colour reaction with iodine solution*[(1)]	*Effect of organic solvents*
Methyl cellulose	Soluble	Gels at >54°C	None	No effect (with current products)
Ethyl hydroxy ethyl cellulose	Soluble	Precipitates >40°C	None	No effect
Hydroxy ethyl cellulose	Soluble	Soluble		No effect
Hydroxy propyl cellulose	Soluble	Precipitates <40°C	None	See appendix 3, figure A3.20
Sodium carboxy methyl cellulose	Soluble	Soluble	None	No effect
Starch	Swells (translucent)	Soluble >80°C	Deep blue	No effect
Dextrin	Soluble	Soluble		No effect
Agar	Swells (translucent)	Soluble >85°C	Crimson	No effect
Gum arabic	Soluble	Soluble	None	No effect
Glue	Swells (transparent)	Soluble >40°C		No effect
Casein	Swells (translucent)	Swells	None	No effect
Poly(vinyl pyrrolidone)	Soluble	Soluble	None	See appendix 3, figure A3.17
Poly(vinyl alcohol)	Swells (transparent), (degree of hydrolysis <92% soluble)	Soluble	Green	Few (section 7.2)
Poly(ethylene glycol)	Soluble	Soluble	Brown precipitate	See appendix 3, figure A3.19
Poly(vinyl acetate)	Swells (white) may disperse	Swells		See appendix 3, figure A3.6

Note
(1) Test solution: dissolve 3.3 g potassium iodide in 40 ml water, dissolve 2.54 g iodine in solution, dilute to 200 ml with water, add to a dilute solution of the polymer.

Table 2.5 Solvents for recent samples of thermoplastics, 10% solution

Ethanol	*Acetone*	*1,1,1-Trichloroethane*	*Toluene*	*Cyclohexane*
Shellac	PMMA	Dammar	Dammar	Dammar
PVB	PEMA	Mastic	Mastic	PBMA
Mastic	PBMA	PEMA	PMMA	PS
Ketone resin	PVAC	PBMA	PEMA	Natural rubber
	CA	PVAC	PBMA	EVA
	CN	PS	PS	
		Chlorinated rubber	PVAC	
		Ketone resin	Chlorinated rubber	
		Beeswax	Natural rubber	
		EVA		
		Natural rubber		
Soluble nylon >40°C		PE >82°C	PE >66°C	PE (hot)

Other polymers: PVC and PVDC only dissolve in a few ketones
PTFE dissolves in nothing

Abbreviations
CA = cellulose acetate, CN = cellulose nitrate, EVA = ethylene/vinyl acetate copolymer, PBMA = poly(butyl methacrylate), PE = polyethylene, PEMA = poly(ethyl methacrylate), PMMA = poly(methyl methacrylate), PS = polystyrene, PTFE = polytetrafluoroethylene, PVAC = poly(vinyl acetate), PVB = poly(vinyl butyral), PVC = poly(vinyl chloride), PVDC = poly(vinylidene chloride).

3 Solvents

A solution may be obtained by a reversible chemical interaction, e.g. dissolving sugar in water, or by an irreversible reaction, e.g. dilute nitric acid on limestone. The solvents discussed below are primarily the mobile organic liquids which undergo reversible interactions with their solutes (the solids that are dissolved). Occasionally the more reactive solvents, particularly the amines, are used to alter a polymer, perhaps by hydrolysis, to ease its dissolution.

Solvents are used for three main purposes in conservation – for cleaning off contaminants, for applying polymers or for removing polymers. When choosing a solvent there are many properties that must be considered: chemical type and purity, solubility parameters, evaporation rate, toxicity and flammability. These properties are dealt with below and listed in Appendix 2. Many other properties such as density, optical properties and diffusion rate can be important and details may be found in standard texts (Duve *et al.*, 1975, 1976; Marsden, 1963; Mellan, 1970; Durrans, 1971).

3.1 Chemical type and purity

Solvents are usually classified by the most reactive portion of the molecule. The most used classes are listed in Table 3.1, and in Appendix 3.1. Each solvent of a class has properties similar to other members of the class. Few industrial chemicals contain only one component. Many solvents, particularly the ethanol and hydrocarbon solvents (Appendix 3.2), are made as mixtures. In addition, solvents contain impurities. For many industrial purposes, high purity (>95%) is not necessary. The purity of solvents used on objects should be at least 98%, and there should preferably be no non-volatile or coloured impurities. The composition and commercial designation of solvents should be checked as far as possible before use by obtaining manufacturers'

Table 3.1 Chemical classes of solvent

Class	*Characteristic group*	*Example*	
Aliphatic (paraffinic)	H–$(CH_2)_n$–H	CH_3-$(CH_2)_5$–CH_3 or C_7H_{16}	(Heptane)
Naphthenic	–C_6H_{11} (cyclohexyl)	CH_3 | CH H_2C CH_2 H_2C CH_2 CH_2	(Methyl cyclohexane)
Aromatic	–C_6H_5 (phenyl)	CH_3 | C HC= CH | ‖ HC= C–CH_3 CH	(*m*-Xylene or 1,3-dimethyl benzene)
Halogenated	Cl | –C– | Cl or F | –C– | F	Cl_3C–CH_3	(1,1,1-Trichloroethane)
Ether	–O–	C_2H_5–O–C_2H_5	(Diethyl ether)
Ester	O ‖ –O–C– (carboxyl)	O ‖ C_2H_5–O–C–CH_3	(Ethyl acetate)
Ketone	>C=O (carbonyl)	CH_3 \ C=O / CH_3	(Acetone)
Alcohol	–OH (hydroxyl)	CH_3–CH_2–OH	(Ethanol)

data sheets. Many solvents, e.g. ethers, propan-2-ol and turpentine, absorb oxygen from the air to form reactive, sometimes explosive, peroxides. Solvents should be kept in full, dark-coloured, glass bottles to reduce their deterioration.

3.2 Solubility parameters (Barton, 1983)

Subjectively, it is appreciated that 'like dissolves like' but this aphorism is insufficient to predict the effect of a solvent on a polymer. Ethanol is a solvent for shellac but is very weak for wax. Hydrocarbon solvents have no effect on shellac yet are solvents for wax. Early attempts to quantify the strength of a solvent used empirical methods. The kauri gum-butanol number (ASTM D1133-83) is obtained by adding a test hydrocarbon (non-solvent) to a solution of the gum in butanol. The number of ml of the non-solvent required to induce precipitation of the gum is the K-B number. This is widely used for assessing the solvent power of hydrocarbons. A series of three solvents, cyclohexane, toluene and acetone, were developed by Feller (1976b) for testing picture varnishes (Table 2.3). Although these schemes work well within the discipline for which they were developed, they are of little general applicability.

'Like dissolves like' is the intuitive realization that the forces between the molecules of a good solvent must be about the same as those between the molecules of polymer (*Figure 3.1*). The

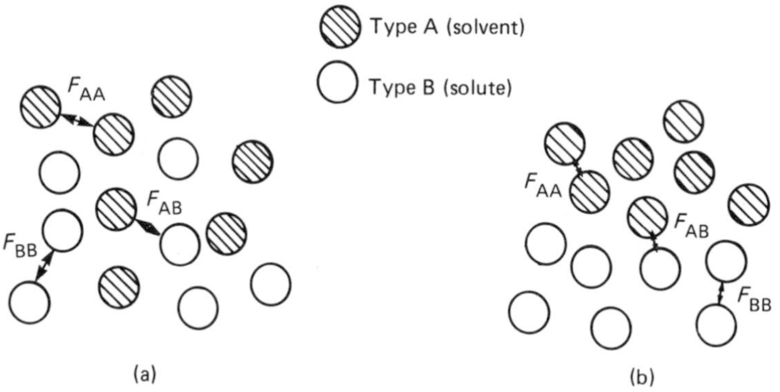

Figure 3.1 Schematic representation of the forces between solvent and solute (Brydson, 1982). F_{AA} = forces between molecules of A, F_{BB} = forces between molecules of B, F_{AB} = forces between molecules of A and B. (a) If $F_{AB} \gg F_{AA}$ and $F_{AB} \gg F_{BB}$, the mixture is compatible and a solution forms. (b) If F_{AA} or $F_{BB} > F_{AB}$, the solution does not form and the molecule types separate out

kauri-butanol experiment starts with a solution and, by changing the composition of the solvent (A), reduces the interaction of the solvent with the gum (B). The solute molecules bind closer to each other than to the solvent and insolubility develops.

If one mixes pure A with pure B, the forces between the molecules of A and B, F_{AA} and F_{BB} respectively, will be broken. Overcoming these forces requires energy. This energy is quantified as the cohesive energy density of the two components, δ_A^2 and δ_B^2, from which are derived the solubility parameters, δ_A and δ_B. Although the development of the new forces between A and B (F_{AB}) produces energy, the net change in energy usually acts against the likelihood of solution. The change from the neatly ordered A and B to a random mixture increases disorder (entropy), which increases with temperature. The increase in disorder increases the likelihood of a solution. One implication is that low molecular weight polymers will dissolve more readily than high molecular weight polymers. Conversely, solvent molecules are likely to be held strongly at high polymer concentrations.

To understand the interactions of solvents, one can start from the intermolecular forces. The forces acting between solvent and polymer molecules may be divided into three types (*Figure 3.2*).

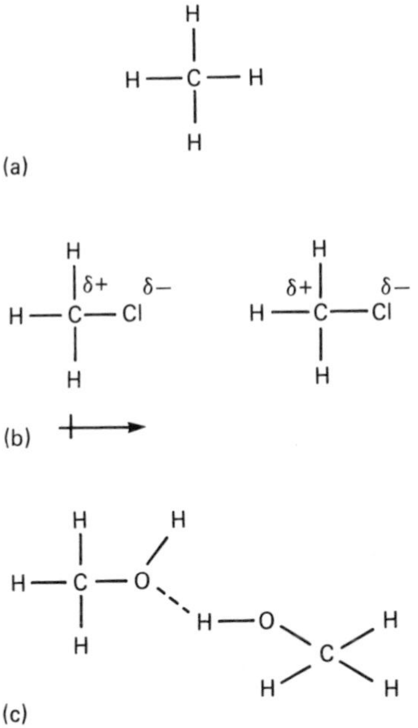

(a)

(b)

(c)

Figure 3.2 The forces between molecules. (a) Methane – a symmetrical molecule attracted only by dispersion forces. (b) Chloromethane – an asymmetric molecule with a permanent dipole. (c) Methanol – hydroxyl groups enable attraction between the oxygen and hydrogen atoms to create a hydrogen bond

(a) Dispersion force arises from the movement of electrons around molecules. This is a very weak force and is the only force which holds symmetrical molecules, e.g. methane, together. Very little energy is necessary to separate the molecules, and this accounts for the low boiling point of methane (−164 °C). This force is present in all substances.

(b) Polar forces arise from non-symmetrical molecules which have an unbalanced distribution of electrons (dipole moment). This imbalance causes further attraction between the molecules, e.g. chloromethane has a higher boiling point (−24 °C) than methane.

(c) Hydrogen bonds are an extreme form of polar attraction and occur when the hydrogen is directly attached to oxygen and nitrogen atoms. The subsequent attraction takes place between, for instance, an oxygen atom of one molecule and the hydrogen atom of another. Methanol has a much higher boiling point (65 °C) than methane or chloromethane.

Methanol would therefore have three components of attraction, dispersion, polar, and hydrogen bond forces; chloromethane would have two components, dispersion and polar; and methane would only have dispersion forces.

The simple description of solubility behaviour using a single solubility parameter, δ, only works in the absence of strong polar and hydrogen bonding forces, which impose a structure on the liquid. Many descriptions using three components have been developed. The most widely used approximation is that of Hansen (Hansen and Beerbower, 1971) who proposed that the forces be considered additively, i.e.

$$\delta_t^2 \text{ (cohesive energy density)} = \delta_d^2 + \delta_p^2 + \delta_h^2$$

where δ_d^2 = contribution of dispersion forces

δ_p^2 = contribution of polar forces

δ_h^2 = contribution of hydrogen bonds

The inadequate one-dimensional ranking of solvents is thus replaced by three partial solubility parameters.

The interactions of small solvent molecules are short-range. However, the polymer molecules are much larger and they do not have sharply defined solubility parameters. The region of solubility can be drawn as a rough sphere in the three-dimensional space of partial solubility parameters. The description of a polymer's solubility characteristics by Hansen has four components – the radius of the sphere and the three values defining the centre. To display these values graphically on a sheet of paper presents severe difficulties. Interpolations are even more difficult.

A way of providing the description in two dimensions is to rank solvents by both solubility parameter and hydrogen bonding ability (Du Pont, no date; ASTM D3132-72). Unfortunately the values of the hydrogen bonding index are based on obsolete data, and this reduces the value of this description.

In an effort to retain the three components in a two-dimensional description, a triangular graph was proposed (Appendix 3.1), using reduced solubility parameters, derived from Hansen's partial solubility parameters. The three components, f_d, f_p and f_h, add up to 1 but are usually expressed as a proportion of 100.

$$100f_d = \frac{100\delta_d}{\delta_d + \delta_p + \delta_h}$$

where f_d = fractional cohesion parameter (dispersion component)
δ_d = Hansen's solubility parameter (dispersion component)
$\delta_d + \delta_p + \delta_h = \delta$ = solubility parameter (total)

f_p and f_h are derived similarly from δ_p and δ_h.

Solubility parameters for mixtures of solvents are derived from the weighted average by volume of the various components. The fractional parameters for a mixture of two solvents would be derived thus:

$$f_d = \frac{v_1 f_{d1} + v_2 f_{d2}}{v_1 + v_2}$$

where f_d = dispersion partial solubility parameter of mixture
v_1, v_2 = volumes of the two components
f_{d1}, f_{d2} = dispersion partial solubility parameter of the components

f_p and f_h are derived similarly.

The outer perimeter of solubility on the solubility chart of a polymer can be indicated by drawing a line outside all those solvents which dissolve the polymer. As the dispersion forces are much the weakest, this plot squeezes the less polar solvents into the bottom right corner and distorts the solubility curve out of the circular shape which is intuitively more likely. The solubility parameters of solvents and polymers have been determined by both empirical and theoretical means. Each set of values is self-consistent but it is unwise to combine sets of data.

3.2.1 Use of solubility charts

On the simplest level the chart, derived from manufacturer's or conservator's data, can provide a visual summary of the solubility of the polymer, of great use when the properties of a number of polymers or solvents are being compared. However, because the charts are approximations, they can be misleading. There is much overlapping of the solvents and non-solvents on the charts. The conclusions must be checked when dealing with unfamiliar materials.

Solubility parameters are valuable in predicting the effects of mixed solvents and in situations where two polymers having overlapping solubility areas are present. These problems are often met with in painting conservation, where the object is itself affected by solvents. Considerable investigations have been undertaken to clarify the response to solvents of varnishes, over-paint and original paint (Ruhemann, 1968; Hedley, 1980; Stolow, 1971).

3.3 Evaporation rate

The boiling point of a solvent gives only an approximate indication of its volatility. The rate at which a solvent evaporates at room temperature is dependent on many factors, such as the vapour pressure, the heat of vaporization, the presence of solute, and the rate of heat supply. Solvents can be divided into three groups according to the evaporation rate (Appendix 2):

(a) high-volatility solvents >1.5
(b) medium-volatility solvents 1.5–0.4
(c) low-volatility solvents <0.4

High-volatility solvents are used to reduce the time for film formation, and so convert the mobile solution into a non-slumping film as soon as possible. Heat is removed by the evaporating vapour, and this cools the solution. The cooling can lower the temperature of the surrounding air below the dew point, causing precipitation of water from the atmosphere. If the condensed water dissolves in the solution, the polymer is likely to precipitate. This results in a white bloom or blush in the film. If the water is insoluble, it will lie on the surface, cause unevenness and create a matte finish, which may be desired. These effects can be countered by incorporating in the formulation medium- or low-volatility solvents which will evaporate after the water has gone. The better of these solvents form azeotropes with water, and this ensures the removal of the water before the film becomes immobile. These solvents include butanol, butan-2-ol, methyl, ethyl and butyl acetates, and 1,2-dichloroethane (Horsley, 1973; Duve *et al.*, 1975). Mixtures of solvents themselves form azeotropes and their suitability must be tested before use.

The selection of solvents for applying a polymer will depend on the method of application. An adhesive or brushing lacquer will have a high proportion of high-volatility solvents. For spraying, such a formulation would give rise to stringing or cobwebbing caused by the premature evaporation of the solvent in flight. A greater proportion of medium-volatility solvents is therefore used. The low-volatility solvents are rarely used as they result in delayed shrinkage of the film.

3.4 Hazards (Sax, 1984; Freeman and Whitehead, 1982; Bretherick, 1981)

All chemicals are dangerous and care is required whenever they are stored (Piptone, 1984), used or discarded (National Research Council, 1983). Fume-extraction facilities should be used whenever necessary. These should be tested and maintained. Sometimes one is able to exchange a dangerous solvent for a less hazardous one which has similar solvent properties. The hazards of solvents fall into two main categories: flammability and toxicity. For more complete listing of the hazards and test methods,

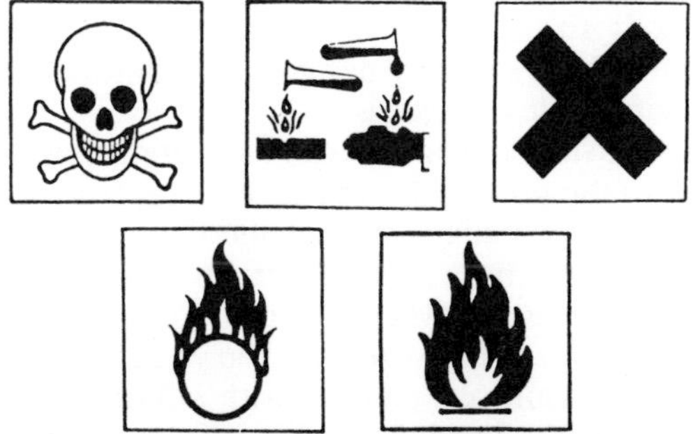

Figure 3.3 Typical hazard warning labels for containers of chemicals, mandatory within the European Economic Community. The label will usually be accompanied by a phrase defining more accurately the particular hazard. The absence of a hazard label on a container does not necessarily mean that no hazard exists – just that no hazard has been legally identified. See Appendix 2.3 for further details

standard texts should be consulted (Sax, 1984; Council of Europe, 1977, 1980). The following is no more than an indication of the possible dangers. Advice should be sought periodically from a local expert as a check against the unconscious introduction or continuation of unsafe practices. Ensuring the safe use of potentially dangerous materials is normally the responsibility both of the person using the material and of the supervisor of the laboratory. The transport, storage and use of solvents is closely regulated in each country. Every container should have the name of its contents clearly and indelibly attached with a label displaying the symbols of the hazards associated with the contents (*Figure 3.3* and Appendix 2.3).

3.4.1 Flammability

All organic solvents, except the highly halogenated ones, are flammable. As any solvent fire must start in the air/vapour mixture, the more volatile solvents are more readily ignited. The flash point is the lowest temperature at which a flame above the liquid will cause the vapour to ignite (Appendix 2). Obviously, the lower the flash point, the more likely is the vapour to ignite at room temperature. Any large containers of solvent, over 1 litre, should be housed in closed steel cabinets. Cabinets should be constructed to prevent leakage of solvent vapour or liquid if a container releases its contents. Only small containers of solvents, less than 500 ml, should be kept on the open shelves, which should be away from sources of heat or direct sunlight. Decanting large volumes of solvents generates static electricity with the possibility of sparks and ignition of the vapour. Whenever more than five litres of a solvent is likely to be stored and transferred, expert advice should be sought. Many specially designed containers for solvents and other flammable materials are now available. Vapours of solvents are heavier than air and can flow along bench tops, into ducting or on to the floor. The vapours can travel some distance from an open vessel containing solvent and hence naked flames, cigarettes, electric switches, static electricity and other sources of sparks must be removed when solvents are used. In general those solvents with a flash point below 21°C are considered most dangerous, while any solvents with a flash point below 32°C are still dangerously flammable. Chlorinated solvents form dangerous byproducts, e.g. phosgene, when heated or exposed to flames.

Solvents do not lose their hazard when work with them has finished. Objects and cleaning materials may be placed in a fume cupboard or well-ventilated area until the solvents have evaporated. Some solvents and oils contain sufficient peroxides to cause wiping rags to ignite while drying. These wastes should therefore be held in fireproof bins until disposal. Solvents should not be washed into the sewage system except with the explicit approval of the water authorities and in a very dilute form. Waste solvent should be collected in fireproof containers for speedy disposal by specialists who will usually require a list of the contents. Chlorinated solvents must be collected separately as they can react with other solvents, e.g. acetone, to create explosive mixtures. Waste and impure solvents must be compatible with the containers – acidic waste could cause disastrous corrosion of steel cans. Ethane-1,2-diol derivatives can react with aluminium to produce hydrogen.

3.4.2 Toxicity

All solvents have some toxicity. Liquid solvents will be absorbed through the skin, will dissolve protective chemicals from the skin, allowing access of infection, and will cause irritation to sensitive membranes, especially in the eyes. These dangers can be reduced by taking commonsense precautions and wearing protective clothing. Perhaps the most insidious damage is caused by breathing the solvent vapours over extended periods. For this reason the effects and relative dangers of solvent vapours have been extensively investigated.

There are two different kinds of vapour toxicity and these may occur with the same solvent. Narcotic effects are those of drunkenness or poisoning which wear off as the solvent is eliminated from the body, e.g. ethanol. Long-term effects may occur long after the solvent has been absorbed, e.g. methanol. With wider use of solvents, it is being found that chronic effects are much more common than had been realized.

The relative danger of different solvents is measured by the Threshold Limit Values (TLV), or Occupational Exposure Limits (OEL). These are the concentrations of vapour, measured in mg/m^3 or parts per million (ppm) by volume of the air, that can be tolerated by the average worker without undue risk (Appendix 2). Two values are commonly listed: one for exposure during the whole of the working week, the Time Weighted Average, TLV-TWA; and the other for short-term exposure, up to 15 minutes, TLV-STEL. National recommendations should be consulted for further details of values and methods of evaluation

(ACGIH, 1983; Deutsche Forschungsgemeinschaft, 1982; HSE, 1984).

Any solvent with a TLV less than 200 ppm should be avoided or treated with considerable caution. Suppliers of chemicals should be able to provide information on the toxicity of any product they supply. It is practically impossible to discover the concentration or toxicity of a material whose chemical composition is not known. The use of such materials presents unknown hazards to the conservator and, incidentally, to the objects. Individuals can vary in their sensitivities to chemicals. When one has been sensitized, irritation can occur at much lower concentrations than the average. To counter the possible dangers, periodic checks on the atmosphere breathed by a conservator are desirable. These should be made in the same conditions as normally found around the face of the worker, with solvent swabs, containers of solvents and solvent-covered object in their normal positions.

The measurement of the concentration of a solvent has been made much easier in recent years by the development of simple and relatively inexpensive instruments. The Draeger system (*Drägerwerk*) uses a hand pump to draw a known amount of air through a tube of chemicals which indicate the concentration of vapour in the air. This method is used by other suppliers of testing equipment who also make more sophisticated systems. One cannot rely on the sense of smell for warning, as many of the solvents have very mild smells. More importantly, the nose rapidly becomes accustomed to a solvent vapour, which may not be smelt at all without considerable effort. The anaesthetic effect of many solvents will ensure a happy ignorance of the increasing danger.

3.5 Solvent–solute interaction

There are two aspects to the interaction: the degree of interaction and the speed of interaction. The degree of interaction is best described by the use of the solubility parameters and the speed of interaction by the size and shape of the molecules.

3.5.1 Solutions (Van Krevelen, 1976)

Polymers form viscous solutions. The viscosity of a solution is increased by various factors: the concentration, the molecular weight of the polymer (*Figure 3.4*) and the viscosity of the solvent. Polymers may not form stable mixtures. When solutions of incompatible polymers are mixed, they separate (Tables 3.2 and

Table 3.2 Compatibility of polymers in organic solvents and of films applied from mixed solutions (Krause, 1978). Incompatible mixtures will separate

	PVAC	*PVbutyral*	*PRA*	*PRMA*	*CA*	*CN*	*Shellac*	*HPC*	*PVP*	*Dammar*
PVbutyral	IC									
PRA	–	–								
PRMA	C(PMMA) IC(rest)	IC	IC	IC (for different R)						
CA	IC	IC	IC	IC						
CN	C	IC	C	C	–					
Shellac	IC	C	–	IC	–	C				
HPC	–	–	–	–	–	–	C			
PVP	IC	C	–	–	C	–	C	–		
Dammar	C	C	–	IC	–	C	–	–	–	
Ketone resin	IC	IC	IC	IC	IC	IC	IC	–	–	C

Key
C = forms compatible solutions and deposits clear films; IC = solutions separate and deposit cloudy or patchy films.

Abbreviations
CA = cellulose acetate, CN = cellulose nitrate, HPC = hydroxypropyl cellulose, PMMA = poly(methylmethacrylate); PRA = polyacrylate polymer, PRMA = polymethacrylate polymer; PVAC = poly(vinyl acetate); PVbutyral = poly(vinyl butyral); PVP = poly(vinyl pyrrolidone).

Table 3.3 Compatibility of water-soluble polymers used in aqueous solution and of the films formed from mixed solutions

	PEG	*PVAL*	*MC*	*HPC*	*HEC*	*CMC*	*Gelatin*	*Gums*	*Starch*
PVAL	IC								
MC	IC	IC							
HPC	C	C	C						
HEC	–	IC	C	C					
CMC	X	?C	–	C	–				
Gelatin	IC	IC	C	C	–	–			
Gums	IC	?C	C	C	C	C	IC		
Starch	?IC	IC	C	–	–	–	–	–	
PVP	C	C	C	–	–	C	IC	C	–

Key
C = forms compatible solutions and deposits clear films; IC = solutions separate and deposit cloudy or patchy films; X = forms a water-insoluble film when dried; ? = conflicting information.

Abbreviations
CMC = sodium carboxymethyl cellulose; HEC = hydroxyethyl cellulose; HPC = hydroxypropyl cellulose; MC = methyl cellulose; PEG = poly(ethylene glycol); PVAL = poly(vinyl alcohol).

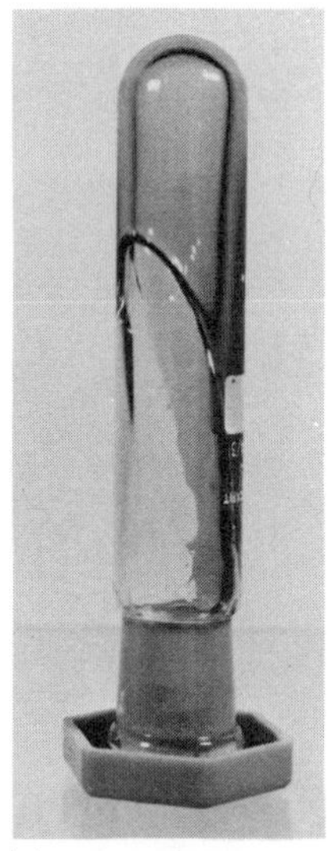

(a)

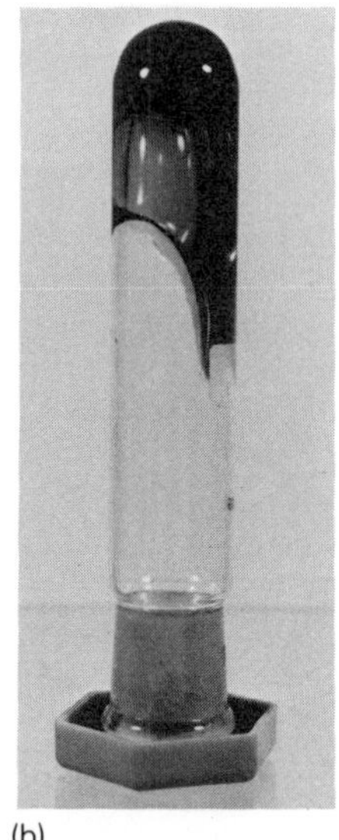

(b)

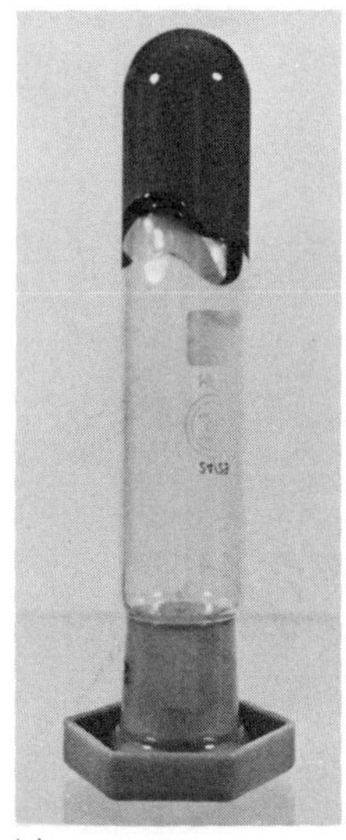

(c)

Figure 3.4 Effect of molecular weight on the viscosity of PVAC solutions. PVAC polymers (Cairn) (Table 8.1) were dissolved in cyclohexanone to form 40% solutions (by weight). These were dyed to aid visibility. The test-tubes were tipped over and photographed after two seconds. The low molecular weight polymer solutions flowed faster: (a) S 2½, (b) S 12, (c) S 27

3.3). On drying, the solutions dry in patches. Although this would be disfiguring if it occurred on objects, no problems seem to have been noticed.

Viscosity values may be quoted using two different scales: dynamic viscosity (Pa.s) and kinematic viscosity (m^2/s). The usual practical units are mPa.s (= 1 centipoise, cP), and $10^{-6}\,m^2/s$ (= 1 centistoke, cSt). The two scales are related by the density of the liquid.

$$\text{Pa.s} = \frac{\text{m}^2/\text{s}}{\text{density (kg/m}^3)} \qquad \text{stoke} = \frac{\text{poise}}{\text{g/cm}^3}$$

Table 3.4 shows a comparison of typical values of viscosity. Viscosity reduces sharply with an increase in temperature.

Table 3.4 Typical viscosities of common liquids

	Dynamic viscosity (mPa.s)	*Kinematic viscosity* ($10^{-6}\,m^2/s$)	
Acetone	0.32	0.25	20°C
Dichloromethane	0.43	0.57	
Toluene	0.58	0.50	
Water	1.06	1.06	
Ethanol	1.22	0.96	
Ethane-1,2-diol	20.8	19.32	
Olive oil	84	77	
Glycerol	1490	1877	
Elvacite 2043 20% solution in toluene	14.4	13	25°C
Elvacite 2043 30% solution in toluene	55	50	
Elvacite 2043 40% solution in toluene	300	300	

A dilute solution of a polymer in a good solvent (one with a good match of solubility parameters) has a high viscosity relative to one in a poor solvent. However, at high concentrations, greater than 15–30%, poor solvents result in higher viscosity solutions than good solvents (Hoernschemeyer, 1974). Good solvents therefore allow the polymer to flow more readily at high concentrations, e.g. during the last stages of drying. An optimum combination of solvents for applying a polymer film might seem to be a mixture of a volatile poor solvent with a small amount of good, slower evaporating, solvent. The same consideration may apply to adhesive formulations. However, it appears that the requirements for consolidation are different. The deepest penetration of objects by polymer solutions is achieved by choosing a solvent with the best match of solubility parameters (Domaslowski and Lehman, 1971; Lewin and Papadimitriou, 1981). The diffusion constant of a polymer in a good solvent is higher than that in a poor solvent.

Polymer solutions differ from simple liquids in the way they react to stirring. Polymer molecules impart a structure to the liquid. The structure is disturbed while the solution is stirred vigorously and in most cases the viscosity drops (Ferry, 1982) (*Figure 3.5*). This is usually not noticeable with polymer solutions

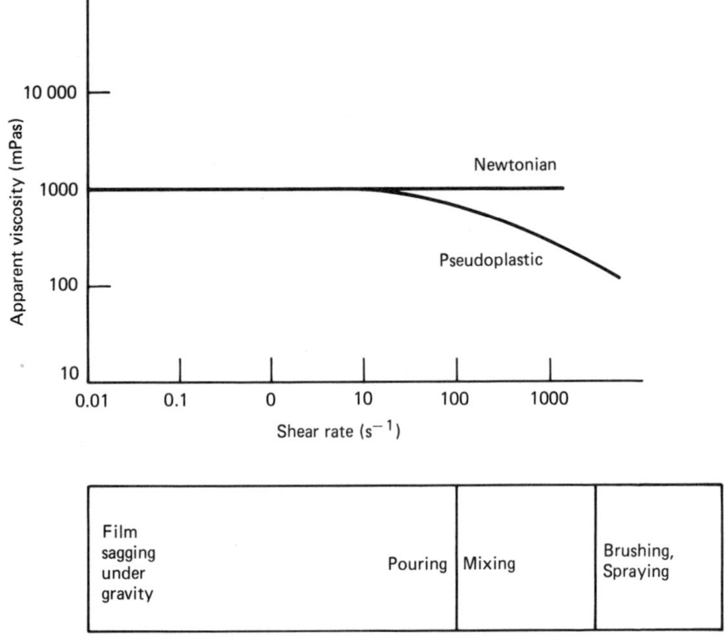

Figure 3.5 The viscosities of simple liquids do not change on increasing the rate of stirring (shear rate), i.e. Newtonian. The viscosities of some polymer solutions decrease when stirred rapidly (pseudoplastic). The pseudoplastic curve is typical of carboxymethyl cellulose solutions (Blanose) (*Hercules*) in water

in organic solvents. Solutions of water-soluble polymers exhibit more extreme properties because of the very strong interactions and structures that are developed by hydrogen bonding. Many of the solutions are thixotropic (the reduction in viscosity persists even after stirring has stopped), because the structure that is broken takes some time to re-establish itself (*Figure 3.6*). A number of water-soluble polymers form a reversible gel in water which can be broken into a liquid by stirring but which will gel again on standing. The use of these gels allows the placing of a polymer solution which will not flow.

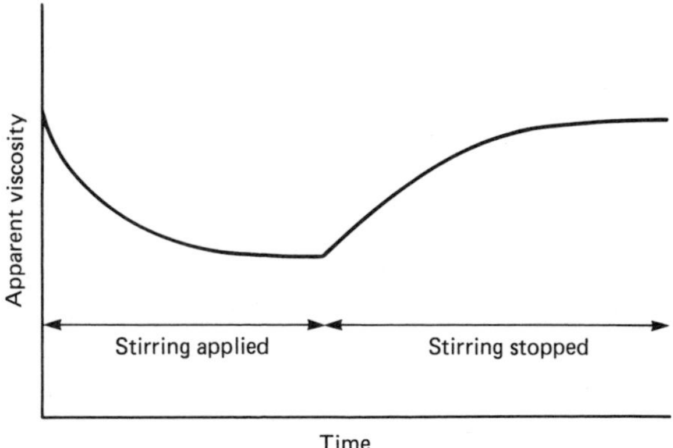

Figure 3.6 The viscosity of a thixotropic solution depends on the rate of stirring and the past history. Stirring will tend to reduce the viscosity until the structure is broken. Once the stirring has stopped, the structure reforms slowly with consequent increase in viscosity

3.5.2 The dissolution process

Cleaning technologists have found that the best solvent for a cleaning task is one in which there is a strong interaction between the soil and the solvent (Jackson, 1979). Solvents are frequently used with special surfactants which must be rinsed off after use (Landi, 1981).

The reaction of a solvent with a polymer to produce a solution goes through four stages (Ueberreiter, 1968) (*Figure 3.7*):

(a) The solvent molecules infiltrate between the polymer chains by diffusion.
(b) The outer layer of the polymer interacts with the solvent and swells.
(c) The outer layer of the swollen polymer absorbs more solvent and becomes a rubbery gel.
(d) The polymer molecules are lost from the surface at a rate depending on the flow of solvent over the surface.

The swelling is a necessary precondition of dissolution. All parts of the polymer molecule must be released from the solid mass before it can escape into solution. The rate of loss of polymer

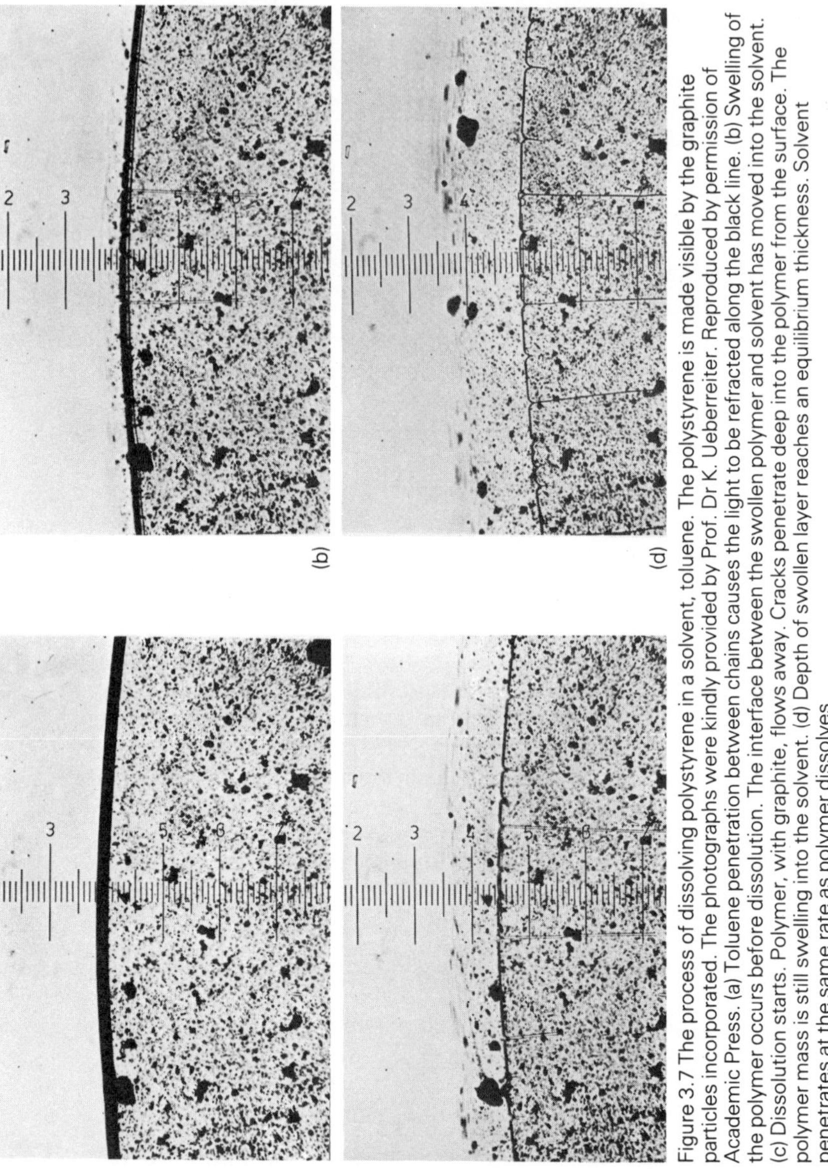

Figure 3.7 The process of dissolving polystyrene in a solvent, toluene. The polystyrene is made visible by the graphite particles incorporated. The photographs were kindly provided by Prof. Dr K. Ueberreiter. Reproduced by permission of Academic Press. (a) Toluene penetration between chains causes the light to be refracted along the black line. (b) Swelling of the polymer occurs before dissolution. The interface between the swollen polymer and solvent has moved into the solvent. (c) Dissolution starts. Polymer, with graphite, flows away. Cracks penetrate deep into the polymer from the surface. The polymer mass is still swelling into the solvent. (d) Depth of swollen layer reaches an equilibrium thickness. Solvent penetrates at the same rate as polymer dissolves

decreases with increasing molecular weight until it comes practically to a halt. The gel thickness increases over time, expanding the object which is embedded in the polymer (Ouano *et al.*, 1977). Increasing the temperature increases the loss of polymer but increases the rate of solvent diffusion even more. While this is useful in preparing solutions, one should reduce the temperature when dissolving polymers off objects. If the temperature of dissolution is much below the glass transition temperature of the polymer, very little gel layer will be formed. The polymer cracks because it is too stiff to stretch (Ueberreiter, 1968). The hard-edge phenomenon noticed during removal of some picture varnishes (Feller, 1981) may result from the high glass transition temperature of the resins used.

When the polymer is cross-linked, it is impossible to pass from the gel state into solution. The swelling action can be so fast that severe stresses build up and parts of the polymer are thrown off violently. This effect is worst with rapidly penetrating solvents (Alfrey *et al.*, 1966).

Mixtures of solvents are often used to achieve a solution in a shorter time. A low molecular weight solvent is chosen to penetrate and swell the polymer. The other component is chosen to have a good match of solubility parameters with the polymer. In many situations where polymers must be removed from objects, a large amount of swelling is undesirable. A paint film varnished with poly(butyl methacrylate) was disrupted by the swelling of the varnish with toluene (Thomson, 1963). A corroded metal object which had been coated with a polyester resin for support was disintegrated by the solvent swelling action necessary to remove it. Solvents should be chosen to cause the minimum swelling necessary to enable the polymer to be dissolved or scraped off. The depth of swelling is reduced by using relatively large solvent molecules at low temperature. The depth of swelling is also reduced by removing the polymer from the film as fast as possible by using a good solvent which is agitated vigorously. Polymers chosen for conservation treatments should have the lowest molecular weight practicable in order to reduce any subsequent strains during removal.

Cross-linked polymers cannot be dissolved using solvents. These polymers may be removed from surfaces by swelling with solvents then mechanically scraping off. They cannot be removed from porous objects. Many proprietory paint strippers or resin disintegrators are available (Williams, 1972), based on penetrating solvents such as dichloromethane combined with undisclosed acid or alkaline additives. It has been shown that home-made mixtures, based on dichloromethane and of known composition, are quite adequate for conservation purposes (Daniels, 1981). A cross-linked polymer may contain low molecular weight portions, plasticizers and degradation products, which will be extracted with solvents. If the solvent evaporates before the polymer is totally removed, the remaining polymer can shrink to a smaller volume than it had originally and may cause further stress on the object.

3.5.3 Film formation from solution

The bulk of a solvent usually evaporates quickly from a wet film according to the evaporation rates given in Appendix 2. However, final removal of the last few per cent of solvent from a dry film can be difficult. Solvent left in the film will cause a gradual shrinkage and change in properties over a period, perhaps many years, of evaporation. Remaining solvents may also cause chemical instability in the film. Linear, unbranched, solvent molecules have less difficulty in passing between polymer molecules, i.e. less steric hindrance (Table 3.5). Branched solvents should be avoided.

Table 3.5 Solvent retention. List of solvents in approximate order of increasing retention in polymer films. Solvents that interact strongly with the polymer will be retained relatively longer (Newman *et al.*, 1975)

(1) Methanol	(8) 2-Butoxyethanol	(15) *m*-Xylene
(2) Acetone	(9) *n*-Butyl acetate	(16) 2,4-Dimethylpentane
(3) 2-Methoxyethanol	(10) Benzene	(17) Cyclohexane
(4) Butanone	(11) 2-Ethoxyethyl acetate	(18) Methylcyclohexane
(5) Ethyl acetate	(12) Dioxane	(19) Cyclohexanone
(6) 2-Ethoxyethanol	(13) Toluene	(20) Methylcyclohexanone
(7) *n*-Heptane	(14) Chlorobenzene	

Solvents with a dipole moment may be more strongly held than symmetrical molecules; e.g. toluene is held for longer than *p*-xylene (1,4-dimethyl benzene) (Dauchot-Dehon and De Witte, 1978). Films cast from good solvents have a greater strength than those cast from poor solvents (Briscoe and Smith, 1983).

The conclusions arising from comparisons of dry-stage evaporation rate are therefore different from those arising from comparisons of solubility parameter; there may be no optimum solvent. In order to reduce the solvent to low levels quickly, one must use a solvent that is relatively poor and that has no side chains. Conversely, to relax the polymer chains into stable conditions, one must ensure that the last solvent to leave the film is closely matched to the solubility parameter of the polymer.

4 Adhesion

Introduction (Wake, 1978, 1982; Allen, 1984)

Joints between different objects can be made in many ways. Carpentry joints are held by mechanical keying; hot-welded iron is held by the merging of the metal from the separate pieces; and dust is held on to the surface of plastics by the electrostatic attraction of dust particles for the surface. These phenomena depend on the physical properties of the objects themselves to create the joint. In conservation an adhesive is employed to bridge and fill the gap between two objects. The adhesive is applied as a liquid which forms a strong bond to the object's surface. The principles of adhesion between a polymer and object surface are relevant to coatings, consolidants and adhesives.

Ordinary water can be used as an adhesive, and water pressed between two sheets of glass will prevent the sheets being pulled apart. However, the sheets can be slid past one another to break the joint. This use of water illustrates the first two essential requirements for adhesion.

(a) The liquid must cover the surface and have a strong attraction for the surface, i.e. it must wet the surface.

(b) The liquid must then set to prevent the relative movement of the objects.

(c) A further requirement is that it must be able to adjust to the stresses which develop during and after the setting of the adhesive.

4.1 Wetting

The best joint between a liquid and a surface is made when the liquid covers the entire surface, i.e. liquid has wetted the surface completely. The extent to which this is achieved depends on the forces within the liquid and between the liquid and the surface.

These forces are illustrated by the concept of surface tension. The surface tension of a liquid is the result of the forces of attraction between its molecules. The molecules in a drop of liquid on the surface of a solid will be subjected to two sets of forces along the interface (*Figure 4.1*):

(a) The attractive forces acting from within the liquid itself.
(b) The attractive forces acting from the surface of the solid.

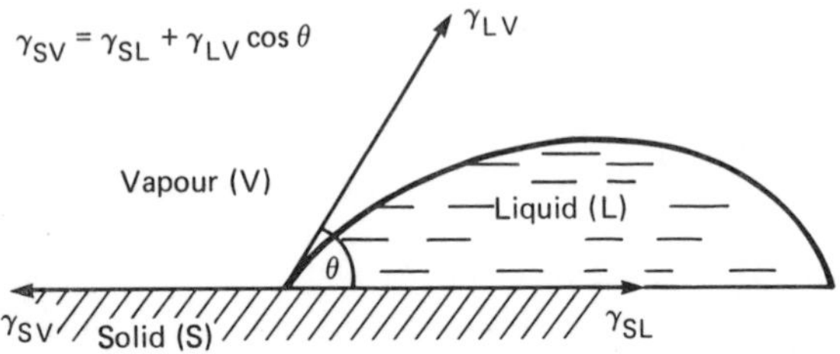

Figure 4.1 The forces in a stable drop of liquid on a surface. γ_{SV} is the surface tension of the solid in the presence of the liquid vapour. γ_{SL} is the surface attraction between the solid and the liquid. γ_{LV} is the surface tension of the liquid in the presence of its own vapour

If the angle θ is more than 90°, liquid droplets will sit on the surface of the solid, e.g. drops of water on polyethylene. If the angle θ is 0°, the liquid will spread out completely and wet the surface spontaneously, e.g. water on clean glass. At intermediate values of θ, i.e. between 90° and 0°, the liquid will spread and wet the surface if force is used to expand the drops. This description of a spreading drop applies only when the surface is absolutely smooth. However, most surfaces contain pores and crevices into which the liquid must flow if complete wetting is to be achieved. Air trapped in a pore will oppose the penetration of the liquid. If the air has time to diffuse out of the hole before the adhesive sets, the penetration will be deeper. This is one cause of the increasing adhesion of self-adhesive tapes with time, since the adhesives used remain liquid. A consolidant or adhesive used in conservation should be given time to penetrate before it hardens. A low-viscosity liquid is obviously more likely to flow readily into the pores.

The liquid adhesives used in conservation have low surface energies, below 10^{-5} N/m. The hard solids such as dry glass or metals have much higher energies, 5×10^{-5} to 10^{-3} N/m, and are termed high-energy surfaces (Zisman, 1977). A low-energy liquid will spread and wet a high-energy solid. Therefore, initial wetting and adhesion is rarely a problem with these materials, provided the surface is free of contaminants. It is likely that the adhesive force in the majority of instances is derived from the physical attractive forces of dispersion, dipolar and hydrogen bonding described in section 3.2.

The wetting description above implies that a polymer in solution should spread easily over a flat surface, although it may need mechanical assistance and/or time to achieve a good coverage over a real object surface. There are two types of situation where this does not occur. The first is when the object surface has been contaminated by a layer of detergent, fatty acid or alcohol. These act like a layer of wax on the surface and so repel most solvents.

The other problem situation is the application of a polymer coating to an organic surface, e.g. a picture varnish over oil paint (Hulmer, 1976; Feller, 1983; Zisman, 1977). To ensure good wetting behaviour on these organic surfaces, the surface tension of the liquid must be slightly but not much higher than that of the substrate. Applying low-polarity solvents to oxidized paint films with relatively high polarity will not produce an even coverage.

4.2 Effects of setting properties on adhesion

The greatest change in property on setting is the transformation from a mobile liquid to a static solid. However, at some point in the setting process, the material is transformed into a gel, a solid swollen with liquid.

A cross-linking resin will form a gel part way through the reaction process. A material that sets by cooling can either precipitate crystals, e.g. wax, or form relatively stable intermolecular bonds, e.g. gelatine. A solution sets when the glass transition temperature rises through ambient temperature as the solvent evaporates (Section 2.3). An emulsion sets when the coalescence of the particles is initiated. All these processes involve a reduction in volume which is initially accommodated by liquid flow. At the gel point, the shape of the gel is fixed. Further shrinkage of the polymer mass cannot be accommodated by flow. Anything embedded in the polymer will be drawn in by the contracting mass. If the shrinkage is restrained by being attached to a substrate, the polymer will, in effect, be stretched by the amount it would otherwise have shrunk. This stretching can only be accomplished when the substrate applies a tensile force to the polymer. The stresses reduce the strength and durability of the adhesive bond.

The shrinkage and stress can be reduced by ensuring that the glass transition temperature of the polymer is around ambient temperature. Polystyrene films (T_g=95 °C) applied from solution may generate stresses up to 10.9 MPa, whereas poly(isobutyl methacrylate) (T_g=55 °C) will produce only 3.4 MPa (Croll, 1980a). The stresses may be eliminated entirely in a thermoplastic with a glass transition temperature at ambient temperature. When applying cross-linking resins, solvents or plasticizers should not be lost after gelation, otherwise large stresses will be generated (Croll, 1981). Damage to an object caused by shrinkage may not be noticed until the polymer is removed.

Polymers which set by chemical reaction may react not only within the components of prepolymer mixtures but also with the substrate. This occurs principally with prepolymers that are sensitive to water, such as isocyanates in polyurethanes and silanes. The chemical links can be deliberately created by using a reactive primer, e.g. a silane coupling agent. Many water-soluble polymers, e.g. poly(vinyl alcohol) and cellulose derivatives, may be expected to adhere more strongly and irreversibly because of the presence of reactive groups on degraded objects.

4.3 Deterioration of the joint

A join can fail in any or all of three distinct ways.

(a) The adhesive material itself may fail because of a weakness in the polymer mass, termed 'cohesive failure in the adhesive'. A brittle coating will tend to crack when applied to a surface that cannot respond to the stresses in the polymer. If the polymer has a low glass transition temperature, e.g. poly(vinyl acetate), flow will gradually allow a join to stretch and distort.

(b) The bond between the adhesive and the object may fail along the interface; this is termed 'adhesion failure'. Many initially good bonds between object and polymer, e.g. glass/epoxy, are affected by water. Adsorption of water from the environment results in the formation of a layer of water at the interface which displaces the adhesive (Wake, 1982).

(c) The object may break, leaving a small portion of the surface attached to the adhesive; this is termed 'cohesive failure in the substrate'. This is to be avoided but frequently occurs due to the inherent weakness of conserved objects.

The failure of a joint is usually caused by stresses in the adhesive and/or object. These may be generated during setting, by deterioration of the adhesive or substrate, or by movement in the joint.

Reversibility of a joint requires that the adhesion failure should be complete, but only when required. If a polymer is chemically bound to an object it is most unlikely that it will be removed without causing physical damage to the surface. A bond that is durable to weathering is probably irreversible.

4.3.1 Surface preparation

The previous discussion has assumed that the polymer has been applied to a clean dry surface. However, a clean surface is achieved with difficulty even in the most advanced industries of medicine and electronics. Common contaminants are oils, air pollutants and greases from the skin. Once a surface has been cleaned it should not be touched. Some contaminants, such as detergents, can form stable chemical bonds with the surface. Industrial methods of cleaning frequently involve removing the surface layer mechanically or with acid or alkaline solutions (Shields, 1984). A less destructive method of cleaning inorganic objects is to use an oxygen plasma (Daniels *et al.*, 1978). Washing with solvents is a more widely used method of cleaning. Solvents or water used for final rinsing must of course be free of oily impurities.

Water is a ubiquitous surface contaminant. Its presence can be reduced by working in warm and appropriately dry conditions. Water may be removed by employing solvents in the adhesive formulation that will dissolve water from the surface as the liquid front advances.

An improvement to the adhesive bond can be made using coupling agents, e.g. silanes. These react both with the substrate and with the applied adhesive. They are usually used to reduce (but will not eliminate) sensitivity to water of the adhesive bond.

5 Uses and requirements of applied polymers – a summary

The specific requirements of materials for conservation must be determined for each object. There are a number of general requirements that can be listed about the products and their usage. These requirements should be set aside only for good, explicit, reasons.

Stability

The following should not be used:

- products which contain plasticizers, e.g. cellulose nitrate adhesives
- polymers which deteriorate rapidly on ageing by yellowing or oxidation, e.g. poly(vinyl chloride), rubber
- thermoplastics which cross-link on ageing, e.g. poly(butyl methacrylate)

Reversibility

- The techniques for reversal should be made explicit during the initial conservation procedures.
- The application of thermoplastics is more likely to be reversible than that of cross-linking resins.
- The lowest practicable molecular weight polymer should be used.

Glass transition temperature

- Thermoplastics which are above or near their glass transition temperature at ambient temperatures, e.g. poly(vinyl acetate), should not be exposed to stress or dirt over the long term.
- Polymers with a glass transition temperature above c.65 °C should not be used.

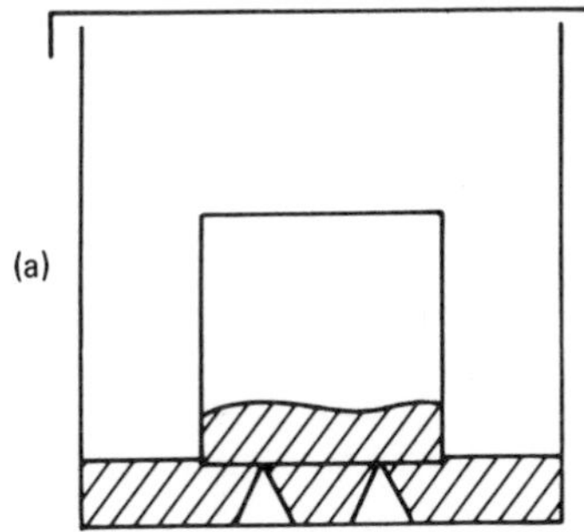

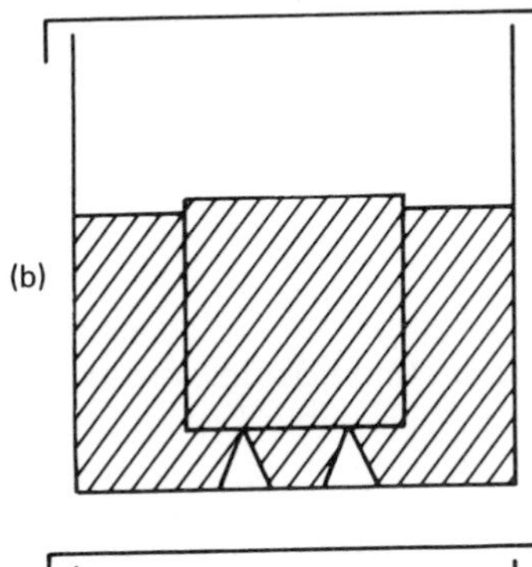

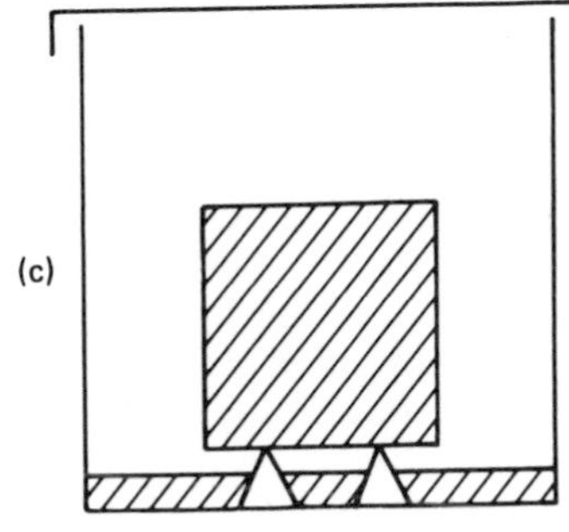

Figure 5.1 A guide to the application of consolidant to an object. If the application is carried out under vacuum, the container should be evacuated before the addition of the liquid consolidant. A cover should be placed over the container to prevent premature evaporation or reaction with atmospheric moisture. The object is lifted off the bottom of the container to reduce the possibility of air pockets. (a) A small amount of polymer in liquid form is added to start the penetration process. This liquid is drawn up into the porous material by capillary absorption. (b) The object is soaked in consolidant to allow time for trapped air to dissolve and the diffusion of the various components in the liquid to approach equilibrium. Any vacuum which has been applied is broken slowly and carefully to prevent sudden stresses being applied to the object. (c) Excess consolidant is allowed to drain out before the drying or setting takes place. This reduces excess consolidant and reduces the formation of a surface skin with solvent-applied polymers

Setting

- Maximum adhesion is obtained by using a low-viscosity liquid on a clean surface.
- Products that react with the object's surface should not be used, e.g. poly(vinyl alcohol), silicone rubbers.
- Products that set with a large amount of shrinkage should not be used, e.g. gelatine, methyl methacrylate polymerization.

Strength

- A product should be slightly weaker than the object to which it is applied.

Consolidation

Consolidation is irreversible, so only materials of proven stability should be used. The minimum amount of consolidant necessary should be incorporated in an object. It is wise to assume that an object weak enough to warrant consolidation is too weak to withstand attempts to remove the consolidant. Objects consolidated with products whose glass transition temperature is below ambient temperature will not be self-supporting. Distribution of the set consolidant in the object should be as uniform as possible to reduce stresses at interfaces (*Figure 5.1*).

Adhesion

An adhesive system should enable the object to be dismantled without damage. A thermoplastic adhesive should normally have a glass transition temperature above 40°C. Flexible thermoplastic adhesives (T_g below 15°C) should be used only where there is no long-term stress or risk of diffusion into porous materials. Cross-linked materials might be used in these circumstances. Temporary adhesives should conform to high standards of reversibility.

Adhesives frequently act as consolidants (*Figure 5.2*). These materials require higher standards of stability than most adhesives. It is often wise to use separate processes for consolidation and adhesion. Similarly, it may be wise to separate the functions of adhesive and gap filler. A two-stage process of a permanently soluble primer with a cross-linking adhesive may ensure reversibility for the process. The use of adhesion promoters such as coupling agents should be considered only in extreme conditions of use.

Adhesive bonds should act over a large area, so reducing point stress.

Coating

It should be expected that all coatings will be damaged and replaced periodically. High standards of reversibility are required. No semi-permanent coating should have a glass transition temperature below 40°C. Oil and wax coatings must be renewed as

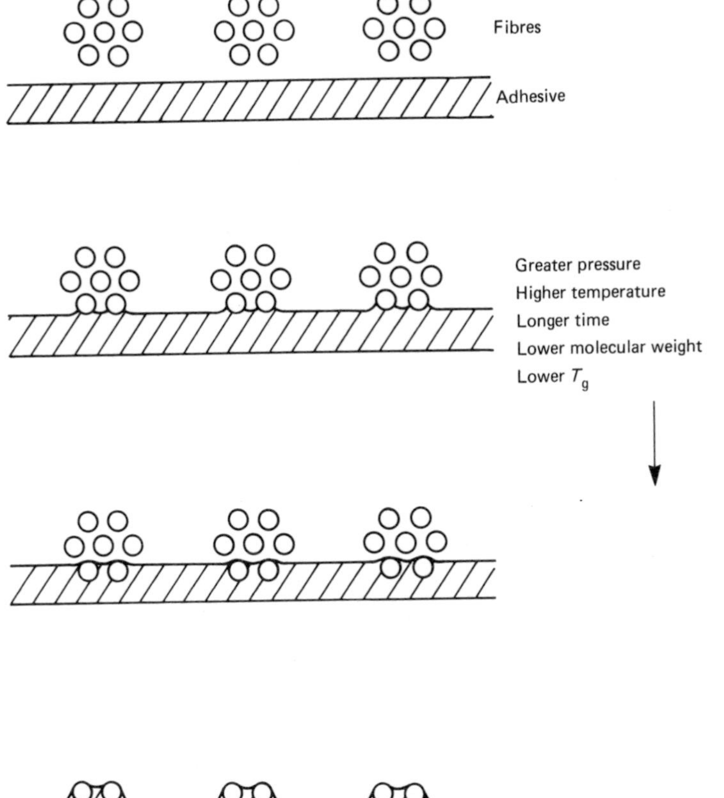

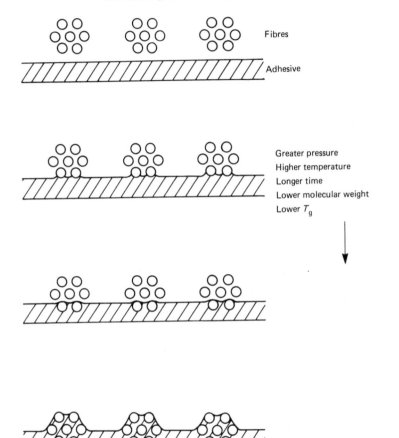

Figure 5.2 Development of an adhesive bond between a textile substrate and a high-viscosity liquid adhesive

they drain off or become dirty. Most complete coverage is ensured by multiple thin coats, preferably sprayed on. No polymeric coating can prevent diffusion of water vapour and other contaminants, though it may slow the rate considerably (Comyn, 1985).

For maximum saturation of a surface colour, the liquid should have a low viscosity and should set to a solid with a good match of refractive index with the surface. For minimum change of colour, the opposite applies even to the extent of using a gelling solution.

Table 5.1 Specifying a product for conservation

Necessary information	*Desirable information*	*Reasons*	*Example*
Product information			
Name of product, declared composition	Batch number, date of supply, independent evaluation, previous references	Product name should be used for referring to the material. Products can change and no untested assumptions should be made about composition	Paraloid B72 changed its formula without notice
Address of supplier/ manufacturer		Product names can differ across frontiers	Blanose (Europe) and Cellulose Gum (USA) are synonymous (Hercules)
	Pack sizes, price, shipping hazards	Some materials cannot be purchased in the small quantities used by conservators	
Properties of Product			
Properties of product as supplied	Solid/ solution/liquid prepolymers, viscosity	These properties, derived from the manufacturer's literature, indicate the limits of usefulness of the material	Epoxy resins are available in many grades, from pastes to thin liquids
Method of setting	How activated (UV, heat, mixing), proportions of components, setting time, shrinkage	Ditto	Silicone rubbers are available as 1 or 2 part, set in 5 minutes to 48 hours and shrink to 3 to 0.5%, depending on grade

Modification of product by conservator	Changing viscosity, pigmentation, de-airing	A material can frequently be adapted to suit its use better	Only a limited range of pigments is compatible with polyester resins
Special requirements	Shelf life, pretreatment of objects	The material may deteriorate before use or may require an unacceptable change to an object	Many PVAC emulsions have a shelf life of only 6 months
Hazards: toxicity, flammability	Precautions necessary	These data will alert the conservator to the dangers	Lacquering objects may produce toxic vapours
Properties of materials which have set			
Role of polymer	Adhesive/coating/consolidant/moulding material	A brief description of the tested conservation application is valuable	Cellulose acetate was rejected as a picture varnish
Physical properties	Tensile strength, hardness, extensibility, glass transition temperature	These data (derived from manufacturer's literature or practical experience) indicate the limits of use	PVAL coatings form strong films but have little adhesion to picture varnish
Optical properties	Colour, clarity, refractive index	The appearance of the object can be improved by educated choice of conservation material	Epoxy adhesives can be chosen to have a matching refractive index to the substrate
Modification when set	Polishing, coating, adhering	The use of a material may prejudice the next stage of treatment	A silicone release agent may prevent any further adhesion to the surface
Reversibility of treatments		All treatments involving added materials should be tested for reversibility before use	Wax impregnation of stone has been found to prevent further treatment

The glossiness of a coating can be adjusted by the spraying conditions or by adding transparent fillers.

Coatings may be used as carriers for chemicals which stabilize objects, e.g. corrosion inhibitors and ultraviolet absorbers.

Moulding

Any separating layers used during moulding should be treated as a temporary coating. Moulding materials should not react with the object nor should any oils be left on the object after removal of the mould. Moulding materials should normally be weaker than the object to reduce the risk of damage during demoulding. Materials with minimal shrinkage should be used.

Specifying a product for conservation

A product has many aspects, each of which may be relevant to its proposed use. The headings in Table 5.1 should be considered when choosing or recommending a product. Although the use of standard methods of reporting properties are most useful, even qualitative descriptions of the properties are more valuable than none at all.

Part II

Survey of Individual Polymers

6 Hydrocarbons

6.1 Polyethylene (PE) and paraffin wax

Background

Polyethylene (*Figure 6.1*), is made by polymerizing ethylene gas. Two main forms are made: a highly branched, low-density, polyethylene, LDPE, and a more uniform, high-density polyethylene, HDPE (Brydson, 1982). When the chains in PE are

```
   H   H
   |   |
 —C—C—
   |   |
   H   H
```

Figure 6.1 Monomer unit of polyethylene

highly regular, they can pack closely together to form crystals. These crystals form within the amorphous polymer mass. LDPE forms fewer and smaller crystals than HDPE. The latter is usually opaque because of light scattering by the crystals. Wax can be considered a low molecular version of PE, with two forms available. Most waxes are derived from fractions of crude oil (Mozes, 1982), though some very low molecular weight PEs are manufactured to fill the gap between petroleum waxes and LDPE. Waxes are found as minerals in rocks, either pure (ozokerite) or impure (ceresin). Microcrystalline wax is composed of mainly highly branched and irregular molecules. The straight-chain alkanes make up the bulk (>90%) of the 'paraffin waxes', defined here as being the straight-chain variety of wax. Paraffin waxes form large crystals when solid and are more brittle than the tougher microcrystalline waxes. A mixture of the two is stronger than either separately.

The physical properties of the polyethylenes depend on both the molecular weight and the crystallinity (*Figure 6.2,* Table 6.1). Petroleum jelly, wax swollen with oil, is a pasty grease at room temperature. On solidification, the paraffin waxes shrink to a greater extent (13–14% by volume) than do the microcrystalline

Table 6.1 Polyethylene properties (*see also* **Table 2.1**)

Material	*Molecular weight*[1]	*Melt flow index*[2]	*Branching*	n_D[3]	*Softening point* (°C)	*Typical products*
Petroleum jelly	450		High	1.43	45–60	Petrolatum, vaseline (*Astor*) (*BDH*)
Paraffin wax	300	2000	Very low	1.53	40–65	
Microcrystalline wax	600		Very high	1.45	55–85	Cosmolloid (*Astor*), Victory (*Petrolite*) (*Reed Wax*)
LDPE	24 000	20	Moderate	1.51	108	
HDPE	200 000	0.02	Very low	1.52	130	

Notes
(1) Approximate molecular weight (M_n).
(2) A measure of the ability to flow at 190 °C; lower molecular weights have higher values.
(3) Approximate refractive index at room temperature.

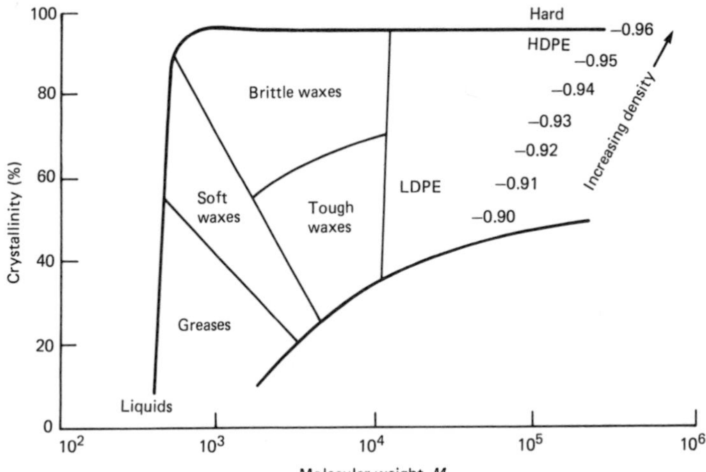

Figure 6.2 Correlation of properties of polyethylene with crystallinity and molecular weight. From R. F. Kratz and E. L. Lyle (1957), *Encyclopedia of Chemical Technology*, First Supplement, Interscience

waxes (9–10%) (Mozes, 1982). PE undergoes about 15% shrinkage on cooling from the molten state (Roff and Scott, 1971).

PE will not dissolve in solvents at room temperature but must be heated in order to melt the crystalline areas (Myers, 1954). The better solvents (tetrachloroethylene, trichloroethylene, methyl cyclohexane, tetrachloromethane) also cause significant swelling at room temperature, up to 40%. Wax is slightly soluble (up to 20%) at room temperature. PE and waxes are inert to aqueous chemicals and to many organic solvents. PE and waxes are subject to photo-oxidation, undergoing degradation, cross-linking, embrittlement and discoloration. PE has a low glass transition temperature and is subject to dirt pick-up.

Ethylene is used as the principal comonomer (c.80–60%) in poly(ethylene/vinyl acetate), EVA copolymers. The vinyl acetate (VAC) component reduces crystallinity and increases flexibility (T_g below 0°C). It also increases the solubility (Appendix 3.3). The presence of VAC in the copolymer reduces the cross-linking tendency under ultraviolet ageing until at 25% VAC this reaction is negligible (Feller and Curran, 1970).

Conservation

Petroleum jelly has been added to organic materials (e.g. leather) to impart flexibility (Leechman, 1931; Yusupova, 1979). The more fluid portions of the jelly are likely to migrate out of the object. Petroleum jelly is very tacky and will hold dirt readily.

Paraffin wax has been used for 100 years as a consolidant for corroded iron (Salzer, 1887; Plenderleith, 1956), later modified with microcrystalline wax (Organ and Shorer, 1962) and graphite (Western, 1972). Wax is not an efficient water vapour barrier (Stevens and Johnson, 1952) for corrosion protection (Keene, 1984). Wax has been used as a consolidant for ivory (Lowe, 1910), wood (Petrie, 1904; Packard, 1971), textiles (Newell, 1933), zoological specimens (Noble and Jaeckle, 1926) corroded copper alloy (Fink, 1933), and frescoes and stonework (Heaton, 1921). Unfortunately the impregnated wax can rarely be removed and prevents the application of other materials for conservation (Johnson, 1984; Berger and Zelinger, 1975; Ashley-Smith, 1978). This use has been largely abandoned except on lead.

Paraffin wax was frequently used as a lifting material on archaeological sites (Droop, 1915) by pouring the molten liquid over objects. Wax has been used for temporary protection for fugitive pigments on paper during aqueous treatments. Advantage is taken of the inertness of wax in moulding. Wax polish provides a very good release agent for most resins.

A mixture of microcrystalline and paraffin waxes made up as a paste in hydrocarbon solvent has been recommended as a polish (Plenderleith and Werner, 1971) (Renaissance Wax) (*Picreator*).

100 g Cosmolloid 80H (microcrystalline wax) (*Astor*)
25 g Wax A (a PE wax) (*BASF*)
Melted together and poured into 300 ml of a high flash point hydrocarbon solvent, stirred constantly until cool.

A harder coating (Larson, 1979) can be made by heating together

90 g Cosmolloid 80H (*Astor*)
30 g Ketone Resin N (*BASF*)
200 ml a high flash point hydrocarbon solvent
This is stirred while cooling with further additions of white spirit to produce a suitable brushing consistency.

The insolubility of microcrystalline wax in cool solvents enables its use as a matting agent in varnishes (De Witte, 1975b). The wax must be dispersed in the varnish by heating the solution. If the varnish has to be removed later, the wax may remain in the object.

Polyethylene was introduced in the 1950s as a moisture vapour barrier for panel paintings (Werner, 1952). PE film was later used for laminating paper by heating and melting the polymer under pressure (Belen'kaya and Strel'sova). A relatively low molecular weight LDPE would be required to ensure good flow and adhesion at moderate temperature (120°C). The polymer may be dissolved in hot (70°C) hydrocarbon or chlorinated solvent (Dadic and Ribkin, 1970). A small amount of surface pigment is lost, presumably due to the shrinkage from the molten state during application and the swelling of the polymer by the solvent.

The major use of EVA polymers in conservation is as additives to hot melt adhesives. Elvax 150 (*Du Pont*) (VAC c.33%) and A-C Copolymer 400 (*Allied*) (VAC c.15%) form the bulk of Beva 371 (*Adam*) picture lining adhesive (Berger, 1976). Elvax 40 (VAC c.40%) has been suggested as a matting agent for varnishes (Hulmer, 1976).

6.2 Rubber

Background

The term 'rubber' can be used in many different senses. The word 'rubber' was first applied to the solid natural polymer which was found to erase pencil marks. Rubber may also mean the cross-linked material that is made by vulcanizing natural rubber, usually with sulphur. By extension the term has come to mean any material that exhibits rubbery properties. This section will deal only with the polyisoprene polymers (natural rubber), cross-linked derivatives (vulcanized rubber) and analogous synthetic polymers.

Natural rubber is contained in the latex obtained by tapping the bark of *Hevea braziliensis.* The rubber is predominantly cis-1,4-polyisoprene (*Figure 6.3,* Appendix 3.4). Polyisoprene has a very

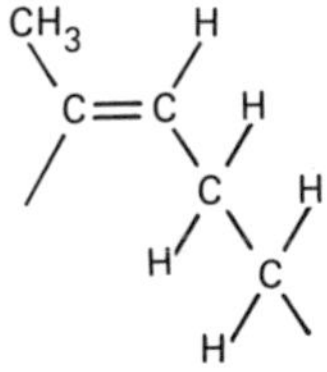

Figure 6.3 Monomer unit of cis-1,4-polyisoprene

low glass transition temperature, enabling it to flow at room temperature. The molecular weight can be reduced sufficiently to create the viscous liquids used in pressure-sensitive tapes. Polyisoprene is also produced by polymerizing isoprene catalytically.

Solid natural rubber has some elasticity, i.e. it will snap back if stretched and released. This rubbery property is highly developed when the chains are cross-linked. The amount of cross-linking is slight for a soft solid such as erasers. Use of larger quantities of sulphur increases the strength and rigidity. The vulcanized rubbers are insoluble in solvents but are swelled by some.

Commercial rubber latex is produced by concentrating the latex drawn from the tree, to 60% rubber, with ammonia added to prevent deterioration. The rubber is vulcanized while in the latex form. This will then dry to form an elastic and strong film.

The double bonds in the polymer create potential sites for rapid oxidation at room temperature. The molecular weight of an unvulcanized rubber will therefore fall rapidly. Vulcanized rubbers may become tacky or even pasty. Antioxidants are widely used to reduce the short-term susceptibility to oxidation. Rubber is especially sensitive to attack by ozone and to the catalytic effects of metal ions.

A material chemically similar to rubber is gutta percha, trans-1,4-polyisoprene, also obtained from a tree. However, the configuration of the molecule is different, leading to plastic, not elastic, properties.

Chlorinated rubber (Parker, 1967), e.g. Duroprene (*ICI*) (Appendix 3.5), is a saturated polymer. Although more stable than rubber, it is sensitive to light and ultraviolet, probably in a similar fashion to PVC, resulting in oxidation and discoloration. Chlorinated rubber can react with various pigments such as zinc oxide, copper salts, Prussian blue (ferric ferrocyanide) and ultramarine to form cross-links.

Conservation

Solutions of natural rubber were used during the 19th century as consolidants for iron corrosion products and textiles (Rathgen, 1905). They have been used as adhesives for paper (Weidner, 1967), textiles (Rice, 1972), facings on paintings (Curister and De Wild, 1939), pottery (Gedye, 1968) and as an isolator during the development of fossil bone (Toombs, 1948). Pressure-sensitive adhesives, based on degraded rubber and rosin derivatives, have been available since the 1920s. The low molecular weight resins migrate into porous substrates. These polymers are not stable and are not designed for long-term use. When a tape is pulled off an object, a small amount of adhesive remains on the object surface. These remnants can result in dirt pick-up or discoloration. Removal of old pressure-sensitive adhesives may require a range of solvents such as (Collins, 1983) denatured ethanol, acetone, 1,1,1-trichloroethane, toluene, and aliphatic hydrocarbon solvent.

If these fail, a mixture of 5 ml 1,1,1-trichloroethane, 5 ml of acetone, 1 ml of 0.88 ammonia solution and 10 ml of ethanol may be successful. Rubber is too unstable for application to objects in conservation.

The sulphur and other vapours given off by vulcanized rubber can cause severe staining (Cooper, 1939) and corrosion of nearby objects (Oddy, 1975a).

Vulcanized rubber is used during cleaning to remove dirt particles from objects. It may be used either as a solid block or as a powder. The soiled powder is removed by brushing or lightly applied compressed air. Being tacky, the very small particles are held in fibrous material. Over time and exposure to light, the powder adheres to itself, forming a film, yellowing slightly at the same time. The rubber is almost totally insoluble in solvents. The sulphur components will discolour brass.

Rubber latex has been widely used since the 1930s as a moulding material (Watkinson, 1982; Schollenberger *et al.,* 1969). The prevulcanized latex is applied to the object, allowed to dry to a film and peeled off the surface. The latex will shrink by c.8% on drying unhindered. The latex, containing ammonia, will react with many metals and alkali-sensitive objects. Rubber latex sheet, when dry, will stick to itself and requires a separator of talc or similar to prevent this. Rubber moulds deteriorate very quickly in light and air, becoming weak and brittle within a couple of months. Gutta percha has been used to make moulds as an impression material (Nimmo and Prescott, 1968).

Chlorinated rubber was introduced as a lacquer for iron, sometimes with graphite added (Scott, 1933), and as a general consolidant for organic materials (Leechman, 1931). Although its susceptibility to deterioration was pointed out in 1931 (Anon, 1931), it continued in use into the 1950s on geological material (Tornesite) (Franklin-Ewing, 1950).

7 Vinyl acetate derived polymers

7.1 Poly(vinyl acetate) PVAC

7.1.1 PVAC homopolymers

Background

PVAC (*Figure 7.1*) is prepared by all of the free-radical polymerization methods: bulk, solution, suspension or emulsion. The polymer is usually slightly branched (Billmeyer, 1971). PVAC homopolymers are available with a wide range of molecular weights (Table 7.1). The glass transition temperature of PVAC is around room temperature, contributing to its toughness and adhesiveness but also to dirt pick-up and cold flow over long periods (Section 2.2). Although pure alcohols are non-solvents (Appendix 3.6), the addition of small amounts of water may convert them to solvents. PVAC is swollen by water, becoming opaque white but reverting to a clear film on drying. Of all the polymers available to conservators, PVAC has been shown to be one of the most stable to light ageing (Thomson, 1963). Although PVAC suffers oxidation and other minor changes, it does not appreciably cross-link or degrade in air (David *et al.*, 1970). PVAC has been shown to be dissolvable from objects after more than 30–40 years (Cronyn and Horie, 1985). PVAC is incompatible with methacrylates in solution (*Figure 3.8*).

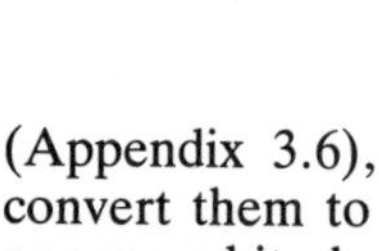

Figure 7.1 Monomer unit of poly(vinyl acetate)

Table 7.1 Commercial poly(vinyl acetate) grades

Trade name	*Manufacturer*	*Grade designations*										
Mowilith	Hoechst		20	25	30	40		50	60	70		
PVAC resins	Cairn	S1½	S2½			S7	S12		S27		S88	
Rhodopas	Rhone-Poulenc	BB	B		30				H	HH	HV1	
Vinac						B-7		B-15	B-25		B-100	B-800
Vinylite[1]	Union Carbide	AYAC				AYAA		AYAF	AYAT			
$10^{-3} M_w$[2]		12.8				83		113	c.167			
Viscosity grade[3]		1.5	2.5		4	7	12	15	25	60	100	800
T_g(°C)[4]		16	17			21		24	26	27	28	29

Notes
(1) Name is no longer current.
(2) Weight average molecular weight.
(3) Viscosity of an 8.6% solution of the polymer in benzene.
(4) Approximate glass transition temperature.

Conservation

The first report of PVAC in conservation was in 1932 as a facing and attaching adhesive for the transfer of a fresco (Stout and Gettens, 1932). The grade of PVAC used was Vinylite A, precursor to AYAF (*Union Carbide*) (Feller, 1971d). PVAC was soon used on frescoes, on wallpaper, on pottery as a glaze, and as lining adhesive for painting (Gettens, 1935) and bone (Woodbury, 1936). Use of PVAC has been extended to most aspects of conservation (Plenderleith, 1956) and was proposed as a picture varnish (Stout and Cross, 1937). PVAC, either as a varnish or as a medium for restoration in paintings, should be overcoated by varnishes of methacrylate polymers (Feller, 1983).

7.1.2 Dispersions

Background

Vinyl acetate monomer lends itself to copolymerization and is used as a minor component in the ethylene/vinyl acetate, EVA, copolymers. Many copolymers are used in the form of dispersions. Dispersions of PVAC homopolymer require relatively high temperatures for good film formation; minimum film-formation temperature (MFFT) is c.20°C. Most current formulations are therefore copolymers with a glass transition temperature and MFFT below 5°C (Table 7.2). Products once used in conservation had plasticizers incorporated. These plasticizers are likely to be lost within a few decades (Barrow, 1965). PVAC dispersions are particularly unstable in storage, releasing acetic acid which can react with objects (Oddy, 1975a; Feast, 1982). Stocks should be kept in cool conditions and be discarded when too old, typically six months after production. The film cast from the dispersion will not be soluble in water, though some formulations will disintegrate on soaking (Bradley *et al.*, 1983). The molecular weight and cross-linking can be varied considerably during manufacture, but details are rarely available from the manufacturer. Yellowing of the cast film occurs far more rapidly than would occur with non-dispersion polymers, because of the relatively unstable emulsifiers used (Howells *et al.*, 1984). The stability of the cast film was reportedly increased by adding a calcium carbonate/acetate buffer (Barrow, 1965) though later work did not confirm the value of a buffer. Few intensive investigations of PVAC dispersions designed for conservation purposes have been carried out. No sets of guidelines in the formulation of conservation products have emerged.

Table 7.2 Some poly(vinyl acetate) emulsions used in conservation

Product	*Manufacturer*	*Declared comonomers*[1]	*Solids content*	*Particle size* (μm)	*Viscosity* (mPa.s)	*pH*	*MFFT*[2] (°C)	T_g (°C) *(brittle point)*[3]	*% soluble in solvents*	*Stabilizing emulsifier*
Vinamul 3250	Vinyl products	Ethylene	55	1–2	14 000	4.5–5	3	(5)	90	PVAL
Vinamul 6515		15% Vcaprate	56	1–2	100	4–4.5	9	(10)	>95	
Vinamul 6525		25% Vcaprate	56	1–2	200	4–4.5	4	(5)		PVAL
Vinamul 6815		15% 2-EHA	55	0.5	300	4.5–5.0	10	(10)	>95	PVAL
Vinamul 8100		None	55		40	6.2	0			
Vinamul 9146		20% DBP	55	1–2	2000	4–4.5	1			
Vinamul 9910		10% DBP	53	1–2	6000	4.5–5.0	4			
Mowilith DMC2	Hoechst	35% dibutyl maleate	55		8000	4.5	10	10		Cellulose ether
Mowilith DM5		35% BA	53	0.2	3500	4–5	3	2		
Mowilith DM22		(4)	50	0.1–1.5	8000	4–5	0	–5		
Mowilith DM155		Ethylene	55	1.3	6000	5	0	10		
Mowilith D50		None	50	0.5–5	25 000	3.5	16	29		PVAL
Flexbond 800		Dibutyl maleate	53	0.7	70	5–6				
Elvace 1874		Ethylene	55	0.2–11	400	5				
Jade 834-403N	Aabbitt	Ethylene	50	6–7						

Notes
(1) Balance of monomer VAC, Vcaprate = vinyl caprate, 2-EHA = 2-ethyl hexyl acrylate, BA = butyl acrylate; DBP (dibutyl phthalate) and dibutyl maleate are plasticizers.
(2) Minimum film-formation temperature.
(3) Glass transition temperature; brittle point is the lowest temperature the film will crack on bending.
(4) Comonomers are vinyl fatty acid ester and acrylate ester.

Conservation

Dispersions of PVAC became widely available in the later 1940s (Corey *et al.*, 1977). By the early 1950s they were proposed as adhesives, plasticized by dibutyl phthalate, for relining paintings (Werner, 1952) and were used occasionally later (Werner, 1968a; King, 1976). Dispersions became widely used for textile and paper conservation. Vinamul 6525 (*Vinyl Products*) was proposed as a heat-set adhesive for attaching fragile textiles to supports (Beecher, 1959, 1963). It was probably too widely used, judging by the difficulties encountered during the re-conservation of objects made necessary by severe changes in flexibility, colour and dirt pick-up. The polymer should be removable, if it remains soluble, by soaking in an ethanol/water mixture (Blum, 1983). PVAC dispersions were investigated for conservation use in the 1960s (Barrow, 1965). The conclusion was that better materials would be needed for long-term use in conservation (Baer *et al.*, 1976). This is confirmed by the regret expressed for the use of PVAC dispersions on globes (Baynes-Cope, 1975).

An emulsion of PVAC formed by mixing a toluene solution of PVAC with a water detergent solution was suggested for consolidating waterlogged archaeological materials (Unwin, 1951). Commercial dispersions have been used to consolidate wet and dry bones from both archaeological (Werner, 1968b) and geological contexts (Rixon, 1976).

7.2 Poly(vinyl alcohol) PVAL

Background (Finch, 1973; Molyneux, 1983)

PVAL (*Figure 7.2*) cannot be made from its nominal monomer, vinyl alcohol, which is not stable. Instead the acetate groups are removed from PVAC and replaced by hydroxyl groups by a process of alcoholysis, similar to hydrolysis but using alcohol instead of water. The reaction need not go to completion. There is thus a choice in the amount of acetate groups left on the molecule, creating what may be thought of as a copolymer between 'vinyl

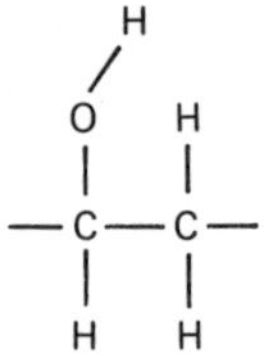

```
   H
  /
 O    H
 |    |
—C————C—
 |    |
 H    H
```

Figure 7.2 Monomer unit of poly(vinyl alcohol) homopolymer. Most polymers are effectively copolymers of vinyl alcohol and vinyl acetate monomer units

alcohol' and 'vinyl acetate'. The proportion of alcohol groups in commercial polymers can be nearly 100% – 'fully hydrolysed' grades – or down to 70%. Various methods are used to describe the alcohol content (Table 7.3). The molar degree of hydrolysis

Table 7.3 Different measures of -OH content in poly(vinyl alcohol)

Hydrolysis mole %[(1)]	*Ester index*[(2)]	*Residual acetate weight % PVAC*[(3)]
100	0	0
98	13	1.9
92	95	14.5
86	157	24.1
81	205	31.4
78	232	35.5
72	281	43.2

Notes
(1) Number percentage of hydroxyl groups formed in the molecule.
(2) The weight, in mg, of potassium hydroxide necessary for complete saponification of 1 g of polymer.
(3) The weight percentage of the vinyl acetate component of the molecule.

will be used here for identification of the polymer type (*Figure 7.3*). PVAL chains pack closely together through the hydroxyl groups along the chain. PVAL with a degree of hydrolysis of c.93% will only dissolve in hot water and, on cooling and standing, will form either a gel or a precipitate. Between 90% and 85% hydrolysis the polymer is most stable in cold and hot water. With less than 80% hydrolysis the polymer will dissolve in cold water only. PVAL has few organic solvents at room temperature. In aqueous solutions PVAL has a pH of 4.5–7 and lowers the surface tension. The tensile strength is greatest with fully hydrolysed material. Oxygen and carbon dioxide permeate at a low rate through PVAL films. Although attempts have been made to utilize this property, the lack of adhesion to most organic coatings has prevented practical applications (Feller, 1983). Films formed when drying from a solution will shrink if the PVAL is a grade which forms a gel at room temperature.

Pure PVAL has been shown to be very stable to ultraviolet/oxygen ageing, undergoing fairly slow chain scission (Ciabach, 1983). It may become insoluble by the formation of ether cross-links on light ageing (Thomson, 1963) or heating. The hydroxyl groups are extremely reactive. In slightly acid or alkaline conditions the chains will cross-link and become insoluble (Billmeyer, 1971). It will react with polyaldehydes or polyacids to form insoluble complexes. It will also react with many inorganic

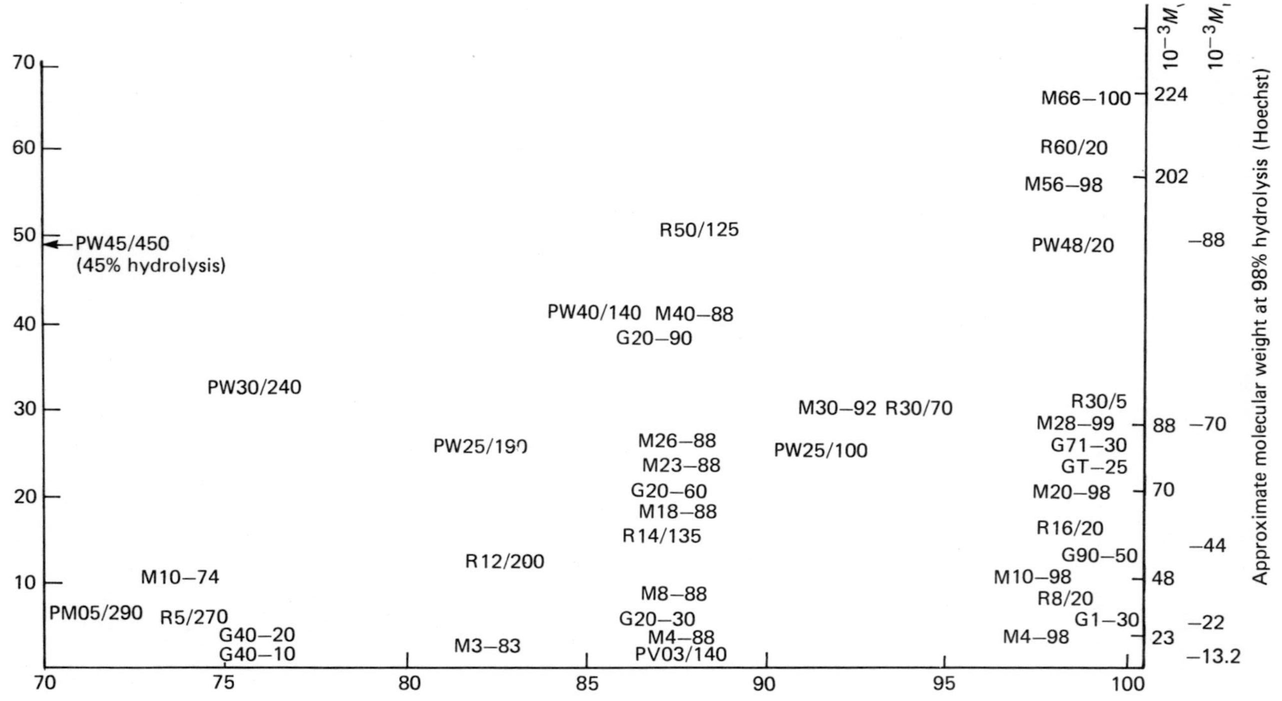

Figure 7.3 Some commercial poly(vinyl alcohol)s after Toyoshima (1973a). E – Elvanol (*DuPont*), G – Gelvatol (*Monsanto*), M – Mowiol (*Hoechst*), R – Rhodoviol (*Rhône–Poulenc*), P – Polyviol (*Wacker*). From manufacturer's information; other grades available

salts and some dyes, becoming insoluble, especially on exposure to light (Corey *et al.*, 1977). These cross-linking habits probably account for the insolubility of films formed from PVAL-stabilized poly(vinyl acetate) emulsions. PVAL is hygroscopic and will absorb water vapour, particularly above 75% relative humidity.

Conservation (De Witte, 1976/7)

The first reports of PVAL use in conservation were in the early 1950s for textiles, as a size (Takakage, 1951) and heat-seal adhesive (Sieders *et al.*, 1956), and as an adhesive for parchment (Gairola, 1958–60). By the early 1960s doubts were expressed about the solubility of PVAL which had been applied, particularly to textiles (Geijer, 1961; Thomson, 1963). It is wise to assume that these treatments are irreversible. PVAL continues to be used as a consolidant for textiles and as a heat-seal adhesive for paper (Griebenow *et al.*, 1982), e.g. Lamatec (*Archival Aids*). Many of the PVALs that have been used in conservation were fully hydrolysed. Redissolving the polymers will involve washing in changes of hot (c.93°C) water (Modi, 1980). Advantage has been taken of the chemical cross-linking. PVAL has been shown to increase the strength of paper considerably when added to the paper as a size (Blank, 1978). The conditions of accelerated ageing lead to cross-linking. PVAL fibres mixed with cellulose fibres have been used in a pulp for strengthening degraded paper (Nyuksha *et al.*, 1975). Neither the cellulose nor PVAL fibres would be removable.

PVAL has been widely used for the fixing of pigments (Savko, 1971; Iwasaki, 1974) and for inpainting (Falwey, 1981). Shrinkage of the drying film on paintings on paper resulted in the curling up and exfoliation of the pigments to which a PVAL/agar–agar consolidant had been applied (Chemical Section, 1968). Reversal of the treatment involved removal of the bulk of the surface coating, facing, and re-adhering the flakes. PVAL will cross-link with many metallic salts, some of which are used as pigments.

PVAL is used widely in industry and in conservation as a release agent during casting and moulding (Wihr, 1968).

7.3 Poly(vinyl acetal)

Background

Poly(vinyl acetals), PVacetal (*Figure 7.4*), are manufactured by reacting PVAL with an aldehyde. The resultant PVacetal is

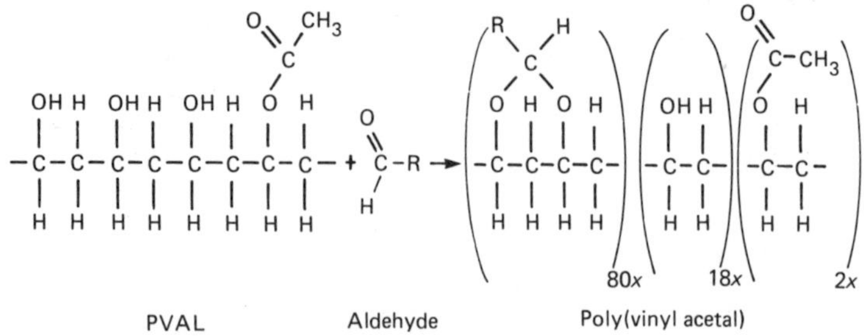

R = –H i.e. poly(vinyl formal)
R = $-CH_3$ i.e. poly(vinyl acetal)
R = $-CH_2-CH_2CH_3$ i.e. poly(vinyl butyral)

Figure 7.4 Structure of poly(vinyl acetal)s with typical proportions of components

essentially a terpolymer of 'vinyl acetal', 'vinyl alcohol' and 'vinyl acetate' monomers. Poly(vinyl butyral), PVB, the most widely used of these polymers in conservation, is available in various molecular weights and proportions of the –OH groups remaining (Table 7.4). PVB with a high proportion of hydroxyl groups (17–21% molar) is soluble in solvents only with a considerable hydrogen bonding capability (Appendix 3.7). Low hydroxyl PVB (9–13%) is soluble in a wider range of solvents and has a lower glass transition temperature. Viscosity of PVB solutions is reduced by using mixed solvents, e.g. 60% ethanol:40% toluene. Difficulties have been found with adhesion of the higher hydroxyl PVB (Howie, 1984), perhaps due to the high glass transition temperature.

PVacetals can be cross-linked by traces of acids and heat (Cohen *et al.*, 1958) and other chemicals such as dialdehydes (Lavin and Snelgrove, 1977). Heat ageing tests (100°C for 14 days) have shown that the solubility of the polymers may be affected. Of the two types tested, Mowital B30H and Rhovinal B10-20, the Rhovinal appeared less suitable as it yellowed, became slightly brittle and lost solubility (Blackshaw and Ward, 1983). Exposure to ultraviolet in air of PVB causes some oxidation (Thomson, 1963). Considerable cross-linking with some degradation leads to an insoluble network under extreme conditions (Ciabach, 1983).

Conservation

Poly(vinyl formal) PVformal was tried as a consolidant for textiles (Geijer, 1961; Leene, 1963) but could not be redissolved.

Table 7.4 Commercial poly(vinyl butyral)s (manufacturers' data)

		Weight proportions of				
Product	*Manufacturer*	*Vbutyral*	*VAL*(1)	*Molecular weight,* M_w	*Solution viscosity* (mPa.s)(2)	*Tg* (°C)
Butvar B-73	Monsanto	80	19	50 000–80 000	87	62–68
Butvar B-74		80	19	100 000–150 000	140	62–68
Butvar B-76		88	11	45 000–55 000	45	48–55
Butvar B-79		88	11	34 000–38 000	25	48–55
Butvar B-90		80	19	38 000–45 000	59	62–68
Butvar B-98		80	19	30 000–34 000	25	62–68
Mowital B20H	Hoechst	76	20		14	
Mowital B30H		76	20		25	
Mowital B30T		70	26		25	
Mowital B60H		77	20		65	
Mowital B60HH		83	14		60	
Rhovinal B 7/20	Rhône-Poulenc	77	19		16	
Rhovinal B 10/20		77	19	30 000–35 000	29	
Rhovinal B 20/20		77	19	ca.55 000	54	
Rhovinal B 50/20		77	19	150 000	140	

Notes
(1) VAL = vinyl alcohol component; vinyl acetate content about 0.5–2.5%. Balance made up in volatiles.
(2) Viscosity of a 5% solution of the polymer in *n*-butanol.

PVacetal itself was used from the 1930s (Woodbury, 1936) to the 1960s (Howie, 1984) for the conservation of geological bone and ivory (Gyermek, 1964). It was replaced in the 1960s by PVB.

PVB has been widely used as a consolidant for textiles (Mowital B60HH) (Leene, 1972), Mowital BH10 (Lodewijks and Leene, 1972), fossils (Butvar B98 and B76) (Howie, 1984), wood (Butvar B90) (Barclay, 1981) and paper (Belen'kaya, no date), and as an adhesive for wood (Mowital B20H) (Cronyn and Horie, 1985), glass (Mowital B60HH) (Vos-Davidse, 1969) and paint films (Kostrov, 1956; Higuchi, 1980). A modelling material (AJK dough) was based originally on poly(vinyl acetal) (Alvar) (Gedye, 1968), later replaced by PVB (Butvar B98) (Patterson, 1978). This kneadable paste is prepared from an emulsion of water in a resin solution to which was added kaolin and jute flock. This models well and produces a strong, lightweight, material. Unfortunately the dough undergoes short- and long-term shrinkage on drying, presumably through the loss of solvent and water.

8 Acrylic resins

Background

Acrylate and methacrylate polymers (Luskin, 1970) The majority of acrylic polymers used in conservation are made from two families of monomers (*Figure 8.1*); the acrylates, derived from acrylic acid, and the methacrylates, derived from methacrylic acid.

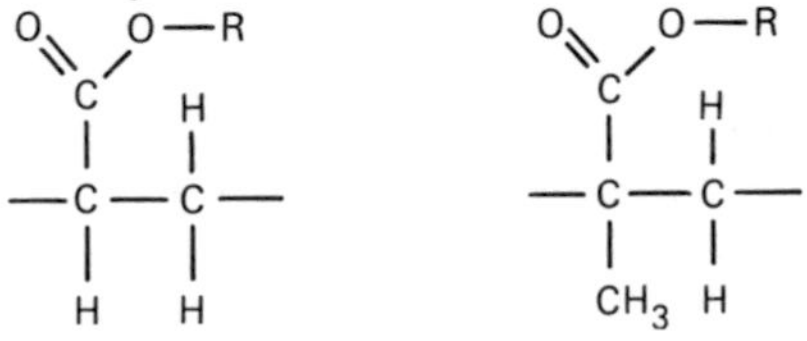

$$-\underset{H}{\overset{C(=O)OR}{C}}-\underset{H}{\overset{H}{C}}- \qquad -\underset{CH_3}{\overset{C(=O)OR}{C}}-\underset{H}{\overset{H}{C}}-$$

Poly(alkyl acrylate) Poly(alkyl methacrylate)

Figure 8.1 Acrylic polymers, monomer units. The alkyl (—R) group can be chosen to produce a range of polymers (Table 11.1)

In addition, two other monomer groups appear in conservation materials, acrylonitrile (the comonomer in vinylidene chloride polymers) and the cyanoacrylates. Abbreviations are used in discussion of the various polymers (Table 8.1). The glass transition temperatures (T_g) of the homopolymers are highest when the side chain is shortest and the T_g of a methacrylate polymer is higher than its acrylate counterpart. It is relatively easy to make copolymers with a chosen T_g by using two or more acrylic monomers (Luskin, 1970). The polymerization of acrylic monomers results in shrinkage, c.20% by volume in the case of MMA. Heat is also generated, c.60 kJ/mole for methacrylate and 79 kJ/mole for acrylate polymerizations.

PMMA is extremely stable to degradation by heat and oxygen/ultraviolet ageing. However, the higher methacrylate polymers cross-link under ultraviolet exposure (Feller *et al.*, 1981; Morimoto and Suzuki, 1972). The cross-linking under light appears to occur through reactions on the side chains (Feller,

Table 8.1 Acrylic homopolymer properties and abbreviations[1]

Side chain radical	Acrylate polymer			Methacrylate polymer		
	Abbreviation	T_g (°C)	n_D (25 °C)	*Abbreviation*	T_g (°C)	n_D (25 °C)
$-CH_3$ (methyl)	PMA	8	1.479	PMMA	105	1.489
$-C_2H_5$ (ethyl)	PEA	–22	1.464	PEMA	65	1.484
$-(CH_2)3CH_3$ (*n*-butyl)	PnBA	–54	1.474	PnBMA	20	1.483
$-CH(CH_3)C_2H_5$ (isobutyl)	PiBA			PiBMA	50	
$-CH_2CH(C_2H_5)(CH_2)_3CH_3$ (2-ethylhexyl)	P2EHA	–55				
$-C_6H_5$ (phenyl)	PPha					
-H (acid)	PAA			PMAA		

Notes
(1) Abbreviations for copolymers are expressed as in P(MMA/EA) for a copolymer of methyl methacrylate (major component) and ethyl acrylate.

1971a) by an oxidation mechanism (Feller, 1976b). The methacrylates are more likely to cross-link if they are exposed above or near their glass transition temperatures. In PEMA the chain scissioning reactions predominate at room temperature but higher methacrylates form insoluble gels. The acrylates all cross-link on ultraviolet exposure (Morimoto and Suzuki, 1972). In copolymers of acrylates with methacrylates, the formation of a gel depends on the proportion of the monomer groups and the temperature of exposure with respect to the glass transition temperatures of the polymer (Grassie, 1982). It is possible to construct copolymers with the required physical properties and with the desired balance of scissioning/cross-linking behaviour. Oxygen is incorporated into the polymer leading to an increase in the polarity of the solvents required for dissolution (Feller, 1963).

Acrylic lacquers have poor solvent release from touch-dry films (Gaynes, 1967) and retain solvents for considerable times. Toluene has been shown to be held very strongly – for much longer than two months in films of Paraloid B72. By contrast, *p*-xylene evaporates more slowly during the initial wet stage of drying but leaves freely during the later stages (Dauchot-Dehon and De Witte, 1978). This was ascribed to the difference in polarity of the solvents.

Commercial reaction adhesives Cyanocrylate polymers (*Figure 8.2*) are polymerized *in situ* from monomers. The reaction is

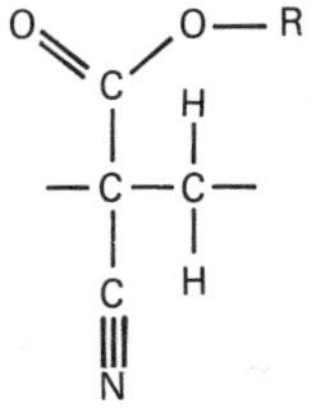

Poly(alkyl cyanoacrylate)

Figure 8.2 Cyanoacrylate monomer unit. The alkyl (—R) group can be varied to modify the polymer properties. R may be methyl, ethyl or butyl

initiated in the film of moisture on the surface. It is thus dependent on the nature of the surface and the relative humidity of the air. Commercial products contain plasticizers or soft polymers, stabilizers to prevent premature polymerization and thickeners to stop the liquid draining out of the joint before setting. Very high molecular weight polymers are formed during setting. These can be dissolved with difficulty in dimethyl formamide or nitromethane (Coover and Wicker, 1964). Soaking in acetone will often break down the joint (Davison, 1978) although prolonged immersion is usually required. Cyanoacrylate adhesives appear to lose strength on prolonged light exposure (A. Moncrieff, personal communication). Cyanoacrylates degrade severely in alkaline conditions by hydrolysis (Leonard *et al.*, 1966).

Many acrylic derivatives are used as prepolymers in thermosetting adhesives. Typical prepolymers are formed by reaction with glycols or isocyanates (*Figure 8.3*). These materials polyme-

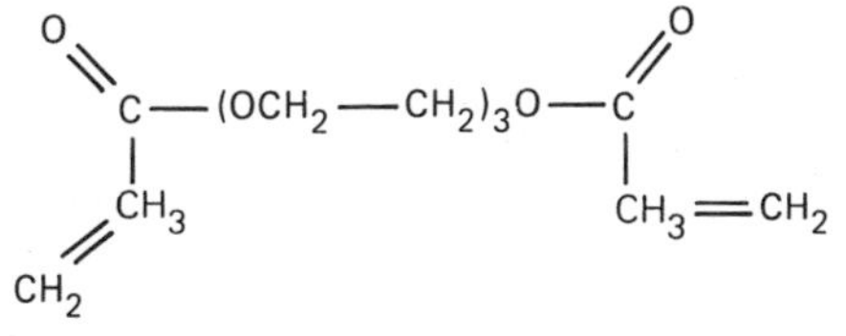

Triethylene glycol dimethacrylate (Martin, 1977)

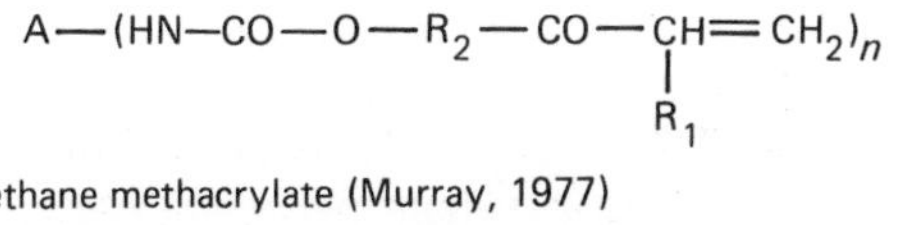

Urethane methacrylate (Murray, 1977)

A = polyisocyanate, e.g. diphenylmethane–4, 4′–diisocyanate

$R_1 = H, CH_3$

$R_2 = -C_2H_4-, -C_2H_4(CH_3)-$

Figure 8.3 Examples of monomers used in acrylic reaction adhesives, e.g. anaerobic and ultraviolet curing types rize to form highly cross-linked structures that will not swell appreciably in solvents. The products can be formulated to set when initiated in the absence of oxygen (anaerobic adhesives), by an activator applied to one surface or by ultraviolet radiation. The few ultraviolet curing adhesives that have been tested for light stability have yellowed and lost adhesion (A. Moncrieff, personal communication).

Conservation

Acrylic polymers: solid or in solution (Table 8.2) During the early 1930s acrylic polymers, Lucite 44 and 45 (now Elvacite 2044 and 2045 (Feller, 1959)) started to be used as picture varnishes (Feller, 1971a). These PBMA polymers were increasingly used for varnishes but about 20 years' experience was gained before this use was published (Werner, 1952; Rawlins and Werner, 1949; Feller, 1971a). PBMA has the advantages of resistance to yellowing, solubility in hydrocarbon solvents (Appendix 3.10), and sufficient flexibility, yet (in the case of PiBMA) a glass transition temperature that will prevent dirt pick-up, and it is commercially available in relatively low molecular weights. Unfortunately PBMA was shown to be unsuitable for long-term use because of the unexpected cross-linking of the polymer under the influence of light (Feller, 1971b). After 22 years' exposure on a laboratory wall, it became about 50% insoluble (Feller, 1971a) and required more polar solvents for removal.

The failure of an apparently excellent material prompted a search for more stable polymers. Paraloid B-72 does not become insoluble or degrade significantly in normal conditions of exposure (Feller, 1978), although oxidation and other changes do occur slowly (Ciabach, 1983). It has therefore become a standard of stability, a Feller Class A material. Although Paraloid B-72 was reported to be a P(MMA/EA) (Feller, 1976a), it has been shown to be P(EMA/MA) with a molar ratio of 70:30 (De Witte *et al.*, 1978). A previous version (ratio 68:32) had a lower molecular weight and was soluble in slightly less polar solvents.

Formulations of Paraloid B-72 with various solvents and matting agents have been suggested. Toluene or xylene are usually the major components (Hulmer, 1976), *p*-xylene probably being the best choice (Dauchot-Dehon and De Witte, 1978). Solutions for picture varnishes are around 20% solids for brushing and 10% for spraying. Matting agents include microcrystalline wax (up to 47% of total solids), aerosol silica (up to 18% of total solids) or ethylene/vinyl acetate polymers, e.g. Elvax 40 W (*Du Pont*) (up to

Table 8.2 Properties of commercial acrylic resins used in conservation[1]

Product	*Manufacturer*	*Monomer composition*	T_g (°C)	*Molecular weight*	*Solubility chart* (appendix 3)	*Comments*
Paraloid B-44	Rohm & Haas	MMA/?	60		A3.11	Used in Incralac (Mander Domolac)
B-67		(iBMA)	50		A3.12	Contains stabilizer
B-72		(EMA/MA 70/30)	40		A3.13	
Elvacite 2043	Du Pont	EMA/?	65	Low	A3.9	
2044		nBMA	15	High	A3.10	Once known as Lucite 44
2045		iBMA	55	High	A3.10	Once known as Lucite 45
2046		nBMA/iBMA 50/50	35	High	A3.10	
Plexigum P24	Röhm	iBMA		Medium		
P26		iBMA		Medium		
M345		MMA		Medium		
Plexisol P550		nBMA/?		Low		
B782						
Pliantex		EA				Waterer (1973)
Synocryl 9122X	Cray Valley	nBMA				was Bedacryl 122X (ICI)

Note
(1) Manufacturers' information. Data from other sources in brackets.

10% of total solids) (Hulmer, 1976). The matteness of a sprayed coating can of course be varied by adjusting the conditions of spraying. There is a gradual loss of gloss over the months of solvent evaporation (De Witte, 1975b).

Paraloid B-67, probably PiBMA (Feller, 1983), is used as a picture varnish. Although it eventually cross-links (Feller, 1976b), it appears to be peculiarly stable and of Class A standard (Feller, 1983). However, as this stability appears to derive from an unknown additive, significant changes in its properties could occur as the secret formulation could easily, perhaps unconsciously, be altered by the manufacturers. It is soluble in less polar solvents than B-72 (Appendix 3.12).

A potentially useful, and somewhat overdue, development is the design of a polymer specifically as a picture varnish (De Witte *et al.*, 1981). The P(MMA/PhA) (ratio 70:30) has a high refractive index, 1.547, slightly higher than dammar, 1.53, and a low molecular weight to improve penetration. Accelerated light-ageing showed that it degraded slightly, but fell within Feller's Class A. Further long-term testing will be required before this encouraging proposal can be adopted by conservators.

Acrylic polymers have been applied in solution to many other types of object. PMMA, the most widely available of the acrylics, has too high a glass transition temperature to be applied successfully. It is likely to separate from the substrate. It was recommended as a coating for glass (Hedval *et al.*, 1951), to consolidate pigments (Takagage, 1951), as an adhesive for paper (Gairola, 1958–60) and as a lacquer for silver (Bhowmik, 1967).

PEMA has been used for the consolidation of wood (Cronyn and Horie, 1985) and PiPMA as a lacquer for mosaic (Stout, 1969). The two PBMAs became increasingly used from the 1930s to the 1960s. Typical uses were for laminating plants (PiBMA) (Wheately, 1941), coating silver (Biek, 1952), consolidating fossils (PnBMA) (Rixon, 1955), pigments (Kostrov, 1956), leather (Waterer, 1973), plaster (Gerassimova and Mel'nikova, 1978), stone (Ageeva *et al.*, 1978) and earth (Natchinkina and Cheinina, 1981; Shorer, 1964), and as adhesive for textiles (PnBMA) (Beecher, 1968) and wood (Angst, 1979). PBMA has been largely displaced by the more stable polymers such as Paraloid B-72 and PVAC. It continues in use for those purposes requiring a low glass transition temperature, low molecular weight and solubility in petroleum solvents, which tend to be cheaper. There are no stable materials which duplicate the useful qualities of PBMA.

Paraloid B-72 was used initially for silver lacquer in 1950 (Anon, 1950; Olson and Thordeman, 1951) and then for textile consolidation (Geyer and Franzén, 1956). Although polymers with more appropriate physical properties could be designed, B-72 remains one of the few polymers that has been tested and cleared for conservation use. The uses suggested for Paraloid B-72 include: hot melt adhesive for paper (Zappala and LaMendola, 1978); consolidant for matte pigments (Welsh, 1980), lacquerwork (Sawada, 1981b) and wood (Serck-Dewaide, 1978); facing for marquetry (von Reventlow, 1978a); and coatings for iron (Evers, 1968) and silver (De Witte, 1973/4). Although Paraloid B-72 has been shown to have poor penetration for stone consolidation (Accardo *et al.*, 1981), it, or something similar, appears to be used in the acrylic/silane consolidant, Racanello 55.050 (once E0057) (*Racannello*) (A. Moncrieff, personal communication).

The solvents providing the best penetration for consolidating solutions have been found to be petroleum solvent for PnBMA (Domaslowski and Lehman, 1971) and dichloromethane for PMMA (Lewin and Papadimitriou, 1981). A limited range of solvents was surveyed. PEA in solution is used as a consolidant for leather (Waterer, 1973).

Acrylic monomers Natural history (and other) specimens were encapsulated in PMMA (Hibben, 1937; Organ, 1963) or PEMA (Puckett, 1940) blocks by both ultraviolet and chemically initiated polymerization. PMMA/MMA slurries are used for restoration of glass (Technovit 4004a) (*Kulzer*) (Jackson, 1983), Plastogen G (*Schmidt*) and other materials. The two parts are a PMMA powder which contains an initiator and MMA liquid. The slurry sets to a translucent solid. The rate of setting and the initial viscosity of the slurry depend on the proportion of powder added.

Consolidation of wood and stone by impregnation and radiation polymerization of MMA was developed for conservation in the 1960s (Moncrieff, 1968; Munnikendam, 1967a). Other monomers such as nBMA (Munnikendam, 1971) and ethylene glycol dimethacrylate (1,2-dimethacryloxyethane) (Munnikendam, 1973) were suggested. This method is extensively used for the consolidation of stone (Wihr, 1979). The specimen is liable to crack, particularly if radiation or low-temperature methods are used (De Witte *et al.*, 1977; Kotlik *et al.*, 1980; Vassalio and Lewin, 1981). The use of higher temperatures and an N_2 blanket reduces the problem. Monomer impregnation and polymerization has been used for consolidating polychrome sculpture. Acrylic monomers are good solvents and could easily damage paint films (Mitanov and Kabaivanov, 1975). The polymer that is formed during the polymerization cannot be dissolved out as it appears to be of high molecular weight and is perhaps chemically attached to the substrate.

Gaseous impregnation of paper and books with an EA/MMA mixture followed by gamma-irradiation has been proposed for the strengthening of paper in bulk (Burstall *et al.*, 1984).

Cyanoacrylates have been suggested for use as adhesives for glass (Ferranzzinni, 1976; André, 1976). However, cyanoacrylates break down in the alkaline conditions on most glass surfaces. Cyanoacrylates have been suggested as temporary holding adhesives for glass before the application of epoxy resins (Turwen, 1983; Kuhn, 1981). Cyanoacrylate adhesives have been found to react with a brass substrate (Williston, 1982) and with minerals in fossils (Howie, 1984). Joins made with cyanoacrylates break down more reluctantly than those of epoxy resins (Moncrieff, 1975), possibly because the joins are much tighter.

Dispersions (Table 8.3) Acrylic dispersions slowly increased in popularity during the 1950s because of the films' greater resistance to yellowing as compared with PVAC dispersion applied films, e.g. PMA (paper) (Yabrova, 1953), PBMA (frescoes) (Frantisek, 1957) and PMMA heavily plasticized (textiles) (Pechova' and Losos, 1957). The dispersions have been recommended for bone (Primal AC-61, AC-634, WS-24, WS-50 (Koob, 1984)) and wall-paintings (Primal AC-33 (Ferragni *et al.*, 1984)). Acrylic dispersions have been much used for heat-set adhesives (Hey, 1970) (Primal AC-634, Plextol B500 (McMullen, 1978)) (Primal AC-61 (Collins, 1983)) (Texicryl 13-002 (Hackforth-Jones, 1981)), liquid adhesives (Primal AC-33/N580 (Hamm and Hamm, 1981)), and consolidants (Texicryl 13-002 (Das Gupta and Whitefield, no date))for paper. Thickened Plextol B500 is used either as a wet adhesive or as a heat-set film applied to relining canvases (Mehra, 1984). Removal of the applied canvas and the adhesive is achieved by softening the polymer. Toluene is wiped over to moisten the canvas, which is then peeled off the painting with the rubbery, solvent-swelled, polymer attached.

Many of the polymers in the dispersions are nominally very close in composition. The polymer contents of Texicryl 13-002, Plextol B500 and various Primals (e.g. AC-634 and AC-33) are P(MMA/EA) copolymers (Howells *et al.*, 1984). Unfortunately the properties of the films formed from these dispersions are extremely variable, presumably from batch to batch. For instance, Texicryl 13-002 has been described both as resistant to yellowing on heat ageing (Das Gupta and Whitefield, no date) and as darkening severely (Collins, 1983). The Primal grades AC-61

Table 8.3 Properties of some commercial acrylic dispersions used in conservation[1]

Product	*Manufacturer*	*Composition*[2]	*pH*	*Particle size* (μm)	*Solids* (%)	*Viscosity* (Pa.s)	*MFFT* (°C)	T_g (°C)	*Comments*
Primal AC-33	Rohm & Haas	(EA(60)/MMA(40)/EMA(?))	9.2	(0.1)	46	6	8	16	Termed Rhodoplex in N. America
Primal AC-61			9.8	(0.1)	46	0.06	18	16	
Primal AC-73			9.5	(0.1)	46	0.25	37	32	
Primal AC-634		(MMA(65)/EA(35))	9.8	(0.1)	46	1.2	12	7	Previously AC-34
Primal N-560		(?BA)	8	(0.1)	55	0.10–0.13	<0		
Primal WS24			7	(0.03)	36		<10	39	
Primal WS50			7.1		38		10	36	
Texicryl 13-002	Scott	(EA(65)/MMA(35)/EMA(?))	9.2	0.25	55	0.75	<0	c. −40	
Plextol B500	Röhm	(EA(60)/MMA(40)/EMA(?))	9.5	0.1–0.2	50	1.1–4.5	7	<29	
Plextol D360			7.5	0.3	60	1–3	0	<−8	

Notes
(1) Manufacturers' information, data from other sources in brackets.
(2) Monomer composition of polymer with percentages, from Howells *et al.* (1984).

(Horie, unpublished research) and AC-634 (Howells *et al.*, 1984; Horie, unpublished research) have been found to be both insoluble and soluble (AC-61) (Collins, 1983; Koob, 1984) (AC-634) (Koob, 1984) in organic solvents. Primal AC-33 (Feller, 1971e; Howell *et al.*, 1984) seems to be more reliably soluble. The differences between nominally identical and similar products make an informed choice uncertain.

Primal N-560 has been used to form a temporary pressure-sensitive film where required (Notman and Tennent, 1980). PBA, probably applied from a dispersion, is the adhesive on a paper tape used for temporary attachement of paper (*Archival Aids*). A specially formulated acrylic/styrene polymer was made and its solution emulsified for textile conservation (Bengtsson, 1975).

9 Miscellaneous synthetic thermoplastics

9.1 Poly(vinyl chloride), PVC

Background

PVC is a thermoplastic made by polymerizing the highly toxic monomer, vinyl chloride (*Figure 9.1*). The polymer is a stiff, hard, material, soluble in a small range of organic solvents (Appendix 3.14). Plasticizers or copolymers are frequently used to reduce the

```
    Cl   H
    |    |
 ---C----C---
    |    |
    H    H
```

Figure 9.1 Monomer unit of poly(vinyl chloride)

stiffness of the material. Although one of the most common polymers, it is one of the most unstable to both heat and light. PVC degrades by loss of HCl from the chain to produce double bonds (Section 2.6). Commercial formulations of PVC have large amounts of stabilizers added.

Conservation

PVC solutions have been used for consolidation of wood (Domaslowski, 1958) and in lifting archaeological objects (Frere, 1958), e.g. Archeoderm (which replaced Dermoplast SG) (*Filoform*) (Wihr, 1977). PVC films were applied with pressure-sensitive adhesives for the lamination of paper (Plenderleith and Werner, 1958; Belen'kaya, no date) as Mipofolie and Genotherm, although their use was discouraged in 1956 (Minogue, 1956). PVC is too unstable to be used on objects. This property has been put to use by following the rapid deterioration of a PVC film as an indicator of the degrading influences of ultraviolet radiation in the museum environment (Tennent *et al.*, 1982).

Plasticized PVC has been used for moulding (Nimmo and Prescott, 1968). A flexible material is melted to a pourable liquid at 120–170 °C. The hot liquid is poured around the object. Even with a release agent such as cellulose acetate, the stress on an object can be very great. An alternative material was a PVC dispersion in a plasticizer, e.g. Vinagel. The paste was kneaded to a soft consistency and an impression taken. The impression was heated in an oven to 140 °C to fuse the particles together. The result was a hard, strong impression. Early workers (Unwin, 1950) did not remove the object before heating and this may have caused damage to the object.

9.2 Poly(vinylidene chloride), PVDC

PVDC (Brydson, 1982) is an intractable thermoplastic (*Figure 9.2*). Vinylidene chloride is therefore copolymerized, frequently with acrylonitrile, to produce polymers that can be used in solution (Appendix 3.15). The major importance of PVDC lies in its very

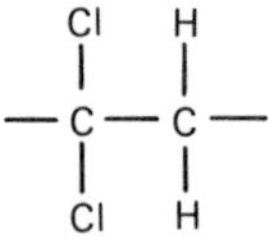

$$-\overset{\text{Cl}}{\underset{\text{Cl}}{\overset{|}{\underset{|}{\text{C}}}}}-\overset{\text{H}}{\underset{\text{H}}{\overset{|}{\underset{|}{\text{C}}}}}-$$

Figure 9.2 Monomer unit of poly(vinylidene chloride)

low permeability to vapours and gases. The polymers are unstable to heat and ultraviolet, degrading in a similar fashion to PVC. PVDC was tested as a moisture vapour barrier in the 1940s (Stevens and Johnson, 1950) to reduce the distortion of panel paintings (Saran F310 (*Dow*)) (Spurlock, 1978). A PVDC copolymer emulsion, Saran 150, has been suggested as a coating on ivory, though some reservations were expressed about its stability (Lafontaine and Wood, 1982).

9.3 Polystyrene, PS

PS (*Figure 9.3*; Appendix 3.16), is a rigid, transparent material that was recommended for optical uses as early as the 1840s. Expanded polystyrene has found uses as a lightweight modelling material and as a support or packing medium. Styrene can be copolymerized, e.g. in polyester casting resins. PS degrades by photolytic oxidation to form conjugated chains of double bonds,

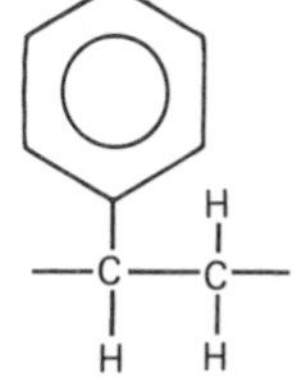

Figure 9.3 Monomer unit of polystyrene

causing yellowing (Grassie and Wier, 1965). It is resistant to water and acids. Polystyrene is in general too unstable and rigid to be used on objects. Because of its high glass transition temperature, it undergoes considerable shrinkage during drying from solution (Croll, 1980b). Perhaps for this reason it was rejected as a picture varnish in the 1930s (Stout and Cross, 1937). PS has been used as a temporary protective resist during acid development of fossils in matrices from the 1940s (Rixon, 1949) to the present (Howie, 1984). In the past PS has been used as a consolidant (Halmagyi, 1958) and an adhesive (Organ, 1959a).

9.4 Poly(vinyl pyrrolidone), PVP (Blecher *et al.*, 1980)

PVP is a stiff thermoplastic plasticized by water (*Figure 9.4*). PVP is soluble in both organic solvents and water (Appendix 3.17). It is insolubilized by polyacids, but is less reactive to cellulose than carboxymethyl cellulose (Trost, 1963). PVP has been suggested for consolidation of ethnographical materials (Schaffer, 1978) and as a washing aid (Wright and Hanlan, 1978).

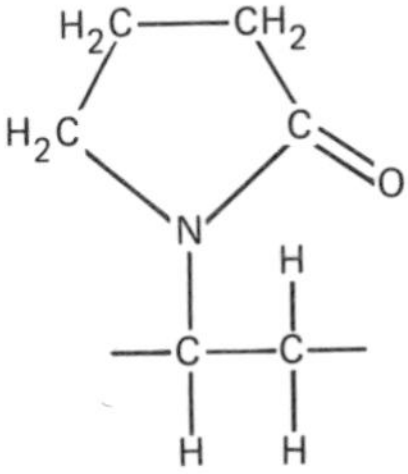

Figure 9.4 Monomer unit of poly(vinyl pyrrolidone)

9.5 Poly(*p*-xylylene), PPX

Poly(*p*-xylylene) (*Figure 9.5*) is deposited in vacuum on to cool surfaces from an unstable monomer vapour (Szwarc, 1976). It is insoluble in solvents and suffers from oxidative degradation on

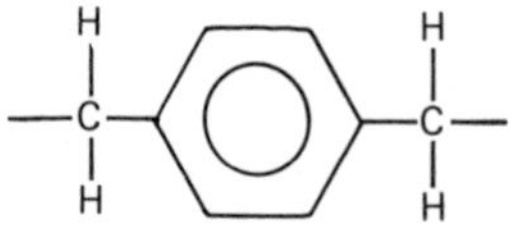

Figure 9.5 Monomer unit of poly(para-xylylene)

ultraviolet exposure. Suggestions have been made that it can be used as a coating for paper and other materials (Parylene) (*Union Carbide*) (Humphrey, 1984), though considerable reservations have been expressed about its reversibility (Pascoe, 1985).

9.6 Ketone resins

Background

Ketone resins are made by heating cyclohexanone (e.g. Laropal K80 synonym Ketone Resin N (*BASF*)), with methyl cyclohexanone for some products (e.g. AW-2 (*BASF*)), with a catalyst (Hill, 1948). About six cyclohexanone molecules join into one molecule. A typical polymer molecule will contain one carbonyl, one methoxy, another ether group and three hydroxyl groups (Roff and Scott, 1971). These contribute to the light absorption and susceptibility to oxidation. The polymer may be hydrogenated catalytically to reduce the carbonyl groups present, e.g. Resin MS2A (Laporte). The removal of carbonyl groups also reduces the sensitivity to water vapour and the tendency to bloom (Thomson, 1963). The polymers are hard, but, because of their low molecular weight, are weak and brittle. Thin films supported on aluminium foil cannot be bent around a 10 cm diameter mandrel without cracking (Feller, 1971a). The low molecular weight of the polymer (that of Resin MS2 (*Laporte*) is c.700) allows high concentration solutions to be made (Appendix 3.18).

Accelerated ageing tests carried out under ultraviolet/air exposure showed that oxygen is absorbed (Thomson, 1963), increasing the polarity of solvents required to dissolve the aged polymers, though no insoluble material is created (Feller and Curran, 1975). Ketone resins have been observed to yellow in dark storage over some years. They are initially more stable than their natural counterparts, dammar and mastic, but eventually become more difficult to dissolve. The formulations of these products have been changed (Mills and White, 1987).

Conservation

Ketone resins have been used primarily for picture varnishes (Werner, 1952) and retouching (Straub, 1962). A typical spraying varnish was made up of 100 g resin in 220 ml of slightly aromatic petroleum solvent (boiling range 150 °C–220 °C). An initial brushing varnish may need a small amount of butanol added to the solution to improve wetting (Lank, 1976). The glossiness of the surface can be adjusted by varying the spraying conditions or by adding a dispersion of microcrystalline wax in solvent (De Witte, 1975b).

Ketone resins have been tried out as varnishes on iron (Barton, 1960). A more important use has been to modify and harden wax (Chapter 6). Ketone resin is added to wax/EVA mixtures used for picture relining adhesives (Beva) (*Adam*) (Berger, 1976).

9.7 Polyethers

9.7.1 Poly(ethylene glycol) PEG

Background (Powell, 1980; Molyneux, 1983)

The term PEG is used commercially as a convenient acronym for the low molecular weight poly(ethylene oxide)s (Table 9.1), polymerized from ethylene oxide (*Figure 9.6*). PEG is used primarily as a solution in water. Both the viscosity in water (*Figure 9.7*) and the solidification temperature of water solutions (*Figure 9.8*) are important in the choice of grade. The penetration of a

Table 9.1 Properties of some poly(ethylene glycol)s used in conservation, manufacturer's data

Molecular weight	*Commercial grades*[(1)]		
	Carbowax (Union Carbide)	(Shell)	*Polydiol/Polywaxes* (Huls)
200	200	200	200
400	400	400	400
600	600	600	600
1000	1000	1000	1000
1450	1450 (was 1540)		1550
3350	3350 (was 4000)		4000
3650		4000	
6750			6000
8000	8000 (was 6000)		12 000
			20 000
			50 000

Note
(1) Grades usually indicate the molecular weight.

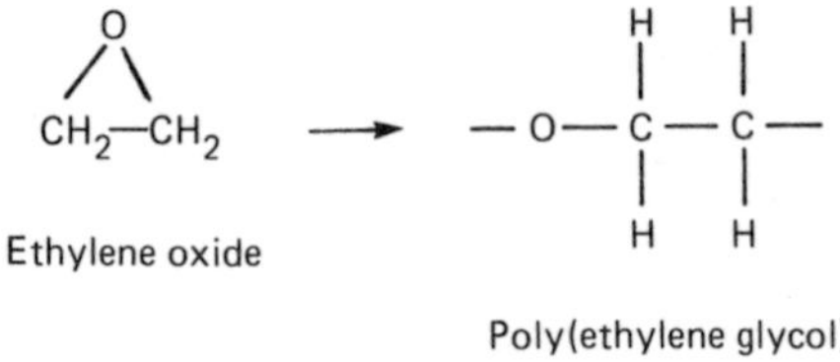

$$\underset{\text{Ethylene oxide}}{\overset{O}{CH_2{-}CH_2}} \longrightarrow \underset{\text{Poly(ethylene glycol)}}{-O-CH_2-CH_2-}$$

Figure 9.6 Monomer unit of poly(ethylene glycol)

PEG molecule into a porous material depends on the size of the molecule and the size of the hole into which it must diffuse. The rate of diffusion of PEG through water is reduced by increasing the viscosity of the solution and the molecular weight, but increased by an increase in temperature and concentration gradient (Brown and Stilbs, 1982).

PEG is hygroscopic (*Figure 9.9*) and there is hysteresis in the response to variations in humidity. Organic solvents (Appendix 3.19) may be used to apply or remove PEG without affecting water-sensitive materials. Many PEG commercial materials produce acid solutions when dissolved in water (pH 4.9–7.2) (Blackshaw, 1975). This acidity could result from incorrect neutralization during manufacture or by oxidative degradation during storage. PEG oxidizes rapidly with a severe drop in molecular weight once exposed to air, a process accelerated by light (McGary, 1960). The most successful stabilizers are likely to be the alcohols (Afifi-Effat and Hay, 1972), e.g. ethanol. Sufficient oxidation can cause initially solid PEG to degrade to a material which will not solidify at room temperature. PEG will, if heated for long periods while exposed to the air, accumulate quantities of highly inflammable vapour (Organ, 1959b). Exclusion of air appears to prevent degradation (Stevens, 1985). Degradation is increased by the presence of metal ions in the solution, even those in tap water. In addition these can react with the acids etc. of the oxidized polymer to form soluble and insoluble salts. Lead, susceptible to attack by organic acids, is attacked very severely. Less severe attack occurs on various aluminium alloys, copper, mild steel and both tin- and zinc-coated steel. Only stainless steel is resistant, although it may be corroded when exposed to the impurities in waterlogged wood as well (Christensen, 1975).

PEG, being well above its glass transition temperature at room temperature, can act as a solvent for inks and paints (Hey *et al.*, 1960) or a plasticizer for polymers, e.g. PVAC, CN or colophony (Powell, 1980). It may cause stress cracking of moulded thermoplastics such as PE. It does not appear to attack beeswax or gelatin.

The presence and quantity of PEG in a solution can be assessed by spot test (Hoffman, 1983).

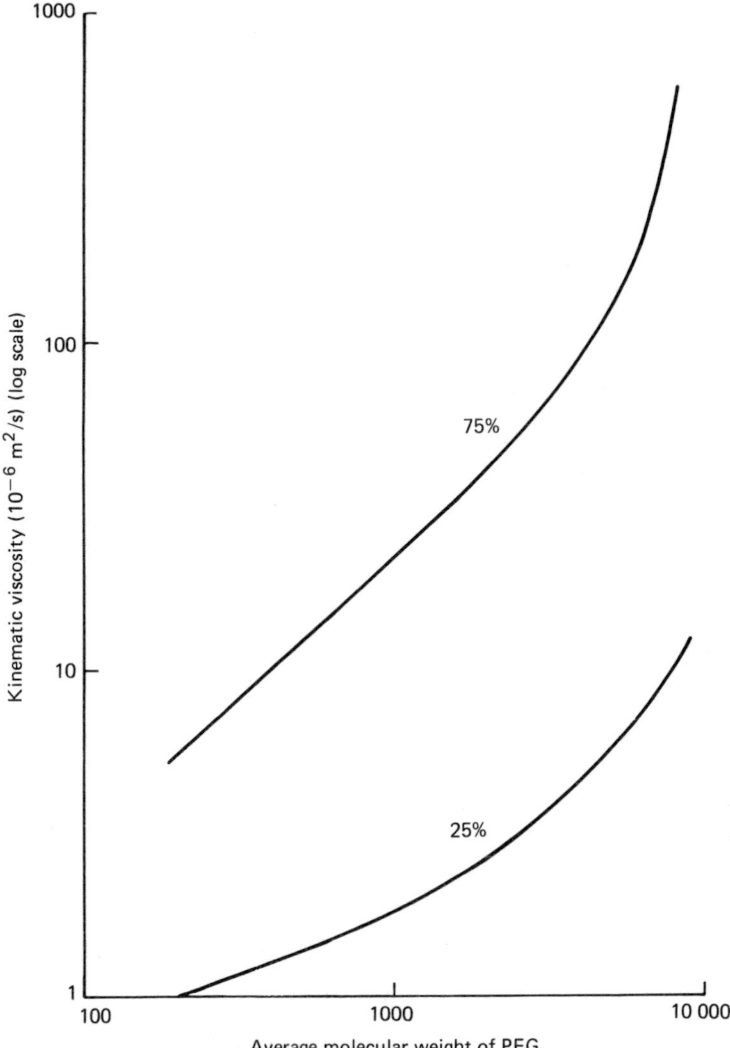

Figure 9.7 Viscosity of 25% and 75% solutions in water of PEG at 60 °C. Data of Carbowax (*Union Carbide*)

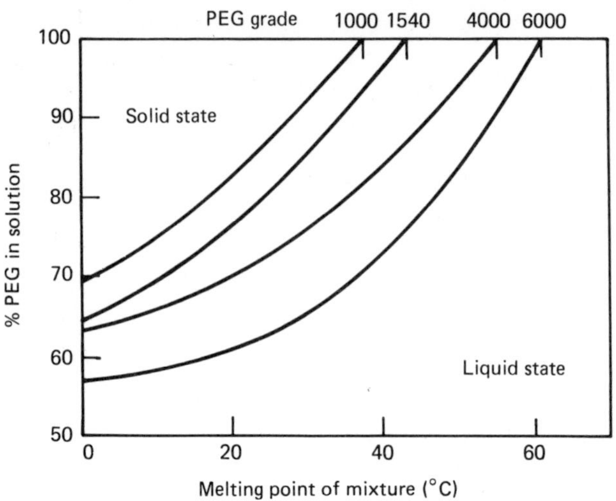

Figure 9.8 Curves of freezing temperatures of solutions in water of various grades of PEG. Data of Carbowax (*Union Carbide*)

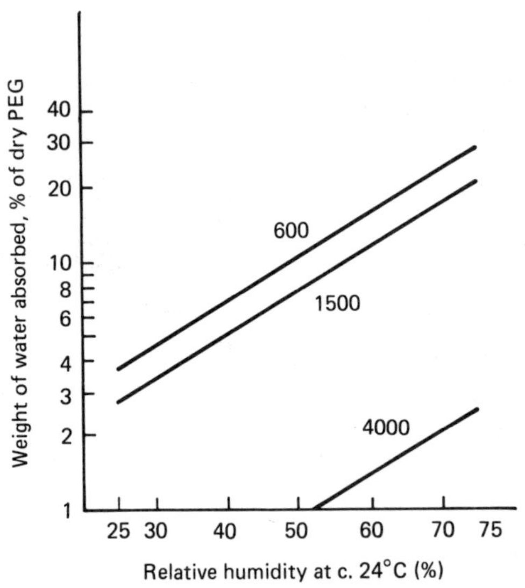

Figure 9.9 Absorption of water by PEGs of various molecular weights over a range of relative humidities, based on Powell (1980) and Blackshaw (1975). Values are approximate, as PEG exhibits hysteresis on absorption/desorption cycles. Products which are nominally similar can differ

Conservation

The major use for PEG as a consolidant for waterlogged wood started in the 1950s (Christensen, 1970). The wet material can be immersed directly in a solution of the polymer in water or, after dewatering, in other solvents, i.e. 2-methylpropan-2-ol or methanol (Grattan, 1982). It has been found that two grades of PEG are needed to achieve stabilization: a low molecular weight material, M_r c.200–400, whose molecules are small enough to displace water in the structure of the cell walls; and higher molecular weight material, M_r c.4000, which bulks the voids in the weakened wood when the PEG solidifies on cooling (Hoffmann, 1984). Although treatments once replaced all the water by molten PEG (Plenderleith and Werner, 1971), many treatments now stop the consolidation process when the PEG solution concentration has risen safely above the solidification point at room temperature (Grattan, 1982). The remaining water is allowed to evaporate naturally from the wood. The PEG appears to attach itself to the wood structure and not all of the polymer can be extracted from treated wood (Barkman, 1975). Relatively high molecular weight PEGs (6000 and 12 000) have been used for consolidating fossil bone (Baumgartner and Lanooy, 1982).

PEG is used as a humectant/lubricant for leather and other skin products (Werner, 1957). Liquid, hygroscopic grades with a molecular weight in the region of 300 to 400 have been recommended. Ganiaris *et al.* (1982) concluded that glycerol provided better results than PEG when leather was treated by freeze-drying or acetone dewatering. Similar grades of PEG have been used for increasing flexibility in cellulose materials such as basketry and tapas (Schaffer, 1978; Bakken and Aarmo, 1981).

9.7.2 Perfluoropolyethers

Perfluoropolyether (*Figure 9.10*) is a very unreactive liquid, being resistant to oxidation and hydrolysis and insoluble in all but fluorinated solvents. A moderately viscous grade (Fomblin YR) (*Montedison*) has been suggested as a water repellent for stone

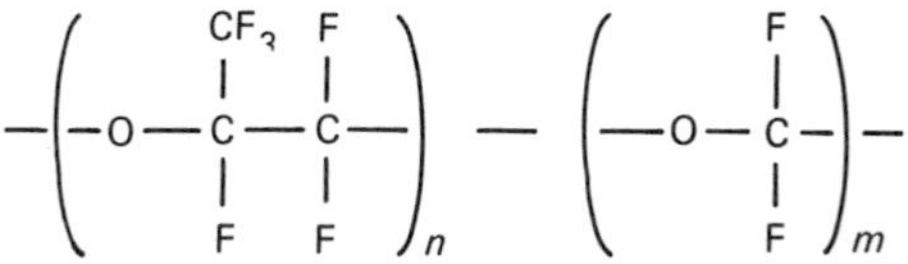

$$-\left(-O-\underset{F}{\overset{CF_3}{C}}-\underset{F}{\overset{F}{C}}-\right)_n-\left(-O-\underset{F}{\overset{F}{C}}-\right)_m-$$

Figure 9.10 Structure of Fomblin Y (*Montedison*), a perfluoropolyether

(Fredani *et al.*, 1982), applied in solution (as Fomblin YMET). It would gradually distribute itself throughout the bulk of porous material, and would therefore require periodic reapplications.

9.8 Soluble nylons

Background

Two forms of soluble nylon are available – *N*-methoxymethyl nylon, which is a substituted nylon, and highly irregular copolymers. Commercial uses are as cross-linking components in coatings. Soluble nylons are soluble in alcohol-based solvents. Nylon is a generic name for a family of polyamides (*Figure 9.11*).

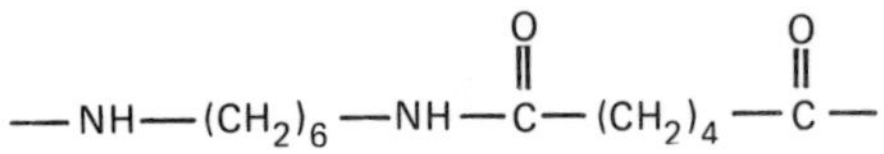

$$—NH—(CH_2)_6—NH—\overset{\overset{\displaystyle O}{\|}}{C}—(CH_2)_4—\overset{\overset{\displaystyle O}{\|}}{C}—$$

Figure 9.11 Monomer unit of nylon 66. The first 6 of the suffix indicates the number of carbon atoms in the diamine component (hexamethylene diamine). The second 6 indicates the number of carbon atoms in the diacid component (adipic acid). Nomenclature: poly(hexamethylene adipamide) and IUPAC poly[imino(1,6-dioxohexamethylene)iminohexamethylene]

The glass transition temperature of nylons is around room temperature at normal humidities and is reduced by moisture absorption. Nylons in general are sensitive to oxidation, particularly photolytic oxidation. They are tough thermoplastics which are highly resistant to solvents because of the strong, regular, hydrogen bonds between adjacent chains. Solvents which can penetrate are phenol, formic acid, 2,2,3,3-tetrafluoropropanol, and 1,3-dichloropropan-2-ol (Roff and Scott, 1971). Two alterations can be made to the structure to produce a soluble polymer. The hydrogen atoms which make the bonds can be replaced. Alternatively the structure of the polymer may be made so irregular that coordinated inter-chain bonds cannot develop.

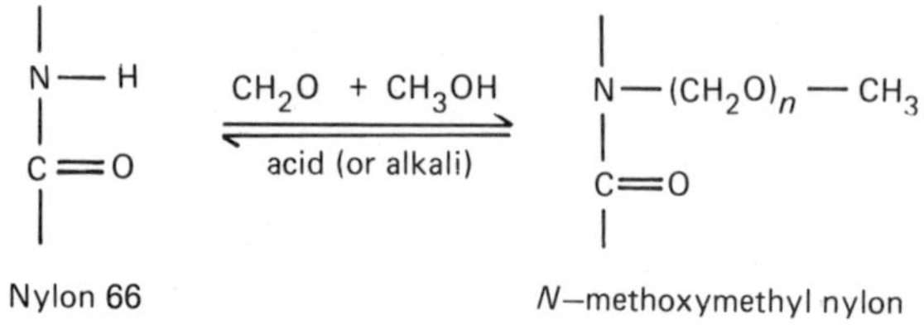

$$\begin{array}{c} | \\ N—H \\ | \\ C{=}O \\ | \end{array} \quad \xrightleftharpoons[\text{acid (or alkali)}]{CH_2O\ +\ CH_3OH} \quad \begin{array}{l} | \\ N—(CH_2O)_n—CH_3 \\ | \\ C{=}O \\ | \end{array}$$

Nylon 66 *N*–methoxymethyl nylon

Figure 9.12 Formation of *N*-methoxymethyl nylon

N-methoxymethyl nylon (Bockoff *et al.,* 1984) is formed by heating nylon 66 with formic acid and methanol to produce short side chains (about 35% substitution) (*Figure 9.12*). This produces a polymer that is more flexible than the original nylon and which is soluble in ethanol or methanol if a small amount of water is added. Soluble nylon dissolves in hot solvent but forms a gel when cooled to room temperature. Films which are formed from the solution shrink on drying. The side chains can be removed by reaction in acidic and alkaline conditions. The film is thus converted back to the original, intractable, nylon 66. The reaction occurs on standing – on opening a container of old *N*-methoxymethyl nylon the methanol can easily be smelled. An additional reaction in acidic conditions leads to cross-linking between the chains, which ensures complete insolubility. The cross-linked film is considerably stronger than the original film (Brydson, 1982). The glass transition temperature of *N*-methoxymethyl nylon is sufficiently low when immersed in water to result in dirt pick-up (De Witte, 1975a).

The unmodified nylons, which are similarly soluble in alcohols etc., are copolymers of widely different monomers (Ultramid 6A (*BASF*) or (Elvamide 8060 (*Du Pont*) series). Films formed from solutions dried at room temperature are usually opaque white and must be heated to c.80°C to ensure transparency. They probably suffer from the degradation reactions of the more common nylons.

Conservation

N-methoxymethyl nylon, Calaton CA and CB (*ICI*) (also called Maranyl C109/P), was recommended in the 1950s (Werner, 1958) for the consolidation of friable stone and pottery surfaces during soaking for removal of salts. By the late 1960s its use was being discouraged because of dirt pick-up (Torracca, 1967), and loss of strength and insolubility (Plossi and Santucci, 1969) after ageing. It has been suggested as a consolidant for paper (Saucois, 1981), pigments (King, 1976), canvas (Berger, 1974), and textiles (Agrawal, 1975), and as an adhesive for leather (Nikitina, 1981). The use of *N*-methoxymethyl nylon in conservation has been strongly discouraged (De Witte, 1975a; Sease, 1981).

Soluble copolymer nylon (Zytel 61 = Elvamide 8061) has been tested as a consolidant for paper (Baer *et al.,* 1972).

10 Polymers derived from cellulose

The ethers covered in this chapter are typical members of a large family of derivatives that have been produced from cellulose (*Figure 10.1*). Abbreviations are used in discussion of the various

$$\text{Cell—ONa} + 2\text{ClCH}_2\text{—}\overset{\displaystyle O}{\overset{\|}{C}}\text{—O—Na}^+ \longrightarrow \text{Cell—O—CH}_2\text{—O—}\overset{\displaystyle O}{\overset{\|}{C}}\text{—}\bar{O}\text{Na}^+$$

Sodium chloroacetate

Sodium carboxymethylcellulose

+

$$\text{HO—CH}_2\text{—}\overset{\displaystyle O}{\overset{\|}{C}}\text{—}\bar{O}\text{Na}^+$$

+

NaCl

Figure 10.1 Formation of sodium carboxymethyl cellulose; impurities are sodium chloride and sodium glycolate

polymers (Table 10.1). Many types of cellulose ether may be formulated, accounting for the large range of different but similar products, many of which are unique to a single manufacturer. Typical reactions are (Greminger and Krumel, 1980):

$$\text{Cell–ONa} + CH_3Cl \rightarrow \text{Cell–OCH}_3 + NaCl$$

or

$$\text{Cell–ONa} + \underset{\diagdown\,O\,\diagup}{CH_2 - CH_2} \rightarrow \text{Cell–O–CH}_2\text{–CH}_2\text{–ONa} \rightarrow \text{Cell–(O–CH}_2\text{–CH}_2)_n\text{–ONa} \rightarrow$$

$$\text{Cell–(O–CH}_2\text{-CH}_2)_n\text{–OH}$$

Table 10.1 Representative cellulose ethers used in conservation, manufacturer's data

Cellulose ether derivative[1]	*Abbreviation*	*Degree of substitution on monomer unit*	*Molar substitution on monomer unit*	n_D *of film at 20 °C*	*Typical products*	*Reference*
Methyl	MC	1.7		1.49	Methocel A (*Dow Chemical*)	Greminger and Krumel (1980)
Ethyl	EC	2.4–2.5		1.47	Etholuse (*Hercules*)	Roff and Scott (1971)
Ethyl hydroxyethyl	EHEC	0.9 (ethyl)	0.8 (hydroxyethyl)	1.49	Bermocoll E (*Berol*) (was Modocoll)	Lindenfors and Jullander (1973)
Methyl hydroxyethyl	MHEC	1.25	0.5		Tylose (*Hoechst*)	Greminger and Krumel (1980)
Hydroxyethyl	HEC	0.9	1.8–2.0	1.51	Natrosol (*Hercules*)	Powell (1980)
Hydroxypropyl	HPC		c. 4	1.56	Klucel (*Hercules*)	Butler and Klug (1980)
Sodium carboxymethyl	CMC	0.9		1.515	Blanose (*Hercules*) Cellulose Gum Cellofas (*ICI* discontinued)	Stelzer and Klug (1980)

Note
(1) Derivatives are designated as methyl cellulose etc.

The number of alkyl groups added to each glucose unit of the chain is described as the degree of substitution, DS. The hydroxyalkyls are usually assessed by the molar substitution, MS, the number of alkene oxide units added per glucose unit (*Figure 10.2*). In general, low degrees of substitution provide water-soluble, rather brittle, materials. Increasing the amount of substitution increases the solubility in organic solvents and the plasticity of the polymer.

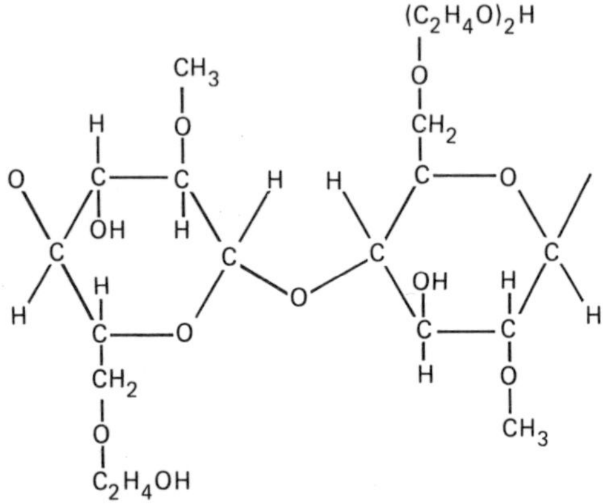

DS, Degree of substitution ($-CH_3$) $= 2/2 = 1$

MS, Molar substitution ($-C_2H_4O-$) $= 3/2 = 1.5$

Figure 10.2 Two monomer units of a hypothetical methyl hydroxyethyl cellulose, showing derivation of the degree of substitution (DS) of the methyl groups and molar substitution (MS) of the ethoxy groups

The granular grades of the polymer dissolve in water more easily than the powdery types, which tend to clump on adding to water. The granules should be added slowly to vigorously stirred water. The stirring should be continued for up to 30 minutes. Alternatively, the powder can be dispersed in a small amount of water-miscible organic solvent, e.g. ethanol or acetone, and added as a slurry to the stirred water.

All cellulose ethers suffer from chain breaking through oxidation (Kozminia, 1968) with an activation energy of 112 kJ/mol (for EC), comparable to cellulose. The CMC and the hydroxyalkyl ethers degrade more quickly than the alkyl. CMC has been found to be less stable than starch (Baynes-Cope, 1975) and MC (Baker, 1984). The oxidation will occur both in bulk storage and *in situ*, especially if there is light exposure. The non-ionic cellulose ethers do not form irreversible, insoluble, complexes with metal ions (in contrast to sodium carboxymethylcellulose), but may be precipitated by high concentrations of salts. All the ethers may be cross-linked in acid conditions through the hydroxyl groups by means of aldehydes and acids which may be found on degraded organic materials.

10.1 Non-ionic ethers

Background

The ethers that are formed with cellulose can be divided into two types, the alkyl and the hydroxyalkyl. Both can occur in the same molecule. Except for EC, the ethers are all soluble in cold water, forming increasingly viscous and then thixotropic solutions (except HPC) at higher molecular weights (Table 10.2). Many solutions

Table 10.2 Viscosity of typical cellulose ethers, 2% solution in water, manufacturer's data

Grade	*Molecular weight*	*Viscosity* (mPa.s)
Methocel A4M		4000
Bermocol E320G		2200
Tylose MH2000		2000
Natrosol 250GR		300
Natrosol 250HHR		100 000
Klucel G	300 000	3000
Klucel E	60 000	7
Blanose 7HF	550 000	13 000
Blanose 7LF	90 000	40

can be spread on with a brush yet thicken when the force is removed (pseudoplastic). The polymers in water solution are distinguished by different responses to heating. MC forms a gel on heating to 50–90°C, depending on the grade. The gels melt on cooling. HPC and EHEC precipitate out of solution on heating to 40–45°C, while HEC remains in solution on heating.

Solubility in organic solvents varies with the type of ether. EC is soluble only in organic solvents. HPC is soluble both in water and in polar solvents (Appendix 3.20). MC, EHEC and HEC are soluble in only a few organic solvents such as dimethyl formamide and dimethyl sulphoxide.

The alkyl ethers, MC and EHEC, are resistant to biodeterioration in water solution whereas the HEC and HPC are susceptible to attack. These latter should be made up just before use. Storage of all the solutions should be in sterile, dark conditions to prevent algal growth.

Conservation

An early (1920s) use for MC was as a lacquer for lead, being a more stable substitute for CN (Jenkinson, 1924). This MC was presumably applied in an organic solvent and so had a degree of substitution (DS) of more than 2.6. Water-soluble MC (DS of 1.5–2.0) is used in paper conservation as adhesives and consolidants (Asher, 1981). MC has been used as a reversible facing on wall paintings (Kottulinsky, 1982); for pigment fixing (Belen'kaya *et al.,* 1965; Ranacher, 1980); as a consolidant for waterlogged wood (Rosenqvist, 1959) and for basketry (Thomsen, 1981); and as an adhesive for textiles (Masschelein-Kleiner and Bergiers, 1984). MC is added to starch adhesives (Anon, 1973) and polymer dispersions (Koller *et al.,* 1980) to improve working properties.

EC is little used in conservation because better solvent-borne polymers are available. EC with a dibutyl phthalate plasticizer has been suggested as a consolidant for leather (Belaya, 1958).

Solutions of HEC in water have been suggested for sizing paper (Santucci and Plossi, 1969), consolidating cellulose materials (Schaffer, 1978) and protecting pigments on unvarnished paintings (Brenner, 1974). HEC (Natrosol 250 GR (De Witte *et al.,* 1984) and Natrosol 250HHR (Mehra, 1984)) are widely used for increasing the viscosity of dispersions, sometimes to form pastes, at a concentration of 1–2%. However, this addition seems to contribute to the yellowing of the dried films (Howells *et al.,* 1984). EHEC has been used for textile consolidation (Geijer, 1961; Lodewijks and Leene, 1972). MHEC has also been used to increase the viscosity of aqueous reagents applied to surfaces (Tylose MH2000) (Hatton, 1977).

HPC (Klucel J (Berger, 1976) and Klucel G (Hofenk-de Graaff, 1981)) as a 2% solution in ethanol has been suggested for pigment consolidation where a non-aqueous treatment is required. HPC, like the other cellulose polymers, does not cause serious darkening of pigments.

10.2 Sodium carboxymethyl cellulose, CMC

Background (Stelzer and Klug, 1980)

Commercial CMC is available in many purities, from 99.5% CMC to 50%, containing as impurities the byproducts of synthesis (*Figure 10.1*). The degree of substitution is normally around 0.7. With increasing molecular weight (up to 1 million), the strength, elongation and flexibility of films increase. Solutions of CMC in water are thixotropic, and high molecular weight materials may form gels on standing. Useful thixotropic solutions form at 2% concentration ($M_r = 7 \times 10^5$) or 5% ($M_r = 2.5 \times 10^5$).

CMC will react with iron, aluminium and other polyvalent ions to form cross-links. The hydroxyl groups of CMC react with aldehyde groups to form cross-links. Films cast from mixtures of CMC and PEG are insoluble in water. CMC is adsorbed irreversibly from solution on to cellulose, especially in the presence of ions (Trost, 1963). Solutions of CMC are susceptible to biological attack. They should be used immediately after preparation. CMC is hygroscopic, having an equilibrium moisture content of c.18% at 60% relative humidity, and becomes increasingly flexible with increase in moisture content.

Conservation

The major use of CMC in conservation has been on paper, as an adhesive (Razdan, 1969), as a moisture-holding gel during aqueous surface treatments, as a pigment fixative (Brenner, 1974) and as paper consolidant by lamination (Raff *et al.*, 1967).

A major commercial use for CMC is to prevent soil redeposition during washing using detergents, though other materials have been used (Trost, 1963). The most appropriate grade seems to have a DS of 0.6–0.8 with a molecular weight of 42 000–106 000. This has been suggested for conservation uses (Blanose 7L) (Smith and Lamb, 1981) at a concentration of 0.005% by weight in the solution. *Figure 10.3* demonstrates the usefulness of including a suspending agent in the wash water.

10.3 Cellulose esters

Various esters of cellulose have been manufactured but only the acetate and nitrate have been used extensively in conservation (*Figure 10.4*). Cellulose butyrate and its copolymer with the acetate do not seem to have been used.

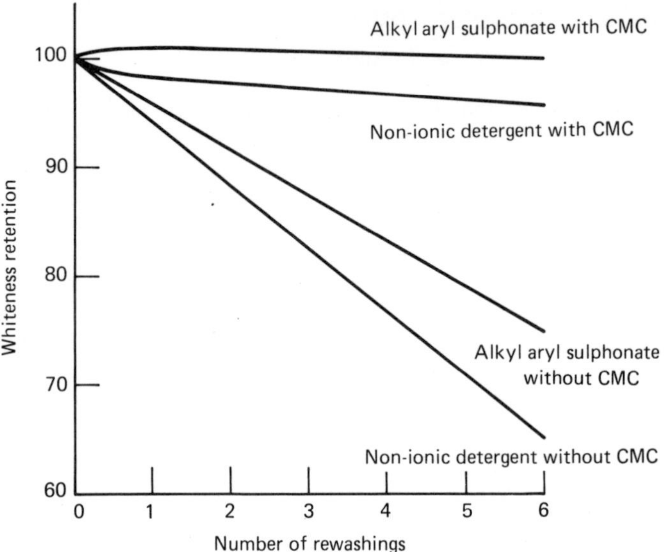

Figure 10.3 Use of sodium carboxymethyl cellulose, CMC, in detergents to prevent soil redeposition during washing of fabrics in dirty water. Redrawn from Stelzer and Klug (1980)

10.3.1 Cellulose-acetate, CA

Background

Cellulose acetate (*Figure 10.4*) is manufactured by heating cellulose with acetic anhydride and a sulphuric acid catalyst. The chemical properties of CA change with increasing degree of substitution, DS. At a DS of about 2.4 (secondary acetates) the polymer is soluble in acetone and similar solvents (Appendix 3.21). As the DS rises towards 3, the polymers require less polar solvents, e.g. chlorinated solvents. The molecular weight of CA, used in solution, is usually below 60 000 (Roff and Scott, 1971).

An intensive investigation into the properties of CA films was made by Wilson and Forshee (1959). CA with a DS of 2.4 will flow at c.150°C, though this is lowered by plasticizers. CA oxidizes at room temperature, the molecular weight is reduced and it becomes weaker and more brittle. Degradation is increased considerably by traces of acid catalysts remaining from manufacture. Old, impure, samples can be expected to have degraded faster than modern equivalents. The process of degradation can be reduced by incorporating an acid acceptor, e.g. a buffer such as

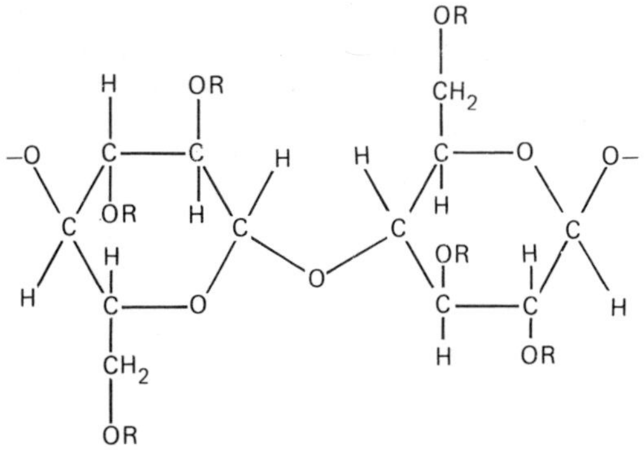

Cellulose diacetate: about 2.4 of the –R groups are $-\overset{\displaystyle O}{\overset{\|}{C}}-CH_3$

Cellulose nitrate: about 2.1 of the –R groups are $-NO_2$
(ca. 12% nitrogen by weight)

The remaining –R groups are –H

Figure 10.4 Two monomer units of a cellulose ester

magnesium acetate. Ultraviolet absorbers and antioxidants can be added where an extended life is desired.

Conservation

Cellulose acetate in an acetone-soluble form became widely available during World War I as a coating for aircraft fabric, 'dope'. CA displaced cellulose nitrate, which was too inflammable. CA was first used, apparently without a plasticizer, in a solution in acetone for fixing pigments on paper and stone (Scott, 1923) and as a consolidant for cloth and other materials (Plenderleith, 1934). It was rejected in 1937 as a possible picture varnish (Stout and Cross, 1937). CA has been largely replaced for conservation uses by modern materials.

The greatest quantity of CA was used in the lamination of paper, starting around 1934 (Kimberly and Scribner, 1934). The heat-lamination process involves heating and pressing the paper between two sheets of CA so that the polymer flows into the paper. The degree of substitution, the molecular weight, the purity of the CA, the type and amount of plasticizer, the stabilizers used and the temperatures and pressures employed have been specified (Wilson and Forshee, 1959). Thin tissue was incorporated into the lamination by some workers to improve the strength (Belen'kaya, no date). Lamination can also be achieved by using solvents instead of heat to soften the polymer. The polymer films were wiped over with acetone then placed over the paper in a press (Kathpalia, 1966; Werner, 1968b).

10.3.2 Cellulose nitrate, CN

Background (Miles, 1955)

Cellulose nitrate, CN (*Figure 10.4*) is prepared by soaking a cellulose pulp in a mixture of concentrated nitric and (usually) sulphuric acids. For use as adhesives and lacquers the degree of substitution, DS, is usually 2.0–2.2 (11.2–12.3% nitrogen by weight). The grade used in recent years for lacquers and adhesives is the '1/2 second' grade, molecular weight c.25 000 (Paist, 1977) (Appendix 3.22). Higher molecular weight materials were used before the 1920s (Roff and Scott, 1971). CN has a high glass transition temperature and is usually compounded with plasticizers such as camphor (forming Celluloid), triphenyl phosphate and dibutyl phthalate. A typical adhesive formulation includes 5% plasticizer, 20% CN and 75% solvent. Camphor is still used as a plasticizer but it volatilizes rapidly, leading to shrinkage of the polymer film. Non-volatile plasticizers may migrate into adjacent porous material, producing similar shrinkage of the film. CN has retained its usefulness as a lacquer and adhesive because it rapidly releases solvents to form a dry, strong, film.

CN is an unstable material, less stable than CA. The grades used for adhesives and lacquers are not supplied dry but are dampened with water or a solvent to reduce the chances of explosion when struck suddenly. This danger is eliminated by compounding with plasticizers. CN degrades at room temperature by a combination of oxidation and hydrolysis, which are catalysed by the presence of acid impurities and accelerated by light. These reactions result in a reduction of molecular weight and in the production of nitric oxides and acids. Yellowing also occurs (Koob, 1982). CN will react in solution, and probably as a plasticized solid, with metal oxides to form an insoluble gel. The reactivity with the metals is greatest with lead, decreasing through calcium, silver, tin, iron, copper and zinc. This became a severe problem during World War II when lead tubes of adhesive were inadequately coated internally. The material inside set to a gel which could not be squeezed out (Anon, 1942). This effect has been noticed on copper alloy objects whose adhesives have had to be removed some years after application.

Conservation

Plasticized cellulose nitrate was first used for the conservation of objects during the late 19th century. Posse (1899) suggested Zapon, a CN/camphor solution in amyl acetate, for the coating of antiquities and strengthening of paper. It remained an adhesive, consolidant and coating of first choice in many applications for the first half of the century (Rathgen, 1905; Plenderleith, 1956). Typical uses were as a consolidant for stone (Zellon) (Rathgen, 1926), earth (von Koch, 1914), wall paintings (Coremans, 1941), pigments (Bailey, 1938), plants (Jackson and Ghose, 1932), wood (Werner, 1978) and general organic materials (Leechman, 1931); as an adhesive for pottery (Miback, 1975); and as a coating for unstable glass (Pauzaurek, 1904), silver (Majewski, 1973) and iron (Western, 1972).

Even in the early stages of its use, reservations were expressed about the stability of the polymer and the effect on objects (Posse, 1899). CN was displaced for some purposes during the 1920s and 1930s by CA (Plenderleith, 1934) and PVAC (Gettens, 1935). Although it has been reported as being used for picture varnishes (Johnson, 1976), few paintings seem to have been subjected to this treatment.

Table 10.3 Some cellulose nitrate adhesives used in conservation

Product	*Manufacturer*	*Plasticizer*[1]	*Relative stability*[2]
Durofix	Rawlplug	DBP (since before 1946)	2
HMG Waterproof adhesive	Guest	DBP (+ levelling agent)	3
Duco Cement	Decon		5
Cement	Randolph		1
UHU Hart	Lingner	DBP	4

Notes
(1) Information from manufacturer or from infrared spectrophotometry; DBP = dibutyl phthalate.
(2) Approximate ordering, 1 being most stable, derived from Koob (1982).

CN continues to be used in conservation, as adhesives (Table 10.3), and for consolidating soil sections (Van Baren and Bomer, 1979). This is probably because of its ease of use. It is packaged conveniently and dries rapidly. It is also, in most cases, readily and completely soluble after long natural ageing. Any proposed replacement must prove to have comparable properties and convenience before CN is displaced completely.

11 Natural water-soluble polymers

11.1 Polysaccharides

There are many types of sugars (saccharides), e.g. glucose, fructose. Polysaccharides are based on sugar monomers but frequently incorporate other components. The term includes cellulose but this chapter only deals with the naturally occurring water-soluble polymers.

11.1.1 Starch

Background (Rutenberg, 1980)

Starch is a polymer made up, like cellulose, from anhydroglucose units (*Figure 11.1*). However, the relationship of adjacent units is different, leading to the very different properties (*Figure 11.2*). There are two types of starch which occur together. Amylose is a largely linear molecule (*Figure 11.2*). The molecular weight of amylose lies between 40 000 and 650 000, being higher for tapioca and rice than for potato starch (Jarowenko, 1977). Amylopectin molecules (*Figure 11.3*), are very large, the molecular weight being typically 10^7 to 10^8. Amylose and amylopectin have different properties, both as dry films and in solution. The highly regular linear structure of amylose allows it to dry from solution to form strong films. Humectants may be added to prevent films becoming brittle at low relative humidities. Amylopectin, being more

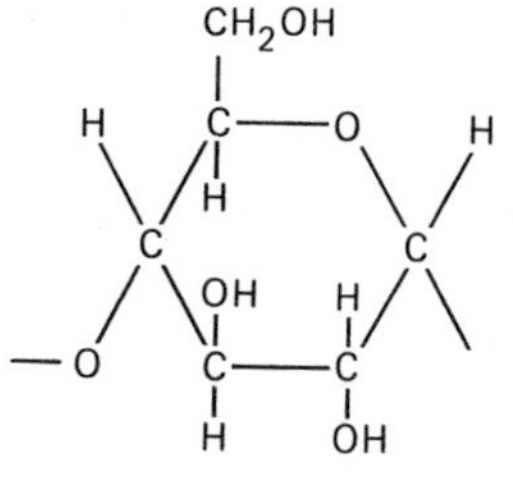

Figure 11.1 Monomer unit of starch (a polyglucose)

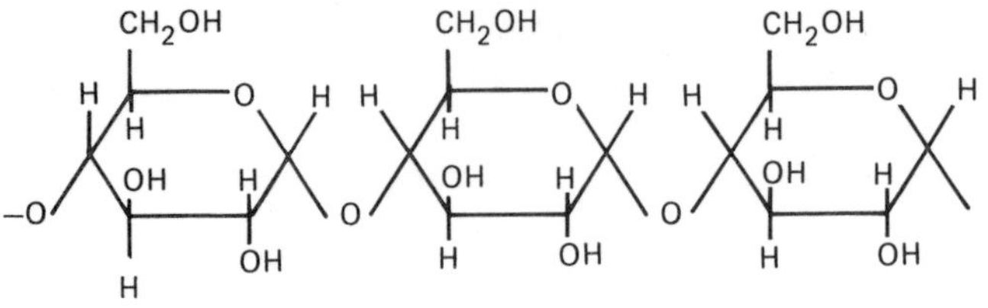

Amylose chain, α–D–glucopyranose units

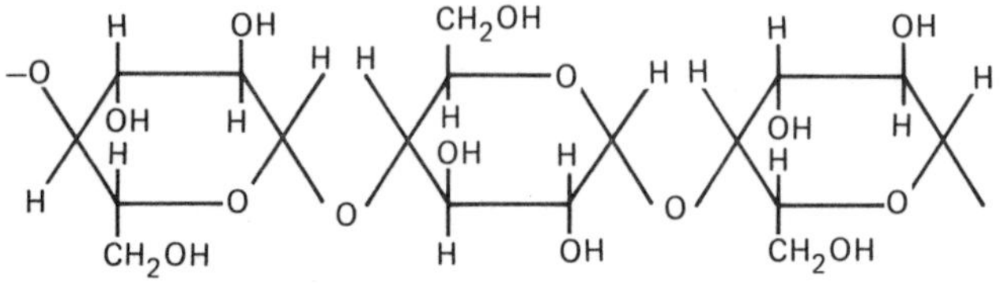

Cellulose chain, β–D–glucopyranose units

Figure 11.2 Starch and cellulose are both composed of the same monomer, glucose, combined in different arrangements. The manner in which the resulting chains can pack together leads to very different physical properties

amorphous, forms weak films. The differences in association are also marked in solution. High temperatures (80–150 °C) are needed to dissolve the amylose in water. In solutions >1%, the molecules align partly, forming a gel when cooled. Films of amylose will absorb up to four times their weight in water without dissolving. Amylopectin will dissolve in cold water to form viscous solutions with little tendency to form gels. Starch dissolves (but may be slightly degraded) in a few organic solvents, e.g. dimethyl sulphoxide and *N*-methyl pyrrolidone (Baynes-Cope, 1972b).

Starch granules are separated by milling the seed, root etc. and washing in water (*Figure 11.4*). The starch is insoluble in water until heated to the gelatinization temperature, 55–80 °C, when the granules swell and start to disrupt. This causes a rapid rise in viscosity which reduces when the granules are completely dispersed. Remains of the original structure of the granule can survive one hour's heating at 100 °C. Constant stirring is needed to prevent lumps forming. Vigorous stirring during cooking also reduces the molecular weight and probably the amount of crystalline material left intact. Agitation should be continued during cooling to reduce the association of amylose molecules.

The proportions and molecular weights of the amylose and amylopectin components determine the properties of the pastes

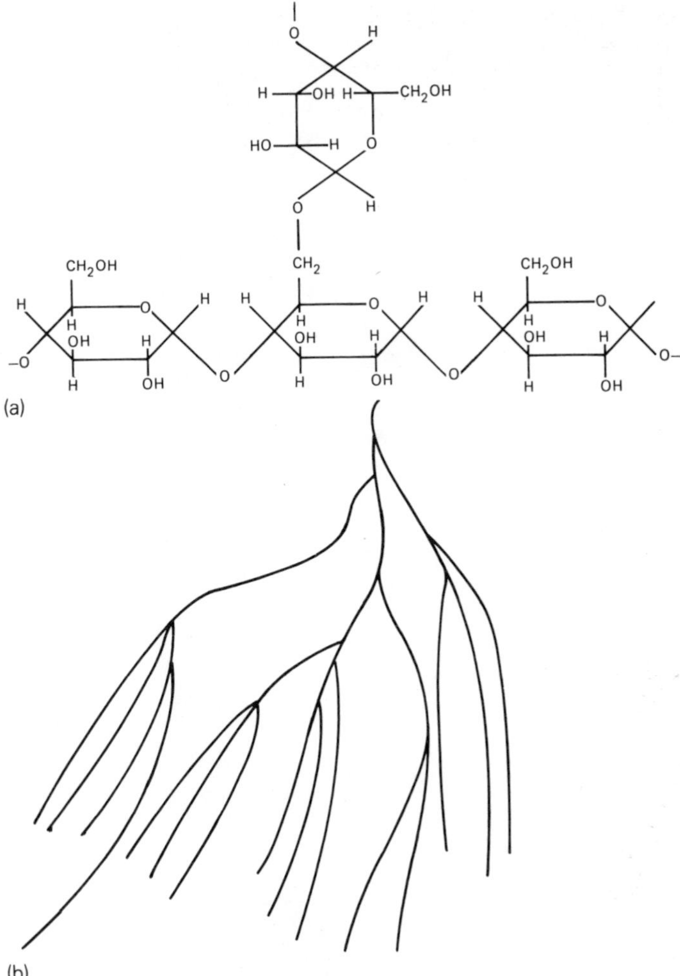

Figure 11.3 (a) Structure of amylopectin at the branch point. (b) Gross structure of amylopectin molecule

and the final film (Table 11.1). A high proportion of amylose, e.g. as in corn and wheat starches, will cause the solution to gel on cooling. A high molecular weight amylopectin will take longer to disperse and will form a high-viscosity solution.

Amylose has been shown to degrade by photo-oxidation and hydrolysis reactions on exposure to ultraviolet (Phillips, 1980), resulting in breaking of the chain and production of organic acids.

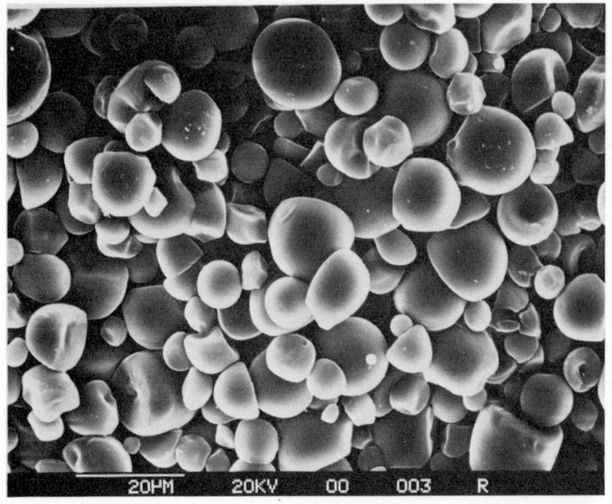

(a)

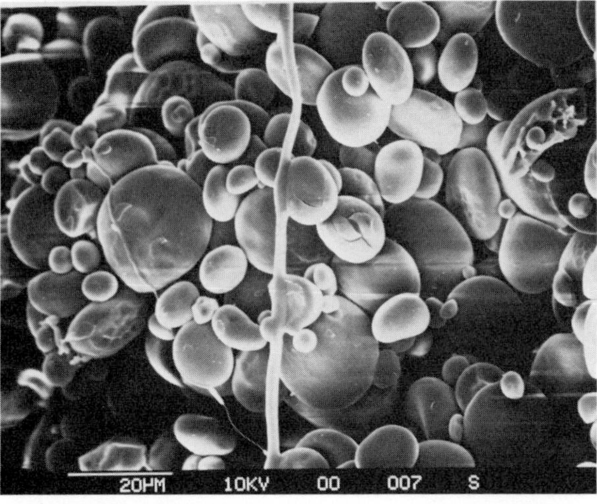

(b)

Figure 11.4 The process of producing starch paste in water from wheat starch. The changes which occur have been followed by extracting samples from the paste at various points in the process. The samples were freeze-dried before taking scanning electron microscope photographs, scale indicated on the illustration. Photographs courtesy of Dr J. Winter, Freer Gallery of Art, Smithsonian Institution. (a) Raw wheat starch granules. These are typical of wheat; different starches have their own characteristic shapes and sizes. (b) Wheat starch heated in water at 50°C. The granules have been swollen and have started to crack.

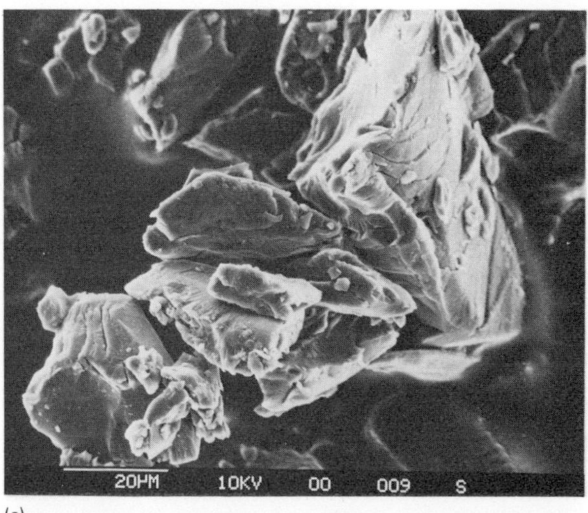

(c)

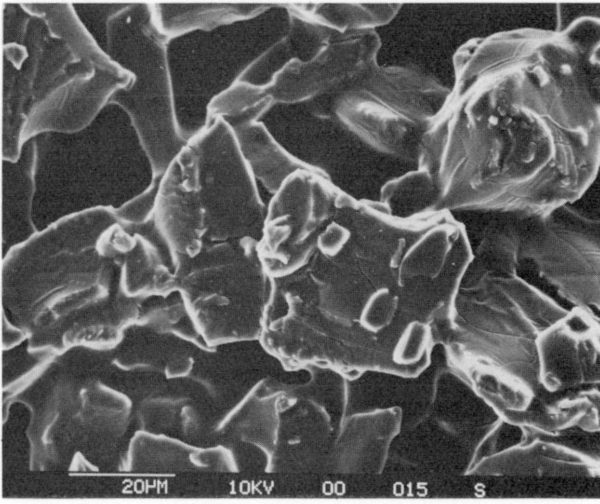

(d)

Figure 11.4 (c) Wheat starch heated in water at 65 °C. The granules have cracked, with layers of starch peeling off. (d) Wheat starch heated in water at 87 °C. The granules have been partly dissolved. Remnants of the granule fragments have been covered and joined with starch which has been dissolved

Table 11.1 Properties of some starches (Jarowenko, 1977; Rutenberg, 1977)

Plant type	*Proportion in starch (%)*	*Degree of polymerization*		*Gel formation on cooling*
		Amylose	*Amylopectin*	
Wheat	17–27			Strong
Rice	16–19			Little
Potato	~23	500–800	~2000	Little
Rye	~27			
Corn	22–28	~480	~1450	Strong
Tapioca	17–22	450–1050	~1300	Little

Empirically, paste films have been found to be more stable if they are made from starch granules rather than flour (Clapp, 1978; Wills, 1984) whose gluten (protein) content will degrade faster (Radley, 1976). The paste made from flour has better properties of slip and adhesion during application than pure starch pastes. Potato and corn starches are more likely to be damaged during cooking, leading to yellowing (Rice, 1972). Rice starch has been found to be less stable than wheat starches on natural ageing (Clapp, 1978).

Starch is modified by hydrolysis and oxidation at elevated temperatures to produce easily soluble British gums and dextrins which have very low molecular weights. The molecular weight of starch can be modified more subtly by controlled hydrolysis of the molecules while still in the granules (Van Steene and Masschelein-Kleiner, 1980). When acid-catalysed hydrolysis is carried out below the gelatinization temperature, the starch molecules are attacked in the amorphous, amylopectin-rich, regions of the granule. This increases the proportion of amylose-type polymer, resulting in an increased tendency to gellation.

Conservation

Flour pastes are traditional adhesives for paper and for use in book bindings, though starch pastes are now preferred. Typical proportions are (British Standards Institution, 1973):

wheat starch	400 g
water	1150 ml

The wheat starch is mixed to a cream in a small quantity of water. It is heated with the remaining water in a double boiler with continual stirring for 10 minutes at a simmer. It is then cooked for a further one hour. The final hour can be replaced by 20 minutes cooking in a pressure cooker at 200 kPa (30 psi). The liquid is decanted into sterile containers. It will set to a firm gel or paste. This can be diluted by working in more water, 200 g paste in one litre of water previously heated to 100°C for a few minutes to sterilize. Starch paste spoils easily. In use the paste should not sink into or release much water into the substrate (Plenderleith and Werner, 1971). A rice starch paste may be made as follows. Rice starch, 30 g, is mixed to a cream with 30 ml water. Boiling water, 600 ml, is poured into the cream with vigorous stirring. It is simmered in a double boiler for one hour.

Wheat starch modified by acid hydrolysis is claimed to provide better qualities as both paste and adhesive for textiles (Van Steene and Masschelein-Kleiner, 1980). Starch has been used as a relining adhesive over many centuries, often mixed with glue (Marijnissen, 1967). A typical formula is (Bergeon *et al.*, 1978):

wheat flour	375 g
rye flour	188 g
skin glue	94 g
Venice turpentine	67 g
phenol	8 g

11.1.2 Gum arabic (Meer, 1980b; Glicksman and Sands, 1973)

Gum arabic is a high molecular weight (c. 580 000) polysaccharide (incorporating calcium, magnesium and potassium) exuded from wounds in Acacia species. It is soluble in water at room temperature and forms viscous solutions with up to 50% by weight of gum. The gum lowers the surface tension of the liquid. Gum arabic probably degrades by hydrolysis and photo-oxidation in a similar fashion to starch. The molecules can be cross-linked and precipitated by trivalent metal ions, e.g. aluminium and iron salts, lead and mercury salts and gelatine. Gum arabic is susceptible to biodeterioration.

Gum arabic has long been the medium in inks and water paints (Lucas, 1932) and it has been suggested as a fixative for pigments (Emmenegger, 1975; Flieder, 1981). The other major traditional use has been as an adhesive for paper tapes and labels, often plasticized with glycerol. Gum arabic has been used in the past as an adhesive for textiles (Lodewijks and Leene, 1972) and insects (Lewis, 1946). It should be removable by washing in water (Flieder, 1981).

11.1.3 Agar–Agar (Meer, 1980a)

Agar is a high molecular weight polymer (incorporating sulphur, sodium and calcium) extracted from the Gelidium and Gracilaria seaweeds. It will only dissolve in near-boiling-point water. At concentrations above 0.7%, the solution will set to a gel on cooling to 32–38°C. However, the gel requires heating to 88–94°C in order to remelt it. On drying, a film of agar undergoes considerable shrinkage. This probably accounts for the exfoliation of a pigment film which had been fixed with an agar/PVAL solution (Chemical Section, 1968).

Agar is likely to degrade by oxidation in a similar manner to other polysaccharides. It is fairly resistant to biodeterioration. Agar gels made with 5–17% by weight of gum in water have been used as moulding material. The warm solution sets to a rigid gel from which casts may be taken (Clarke, 1936).

11.1.4 Funori (Sands and Glicksman, 1973; Winter, 1984)

Funori is the polysaccharide extract from *Gloiopeltis furcata* seaweed found in the waters off Japan. Funori is obtained by dissolving the seaweed in warm-to-hot water. A small amount of the seaweed does not dissolve and is filtered off. Unlike agar, funori solutions do not gel on cooling. Funori probably degrades on ageing in a similar fashion to the other polysaccharides. It is susceptible to mould growth. Funori has been used traditionally in Japan as an adhesive and for refixing pigment (Winter, 1984).

11.2 Proteins

11.2.1 Glue

Background (Ward and Courts, 1977)

Connective tissue in skin, bone and other tissue, is made up of proteins (polyamides), principally collagen with many other components. Collagen molecules are held to each other by a few covalent and many hydrogen bonds. The molecules are partly hydrolysed on heating in water to produce a soluble product with a molecular weight in the range 20 000–250 000 (Hubbard, 1977) though 40 000–50 000 is around the normal value (Roff and Scott, 1971). Skin glues are derived from cattle and sheep hides (parchment glues) but may contain contaminants from skin preservatives and tanning agents. Hide glues have the highest molecular weight and strength, both as gels and as films. Bone glues are derived from most farm animals. Fish glues are made from skins (Norland, 1977) or from swim bladders (isinglas). Gelatine is a purified form of glue. Glue will swell in cold water to form a gel. The minimum amount of swelling occurs around pH 4.8. The gel will melt on heating, about 6°C for fish glues and 30–50°C for animal glues. Gelatine is soluble in few solvents at room temperature, e.g. 2,2,2-trifluoroethanol, and formamide. Water, glacial acetic acid, ethane-1,2-diol and dimethyl sulphoxide require heating (Umberger, 1967). Gelatine can be insolubilized by reacting it with trivalent metal ions, tannins or aldehydes. It is degraded rapidly in acid (pH <3) or alkaline (pH >9) conditions and by enzymes.

Gelatine is applied from warm solutions in water. The liquid sets first by cooling to a gel and then by evaporation of water. This results in a large shrinkage of the film. The glass transition temperature of gelatine is around 210°C (Kozlov and Burdygina, 1983) though, at 25% moisture content, gelatine is rubbery at room temperature. Slight heating can create severe increases in internal stresses; a 10°C rise at constant relative humidity can generate 1 MPa. Moisture content can be increased in a film by incorporating humectants, which serve the role of plasticizers.

Conservation

Glue was one of the strongest adhesives available before the development of synthetic materials. Glue/starch pastes were introduced for the relining of canvas paintings in the 18th century (Marijnissen, 1967) and have been used on other textiles (section 11.1.1). Glue is still the usual adhesive for the conservation of furniture (Hayward, 1976; von Reventlow, 1978b), following traditional methods in its construction. Glue is also used for the production of Japanese art materials (Winter, 1984; Morita, 1984). The shrinkage of glue has been employed to remove paint layers from substrates from the 17th century (Marijnissen, 1967) to the present, especially during the transfer of wall paintings (Mora *et al.*, 1984). These facing adhesives incorporate considerable amounts of plasticizing materials such as molasses in order to increase impact strength and flexibility.

Gelatine solutions were used widely for adhering and consolidating objects: ivory (Anon, 1852; Lowe, 1910), palaeontological bone (Howie, 1984), wood (Petrie, 1904; Cronyn and Horie, 1985), shale (Plenderleith, 1934), pottery (Rathgen, 1905) and porcelain (Thiacourt, 1868). Glues may have been protected from mould growth with mercuric chloride (corrosive sublimate) or formaldehyde (Rathgen, 1905). The former would remain as a toxic impurity and a contaminant for analysis; the latter would cause cross-linking and insolubilization of the gelatine. The insolubilization reaction between glue and tannins was proposed as a method of consolidation of waterlogged wood (Augusti, 1959).

11.2.2 Casein

Background (Salzberg, 1977)

Casein is the main milk protein precipitated from skimmed milk as curds or cheese by acidifying. The molecular weight of casein is about 30 000 (Roff and Scott, 1971). Casein films deposited from dilute sodium and potassium hydroxide solutions will redissolve on warming, though ammonia solutions dry to insoluble films. Calcium and similar multivalent alkalis create cross-links, forming an insoluble product. Calcium caseinate is the most usual form for adhesives. Mediaeval and 19th century recipes involved mixing dispersions of casein and slaked lime in water (Gettens and Stout, 1965; Spon, 1888). Modern formulations employ mixed dry ingredients to which water is added when required. Casein films are brittle but can be plasticized with glycerine or sugars. Casein supports mould growth and cannot be used in a damp environment, even if fungicides are added. The alkaline film prevents enzymes being effective in breaking down films of casein in short periods.

Conservation

Calcium caseinate is a traditional adhesive (Lucas, 1932) for wood (Hayward, 1976) and plaster restoration (Philipott and Mora, 1968). A similar adhesive, calcium albumate, made from white of egg, has also been used (Standage, 1931). The most frequent use has been as an adhesive for detached wall paintings (Filatov, 1975; Mora *et al.*, 1984). Skimmed milk has been applied to lime plasters and will form a cross-linked film. Casein has been used as a surface consolidant for stone (Plenderleith, 1955) and for pigments on paper (Kishore, 1952). The shrinkage of the calcium caseinate gel applied to pigments on wall paintings has created damage and difficulties in reversal (Nisbeth, 1980).

12 Natural resins

Many natural resins (*Suter*) are obtained as exudates from trees. These plant resins are based on the terpene skeleton, which contains ten carbon atoms. This can be arranged in a large variety of ways (*Figure 12.1*). Oleoresins can be extracted from most conifers but the resins display characteristic differences in chemical composition and properties. Those resins which are likely to have been used in the manufacture or conservation of objects have been well reviewed (Mills and White, 1987; Masschelein-Kleiner, 1978).

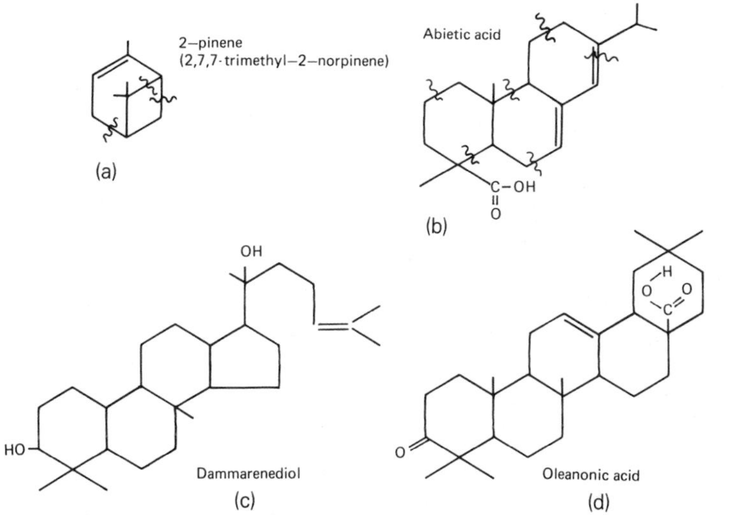

2–pinene
(2,7,7-trimethyl–2–norpinene)
(a)
Abietic acid
C–OH
O
(b)
OH
HO
Dammarenediol
(c)
O
H
O
C
O
Oleanonic acid
(d)

Figure 12.1 Typical terpenes. Many plant resins are terpene resins: (a) is the monoterpene making up the bulk of turpentine oil; (b) is a diterpenoid from rosin; and (c) (Mills, 1956) and (d) (Mills and White, 1987) are triterpenoids typical of dammar and mastic respectively. The wavy lines in (a) and (b) indicate the junction between the five carbon atom monomer units, isoprene, two of which are necessary to form a terpene

12.1 Dammar

Background

Dammar is a hydrocarbon, triterpenoid resin, obtained from various species of the *Diptocarpaceae.* Dammar, like other natural resins, is composed of a mixture of similar molecules whose proportions vary from sample to sample (*Figure 12.1(c)*). As collected, dammar contains about 10% dammar wax, which dissolves only in hydrocarbon solvents. This is removed before the resin is made up into a varnish (Mantell *et al.*, 1942). Dammar is a hard brittle resin, is easily scratched and has little flexibility, though more than ketone resins (Feller, 1971a). The low molecular weight allows mobile solutions to be prepared at much higher solids content than with high molecular weight polymers, and in a wider range of solvents (Appendix 3.23). The mobility of the molecules in solution is also much greater. This, combined with the high refractive index of dammar, makes pigments to which it is applied appear more saturated in colour (Feller, 1957) than do those subjected to high molecular weight polymers. Solvent is retained in dammar varnishes for upwards of six months, during which time hardness and brittleness gradually increase.

When a solution of dammar dries in high relative humidities, a bloom made up of small crystals of ammonium sulphate can occur on the surface. Dammar films can develop wrinkles during drying. The wrinkling appears to be the result of an initial oxidation of the resin combined with movement of the underlying solution. Mastic, which develops fewer wrinkles than dammar (Thomson, 1957), retains less solvent than dammar (Feller, 1957, 1958).

Each molecule of dammar absorbs about two molecules of oxygen during exposure to ultraviolet in air (Feller, 1977). This in turn increases the polarity of the solvents needed for dissolution (Appendix 3.23). Neither degradation nor cross-linking is noticeable during photo-oxidation, though the films do become more brittle. The yellowing of dammar has been shown to occur largely by thermal oxidation (Lafontaine, 1979a). The thermo-oxidation process does not appear to lead to increased polarity of the resin (Lafontaine, 1979b), which indicates that little oxygen is incorporated during dark-ageing. Exposure to ultraviolet causes bleaching of the chromophores. The yellowing (and to a lesser extent the increase in polarity) can be reduced significantly by an antioxidant (Irganox 565). With 0.75% Irganox/dammar resin applied in a stable solvent such as toluene, the projected time to yellow unacceptably was increased from 22 years to about 350 years. When the implications and extended ageing tests have been reported, significant improvements in the useful life of conservation materials should be possible.

Conservation

Dammar was introduced by German restorers as a more stable material than mastic for picture varnishes (Feller, 1966). However, the friability of dammar prompted the incorporation of plasticizing materials, e.g. rubber solutions and drying oils. Both of these will oxidize, rapidly becoming insoluble. They also require increasingly polar solvents, e.g. acetone, for removal (Feller and Bailie, 1972). Various solvents which have been used to apply films have been shown to increase the rate at which yellowing occurs, e.g. turpentine (Feller, 1976b) and Stoddards solvent (Lafontaine, 1979a).

Dammar applied in solution has been used for the consolidation of iron (Rathgen, 1905), wood (Barker, 1975; Blackshaw, 1974) and other materials (Plenderleith, 1934; Hübner, 1934). Dammar should remain soluble.

12.2 Mastic

Background

Mastic is exuded and collected from a bushy tree, *Pistacia lentiscus* (Mantell *et al.*, 1942). The solid resin is composed of a mixture of triterpenoids; *Figure 12.1(d)* is typical. Having a low molecular weight, the resin is brittle with little extensibility, though it forms solutions with high solids content. Portions of the resin are soluble in all the organic solvents (Appendix 3.24), but complete solution requires moderately polar solvents (Mantell *et al.*, 1942). Mastic films applied from solution release solvents relatively quickly and approach their final properties of hardness and brittleness in upwards of a month (Feller, 1957). They are less likely to wrinkle than are dammar films (Section 12.1). On photo-oxidation under daylight fluorescent lamps, mastic absorbs oxygen and becomes more polar, thus requiring more polar solvents for dissolution (Feller and Curran, 1975). Mastic is less stable than dammar in this respect.

Conservation

Mastic was the picture varnish material of first choice for many years (Hendy, 1947) because of its good working and film properties. However, it has been increasingly replaced by dammar (Lucas and Brommelle, 1953) since the early 19th century (Brommelle, 1956). A major deficiency of mastic as a varnish is its brittleness. This can be counteracted by adding a drying oil, but this creates the same types of problem as it does with dammar (Section 12.1). Its brittleness could be an asset during removal, as the film can be powdered on the painting by scraping or crushing (Ruheman, 1968). Mastic mixed with the oleoresin of *Larix decidua*, Venice turpentine, was used in the 19th century as a hot-melt adhesive for ceramics (Thiacourt, 1868).

12.3 Rosin

Background

Trees of the Pinus genus exude a thick liquid, once called common turpentine. A similar material is extracted from waste products of the forestry industry. Oil of turpentine (c. 30%) is distilled off by heating, leaving the highly modified solid rosin. Rosin is composed of a number of diterpenoid molecules, predominantly abietic acid (*Figure 12.1(b)*) (Joye and Lawrence, 1967). This acid reacts by oxidation to form hydroabietic acid and then 7-oxodehydroabietic acid. Rosin is initially soluble in a wide range of solvents which evaporate to deposit glossy clear films. The rapid oxidation of the resin causes loss of gloss, yellowing and increased water sensitivity. Because of its small molecular size, rosin is very brittle. Rosin may be modified by hydrogenation to reduce yellowing and oxidation, or reacted to produce esters.

Conservation

An early conservation use of pine resin was as a hot-melt coating applied to degraded wool in the 11th century (Cronyn and Horie, 1985). The oleoresin and the rosin derived from it have been included in recipes for artistic materials since the 9th century (Gettens and Stout, 1965). Picture varnishes and media were made by mixing oil and resin with or without heating (Van Schendel, 1958). Later, rosin was used as a spirit varnish, being found on globes (Mills and White, 1987), and was probably an adulterant of more expensive resins such as mastic (Brommelle, 1956).

The solubility of rosin in acetone increases from 40% at room temperature to 67% at 52°C (Bryce *et al.*, 1975). This property is the basis for the consolidation with rosin of waterlogged wood which has been dewatered in baths of acetone. After the wood has reached equilibrium with a saturated rosin solution at 52°C, the impregnated wood is allowed to cool. About 40% of the rosin precipitates during cooling. Setting of the other 60% occurs during subsequent evaporation of the acetone. The solvent takes some months to evaporate, during which time the consolidant is still flexible (Oddy, 1975b).

Cellolyn 21 (*Hercules*) (phthalate ester of abietyl alcohol), is used as a relatively stable (Autenreith, 1977) tackifying resin for BEVA 371, a hot-melt adhesive for canvas pictures (Berger, 1976). Rosin and its derivatives are widely used, as in pressure-sensitive adhesives based on rubbers (Autenreich, 1977). Up to 60% of the composition may be rosin derivatives. Adhesives incorporating rosin derivatives are not designed for long-term use and should be avoided in conservation (Magnelli, 1982).

12.4 Shellac

Background (Misra and Senguptal, 1970)

A scale insect (*Tacchardia lacca*) of south Asia secretes a protective covering on twigs. The twigs, sticklac, are collected and the resin is extracted by melting and cooling in various shapes, shellac and beadlac. Shellac is available in various grades – filtered resin (button lac), dewaxed or bleached. Some 30–40% of shellac is aleuritic acid, (9,10,16-trihydroxyhexadecanoic acid) (*Figure 12.2*), which is combined with sesquiterpene acids. The latter are

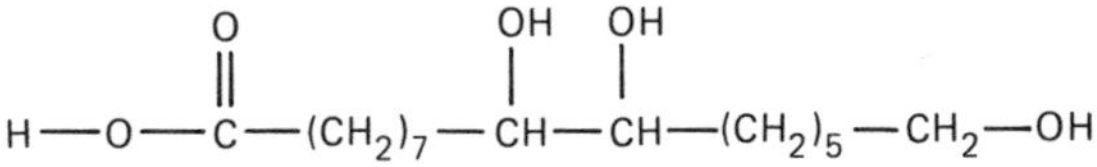

$$H{-}O{-}\overset{\overset{\displaystyle O}{\|}}{C}{-}(CH_2)_7{-}\overset{\overset{\displaystyle OH}{|}}{CH}{-}\overset{\overset{\displaystyle OH}{|}}{CH}{-}(CH_2)_5{-}CH_2{-}OH$$

Figure 12.2 A major constituent of shellac is aleuritic acid (9,10,16-trihydroxyhexadecanoic acid) which is esterified to form a complex polyester

unsaturated as well as having alcohol and aldehyde groups. Shellac dissolves in hydrogen-bonding solvents (Appendix 3.25). The solutions dry to glossy films with good adhesion and toughness. The molecules can be degraded by hydrolysis, e.g. in dilute alkali or by autoclaving with water. Shellac cross-links by two mechanisms. On heating, acetal links are formed. On prolonged room-temperature storage, a different mechanism results in insolubility in cold alcohol, though heating may cause dissolution (Roff and Scott, 1971). Pyridine may disrupt intractable films (Koob, 1979).

Conservation

Shellac has been used from the 19th century for the finishing and refinishing of woodwork, as French polish (Hayward, 1960), a solution of approximately 30 g of shellac in 100 ml of denatured alcohol. It has been applied as a molten liquid to heated ceramic sherds (Koob, 1979) either alone or fused with sulphur (Thiacourt, 1868). Alternatively it has been used as a viscous solution (Thiacourt, 1868; Petrie, 1888). Heat-activated films of shellac have been used for commercial 'drymounted' paper-laminating processes. The adhesive becomes insoluble in alcohol but may be broken down in 2-methoxyethanol (Baynes-Cope, 1972a).

12.5 Beeswax

Beeswax is obtained from the hives of honey bees and is usually purified by melting (m.p. 63 °C) and filtering. It is a complex mixture of hydrocarbons, esters and free fatty acids. It is slightly soluble in a small range of solvents (Appendix 3.26). The solubility increases considerably with temperature. Although it will yellow, presumably due to oxidation, it can remain soluble over millenia in Egyptian tombs. Beeswax has been widely used, mixed with natural resins and fillers, for relining paintings (Marijnissen, 1967). Beeswax has been used for consolidation, like paraffin wax, and as a matting agent for varnishes. This latter addition appears to have a welcome side-effect of reducing the oxidation of cyclohexanone resin varnishes (Raft, 1985).

12.6 Oils and alkyds

Background

Triglycerides (*Figure 12.3*) (Hilditch and Williams, 1964) are the esters of glycerol with a wide range of fatty acids (Tables 12.1 and 12.2). The difference between beef fat and linseed oil is largely caused by the different compositions of the fatty acid components. Most fatty acids are linear carbon chains with 18 carbon atoms. The drying of the oil, polymerization, to a solid is by oxidative cross-linking. This process is initiated by the double bond (*Figure 12.4*), so the reactivity of the fatty acid with oxygen is increased by the number of double bonds present (Wexler, 1964).

$$\begin{array}{l} H_2C-OH \\ \;\;| \\ HC-OH \\ \;\;| \\ H_2C-OH \end{array} \quad + \quad 3HO-\overset{\overset{\displaystyle O}{\|}}{C}-R$$

Glycerol — Fatty acids

$$\downarrow$$

$$\begin{array}{l} H_2C-O-\overset{\overset{\displaystyle O}{\|}}{C}-R' \\ \;\;| \\ HC-O-\underset{\underset{\displaystyle O}{\|}}{C}-R'' \\ \;\;| \\ H_2C-O-\underset{\underset{\displaystyle O}{\|}}{C}-R''' \end{array}$$

Figure 12.3 Triglycerides are esters of three fatty acids with glycerol

Table 12.1 Typical fatty acids in fats and oils

Fatty acid component	*Formula of acid*
Palmitic	$HOOC(CH_2)_{14}CH_3$
Stearic	$HOOC(CH_2)_{16}CH_3$
Oleic	$HOOC(CH_2)_7CH{=}CH(CH_2)_7CH_3$
Linoleic	$HOOC(CH_2)_7CH{=}CHCH_2CH{=}CH(CH_2)_4CH_3$
Linolenic	$HOOC(CH_2)_7(CH{=}CHCH_2)_3CH_3$
Elaeostearic	$HOOC(CH_2)_7(CH{=}CH)_3(CH_2)_3CH_3$

Table 12.2 Major components of some triglycerides (Hilditch and Williams, 1964)

Source of oil	*Major fatty acid components, typical values*	*Type of oil*[(1)]	*Iodine number*[(2)]
Cow/sheep	30% palmitic, 30% stearic, 35% oleic	N	
Olive	13% stearic, 69% oleic, 13% linoleic	N	
Cottonseed	20% stearic, 33% oleic, 44% linoleic	S	
Poppyseed	10% palmitic, 16% oleic, 72% linoleic	D	135
Walnut	5% palmitic, 18% oleic, 73% linoleic	D	140–150
Linseed	10% palmitic, 15% oleic, 16% linoleic, 56% linolenic	D	170–190
Tung	9% oleic, 10% linoleic, 79% eleostearic	D	145–175

Notes

(1) N = non-drying oil; S = semi-drying oil; D = drying oil.

(2) The iodine number is a measure of the degree of unsaturation in the oil. Higher values indicate greater unsaturation.

$$R-O-\overset{\displaystyle O}{\overset{\|}{C}}-(CH_2)_6\,CH_2-CH=CH-CH_2-(CH_2)_6\,CH_3$$

$\downarrow$ O_2 (Catalysed by metal ions)

$$R-O-\overset{\displaystyle O}{\overset{\|}{C}}-(CH_2)_6\,CH_2-\overset{\displaystyle OOH}{\overset{|}{C}H}-CH=CH-(CH_2)_6\,CH_3$$

+

$$R-O-\overset{\displaystyle O}{\overset{\|}{C}}-(CH_2)_6\,CH=CH-\overset{\displaystyle OOH}{\overset{|}{C}H}-CH_2-(CH_2)_6\,CH_3$$

$\downarrow$ Low temperatures $< 100^\circ C$

$$\sim CH_2-CH-CH=CH\sim$$
$$|$$
$$O$$
$$|$$
$$\sim CH_2-CH-CH=CH\sim$$

Ether cross-links and decomposition products,
e.g. dicarboxylic acids, acetic acid and aldehydes

Figure 12.4 Oxidative cross-linking of drying oils (Wexler, 1964)

Degradation products, e.g. carboxylic acids and aldehydes (Rasti and Scott, 1980) are also produced; these may evaporate or be extracted by washing, e.g. with solvents (Stolow, 1971). The oxidation reaction is catalysed by metal ions which are added as driers or as pigments, e.g. verdigris. The drying reaction can be speeded up by heating the oil with oxygen (boiled or blown) as a pretreatment. A vinyl-type polymerization can be achieved by heating the oil in the absence of air (stand oils). This increases the molecular weight and reduces the susceptibility to oxidation. Yellowing occurs when oxidation is in the dark or under low illumination (Chandok and Gupta, 1964). The yellowing can be bleached by sunlight and oxidizing agents. Less highly unsaturated oils yellow less.

The cross-linked oil will continue to oxidize. The physical state changes from a mobile liquid to a gel to a tough film. This is insoluble but is swollen by solvents (Appendix 3.27). Both the density and the refractive index increase. Subsequently the film will become brittle and finally friable as the structure starts to break down. The loss of degradation products and consequent shrinkage of the film causes cracking.

Oxidation of non-drying and semi-drying oils also takes place but without causing the formation of an insoluble network. The resulting oxidation products, such as acids and aldehydes, are the cause of rancidity in fats and oils.

Alkyd resins (Kraft *et al.*, 1967) are formed by reacting drying oils with polyols, typically pentaerythritol $C(CH_2OH)_4$, and phthalic anhydride. A polymer is produced with a much higher molecular weight than the oil. The number of cross-links and therefore the amount of unsaturation required for the insolubilization of the film is reduced. This improves the resistance to oxidation, degradation and yellowing. Because of the higher molecular weights, the alkyds are usually applied as a concentrated, e.g. 50% solids, solution in hydrocarbon solvents. Setting is thus a two-stage process. Viscosity increases during evaporation of the solvent, and this is followed by a slow cross-linking and insolubilization. During manufacture, the viscosity of the resin, drying time, hardness and stability of the film can be optimized to suit a particular application.

Conservation

Walnut and linseed oils have long been used in the creation (Gettens and Stout, 1965; Mills and White, 1987) and restoration (Marijnissen, 1967) of paintings. Walnut oil was often preferred for paints, especially light colours. However, its slow drying and instability in storage has reduced its use. Linseed oil has been used for consolidation of iron corrosion products (Rathgen, 1905) and stonework (Stois, 1937; Rathgen, 1905). The latter use was criticized in the 1920s for its harmful effects on stone (Warnes, 1926). Linseed oil emulsions with vinegar and turpentine were suggested as a polish and dirt remover for furniture (Plenderleith and Werner, 1971). A mixture of ethanol, aliphatic solvent and glacial acetic acid was found to remove the tacky deposit effectively (Martin, 1978).

Animal fat (tallow) was used as a consolidant in the 19th century for preserving iron objects (Rathgen, 1905). Lanolin, the grease derived from sheep fleeces, is, after thousands of years, still employed as a corrosion-inhibiting coating on iron objects. It is not a triglyceride but a lipid, a mixture of esters of fatty acids and long-chain alcohols.

13 Cross-linking polymers

13.1 Silicon-containing polymers

Background

The chemistry of silicones is potentially as diverse as that of carbon-based organic compounds. The scientific nomenclature is derived from silane, SiH_4, analogous to methane. Thus a typical compound might be methyltriethoxysilane (*Figure 13.1*). Silicon atoms form chains not by simple Si—Si bonds but with linking oxygen atoms, i.e. Si—O—Si.

Monomeric silane derivatives used in conservation are tri- or tetrafunctional derivatives, such as tetraethoxysilane (synonyms ethyl silicate, tetraethyl silicate, TEOS). The polymerization,

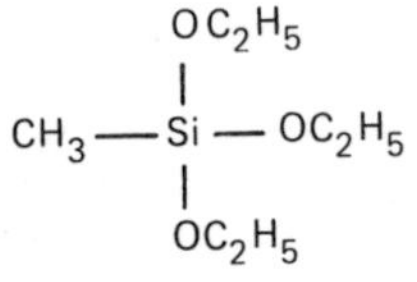

$$CH_3-Si(OC_2H_5)_3$$

Figure 13.1 Methyl triethoxysilane

$$-\overset{|}{\underset{|}{Si}}-O-C_2H_5 \quad + \quad C_2H_5-O-\overset{|}{\underset{|}{Si}}- \xrightarrow{2H_2O} -\overset{|}{\underset{|}{Si}}-O-H \quad + \quad H-O-\overset{|}{\underset{|}{Si}}- \quad + 2C_2H_5OH \text{ (ethanol (evaporates))}$$

$$\longrightarrow -\overset{|}{\underset{|}{Si}}-O-Si- \quad + H_2O$$

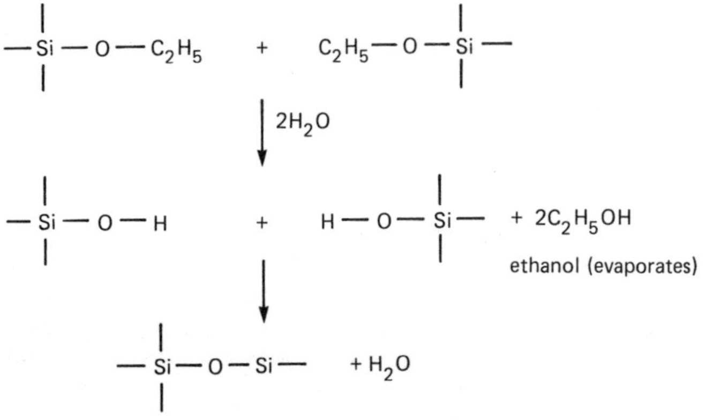

Figure 13.2 Condensation polymerization of ethoxysilanes in the presence of water

Table 13.1 Silane coupling agents. The coupling agents are usually applied to a cleaned surface as dilute solutions in water or alcohol

Name	*Chemical formula*	*Application*	*Trade name* (Union Carbide)[1]
γ-methacrylopropyl trimethoxysilane	$H_2C{=}C(CH_3)COO{-}(CH_2)_3{-}Si(OCH_3)_3$	Polyester resin	A-174
γ-glycidoxypropyl trimethoxysilane	$H_2C\overset{O}{—}CH—CH_2O—(CH_2)_3—Si(OCH_3)_3$	Epoxy	A-187
γ-aminopropyl trimethoxysilane	$H_2N{-}(CH_2)_3{-}Si(OCH_3)_3$	General purpose	A-1100

Note
(1) Other manufacturers, e.g. (*Dow Corning*), supply similar materials.

initiated by traces of water, is by hydrolysis and condensation (*Figure 13.2*). Not all the silanol Si—OH groups will condense to form cross-links (Amoroso and Fassina, 1983). The polymer formed from a tetrafunctional monomer will be similar to silica gel. Care must be taken to ensure anhydrous storage of silanes to prevent premature polymerization. Trifunctional monomers such as methyltrimethoxysilane react in a similar fashion but retain the Si—C bond. The polymer formed from this monomer is resistant to solvents and photo-oxidation. It is tough but not flexible (Moncrieff, 1976). The silanol groups will react with—OH groups on a surface to create chemical links. By using trialkoxysilanes with organic groups that interact with organic adhesives (coupling agents) (Table 13.1), a chemical bond between the surface and the adhesive can be ensured. The bond thus formed is more stable to failure. Coupling agents are therefore used to achieve adhesion on glass (Horie, 1983b). The chemical link between the silicon atom and attached carbon chain will eventually hydrolyse.

The usual chain-forming unit of silicone oils and rubbers is dimethylsiloxane (*Figure 13.3*). Organic substituents other than methyl groups are used for special purposes, e.g. phenyl and fluorinated alkyls. The silicones are made with various molecular weights, from thin fluids (degree of polymerization, DP c. 3) (antifoaming agents) to viscous semi-liquids (DP c. 20 000) (release agents).

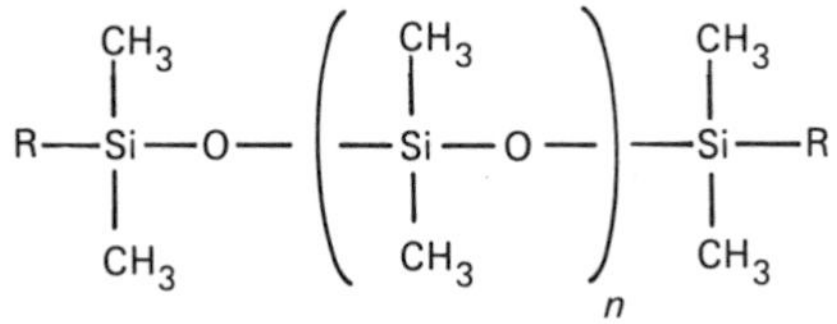

$$R-\overset{CH_3}{\underset{CH_3}{\overset{|}{\underset{|}{Si}}}}-O-\left(-\overset{CH_3}{\underset{CH_3}{\overset{|}{\underset{|}{Si}}}}-O-\right)_n-\overset{CH_3}{\underset{CH_3}{\overset{|}{\underset{|}{Si}}}}-R$$

Figure 13.3 Monomer unit and end groups of dimethylsiloxane polymers. Dimethylsiloxane is the common unit of most silicone polymers. If R = —CH_3, the end groups are trimethylsilane. The polymer is an unreactive silicone oil or grease, depending on the molecular weight. If R = —OH, the end groups are dimethylsilanol. The polymer will react and cross-link with suitable reagents to form a rubber (condensation type). If R = —H, the end groups are dimethylsilane. The polymer will react and cross-link with suitable reagents to form a rubber (addition type)

The chains can be cross-linked if suitable reactive groups are incorporated in the molecule. Most room-temperature vulcanizing (RTV) rubbers set by a condensation reaction (Beers, 1977) (*Figure 13.4*, Table 13.2). RTV rubbers are available either in two parts which are mixed or in a single pack whose setting is initiated

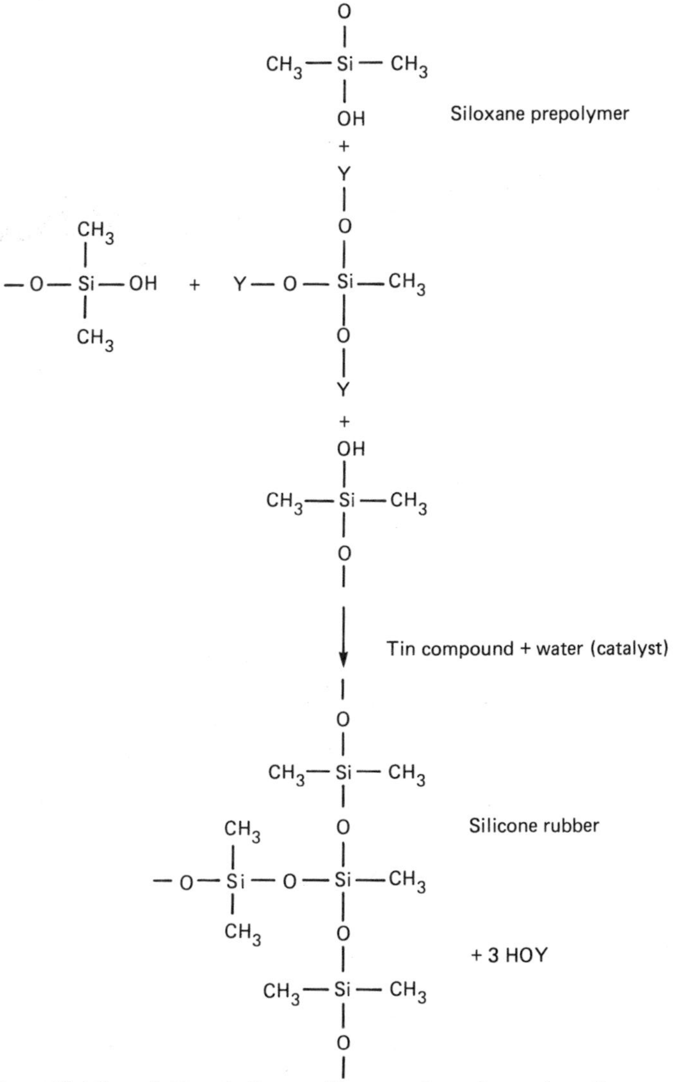

Siloxane prepolymer

Tin compound + water (catalyst)

Silicone rubber

+ 3 HOY

Figure 13.4 Cross-linking of silicone rubber prepolymer by condensation polymerization

by the diffusion of water vapour into the liquid. The volatile fragment evaporates, resulting in shrinkage on setting, up to 2% linear, which increases on ageing (Waters, 1983). The one-part adhesives frequently exhibit adhesion to surfaces on setting, presumably because of the reaction with water on the surface, and

Table 13.2 Some typical cross-linking agents

Reactive group, Y	*Curing rubber gives off*
$-O-C(=O)-CH_3$	Acetic acid
$-OC_2H_5$	Ethanol
$-O-N=C(C_2H_5)(CH_3)$	Methylethyl oxime

this can be increased by coupling agents. These rubbers have low strength and extensibility compared to hydrocarbon rubbers. New varieties of the silicone rubbers show considerable improvements over the very weak original materials (Brydson, 1982). Another group of RTV rubbers set by an addition reaction (Meals, 1969) (*Figure 13.5*), though this cross-linking reaction may be inhibited by many substrates, release agents etc. (Waters, 1983). These materials are notable for having much lower shrinkage on setting, typically 0.3%, as no volatile products are produced.

All silicone rubbers are compounded with fillers to increase their strength and reduce the cost. Silicone rubbers allow fast diffusion of gases through the flexible structure. The rubbers have

$$-O-C(CH_3)_2-CH{=}CH_2 \quad + \quad H-Si(CH_3)_2-O-$$

$$\downarrow \text{Platinum compound catalyst}$$

$$-O-C(CH_3)_2-CH_2-CH_2-Si(CH_3)_2-O-$$

Figure 13.5 Addition cross-linking of silicone rubber achieved by incorporating vinyl groups in the prepolymer

a very low glass transition temperature and are therefore likely to pick up and hold dirt particles. The cross-linked polymers can be swollen by solvents (Appendix 3.28).

Conservation

Silanes Silanes are used in conservation (Grissom and Weiss, 1981) particularly for the consolidation of stone (Amoroso and Fassina, 1983). Tetraethoxysilane (TEOS) (*Wacker*) has been used for stone consolidation because of the similarity of the polymerized gel to many stone materials. Deep penetration may have been prevented in the past because of the presence of prepolymerized silane of high molecular weight. From the 1960s, methyltrialkoxysilanes (*Dow Corning, Dynamit*) were used to make the stone water-repellent. Monomeric silanes are likely to be lost from the surface by evaporation before hydrolysis can take place. The penetration may be improved by employing slow evaporating solvents that accumulate at the surface (Moncrieff and Hempel, 1977), by bathing the surface in consolidant (Wihr, 1976) or by covering the surface with an impermeable membrane (Hempel, 1976). Improved penetration and setting of a silane treatment is claimed for Brethane (*Colebrand*), which is made up of three components mixed just before application; the alkyltrialkoxysilane, water and solvent, and a lead catalyst. The mixture remains mobile for some hours and then suddenly gels (Price, 1981).

Although silane polymers may coat the surfaces of the particles (Snethlage and Klemm, 1978; Mavrov, 1983) they do not provide bulking of the friable stone. Silanes have been modified to increase surface strength with acrylic polymer (Racanello E55050) (*Raccanello*) (Larson, 1980b), or epoxy resin (Rossi-Manaresi, 1976). However, the use of silanes is still in the development stage. While polymerization in stone and ceramics appears to work well in uncomplicated situations (Nishiura, 1981b; Rossi-Manaresi, 1981), the more intractable problems of large stone structures in the open air are still under active research.

Treatment using TEOS has been attempted on organic objects such as wood, basketry and paper (Paleos *et al.*, 1981) though with limited success (Grattan, 1982a; Jespersen, 1982). The polymerization of silanes that lead to more flexible polymers, e.g. using a mixture of difunctional and trifunctional silanes, has been suggested. All silane treatments are irreversible.

Silane coupling agents (Table 13.1) have been widely used to increase the durability of the adhesion between an adhesive and glass. Once the silane end has reacted with the glass (or other substrates), the organic component may be reacted with the adhesive, e.g. epoxy or polyester, or be used to increase the wetting of the surface by a thermoplastic in solution (Errett *et al.*, 1984).

Siloxanes Silicone oils have been used in conservation to reduce the foaming of polymer emulsions (Werner, 1952). They have been suggested as protective coatings for metal objects, e.g. iron (Gyermek, 1964), copper and zinc (Cějka, 1975), and as liquid storage media for fossils (Rixon, 1976). However, silicone liquids are likely to drain away over time, leaving surfaces uncovered. Advantage is taken of the lack of adhesion in the use of these oils as release agents (Rixon and Meade, 1956; Wang, 1977; Ketnath, 1978). They should not, of course, be used on materials which absorb them, e.g. rubber and porous materials. Silicone liquids are notorious for being difficult to remove from substrates, where they prevent the adhesion of another surface coating. Repeated washing with solvents such as toluene is usually necessary.

Silicone RTV one-part rubbers have been widely adopted for adhesive work with stained glass that is to be replaced *in situ* (Bettembourg, 1975). However, the silicones will not dissolve (Erhardt, 1983) and the bond with glass will only be broken by chemical degradation of the polymer and/or glass surface, this being the corollary of its stability. The low glass transition temperature enables the polymer to absorb dirt. Uncured silicone adhesive must not be allowed to come into contact with anything other than the surfaces to be bonded. The range of silicone rubbers are being improved and non-corrosive products with better adhesion properties are becoming available. Although the acetic acid byproduct of many RTV silicones does not seem to have caused corrosion of lead cames in stained glass windows, one case has been noted of a silicone adhesive apparently absorbing manganese colorant from a glass (Cole, 1977). Silicone rubbers contain a small proportion, typically 2–6%, of unreacted silicone oil. This will tend to migrate into porous materials (*Figure 13.6*) and may creep out of joints on to exposed surfaces. Silicone rubbers have been developed as pressure-sensitive adhesives (Fabri-sil) (*Shelley*) (Fieux, 1984). A thermoplastic silicone resin (Vani-sil) (*Shelley*) (Fieux, 1984) has been suggested as a picture varnish, though its T_g (137°C) appears too high for this purpose.

Some silicone adhesives can be modified by thinning with anhydrous hydrocarbon solvents such as toluene or cyclohexane. The moisture-activated curing will be retarded as the solvent

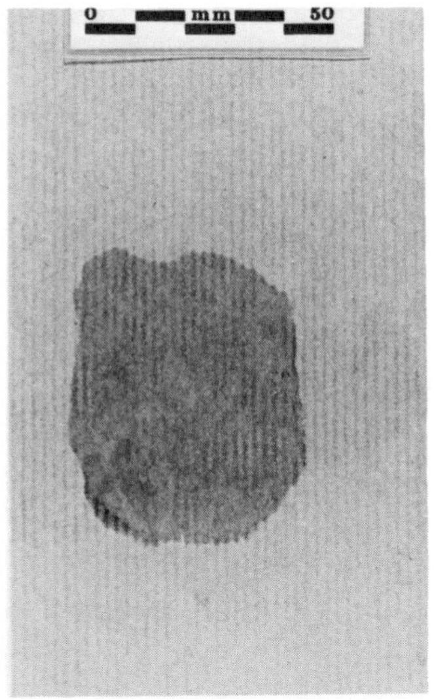

Figure 13.6 Silicone rubber prepolymers are liquid and contain small amounts of unreactive impurities. These will be absorbed into porous materials, causing staining. A useful test is to allow a small sample of the polymer to cure on brown paper. The illustration shows the stain occurring on the reverse side of the paper caused by the migration of the silicone liquids

evaporates. Pigments (*Rhodia*) may be incorporated into the thinned adhesive.

Silicone rubbers are increasingly used for taking moulds of objects because of their ease of use and excellent detail reproduction (Table 13.3). The strength of silicone rubbers can be assessed in various ways but the three most important for conservation use are the tear strength, elongation at break and hardness. By choosing a low tear strength material one can reduce the possible stresses on the object. A rubber which has a high elongation at break is likely to withstand pulling out of deep undercuts or doubling back on itself in a sleeve mould. The harder rubbers are more rigid and more likely to be self-supporting in thin sheets than the softer polymers. As silicone rubbers have a high oxygen transmission rate, the setting of some polymers, especially polyester resins, can be inhibited. Special measures such as curing in vacuum or nitrogen or the use of carefully chosen polyester resins may be employed.

13.2 Polyester resins

Background (Bruins, 1976)

The basis for polyester resin formulations is the polyester resin prepolymer (Brydson, 1982) (*Figure 13.7*). This prepolymer is

Table 13.3 Typical silicone rubbers (manufacturers' information)

Product	*Manufacturer*	*Cross-link type*[1]	*Viscosity* (mPa.s)	*Pot life/ handling hours*[2]	*Elongation at break* (%)	*Tear strength* (N/mm)	*Hardness Shore A*	*Shrinkage (1 week)* (linear %)	*Colour*	*Use with casting materials*[3]	
										Recommended	*Unsuitable*
Silastic 3110	Dow	Cond	12 500	0.1–4/0.3–48	180	22	45	0.6	White	PE	PU,E,M
Silastic 9161	Corning	Cond	16 000	0.1–1/24	150	22	38	1	Off-white	M	
Silastic E		Add	60 000	2/24	400	160	35	0.1	White	PE,PU	E
Silastic J		Add	100 000	2/24	250	150	60	<0.1	Green	PU	M
RTV-ME426	Wacker	Cond	10 000	0.3–1.5/4–24	120	5.3	60		Red	M,PU,PE	
RTV-M531		Cond	28 000	0.5–1.5/15	380	20	19		White	PE,E,PP	
RTV-M533		Cond	35 000	0.5–1.5/8–20	350	20	25	0.4l	Pearl	PP,PE,E	A
RTV-M539		Cond	>100 000	0.5–3/6–24	600	28	20	0.6	Milky	PP,PE	A
RTV-M540		Cond	48 000	0.1–1/15–20	300	20	38		White	PU,E	
Rhodorsil RTV5335	Rhône-Poulenc	Cond	60 000	0.5–2/18	130	32	60	0.5	Beige	PP,PE	
CAF3		Cond	150 000	(4)	300	4	30		Translucent		

Notes
(1) Cond = condensation; Add = addition.
(2) Usually depends on the choice of catalyst
(3) PP = plaster of Paris; PE = polyester resin; PU = polyurethane resin; E = epoxy resin; A – acrylic resin; M = low melting point metals.
(4) Cures on contact with atmospheric moisture to give off acetic acid.

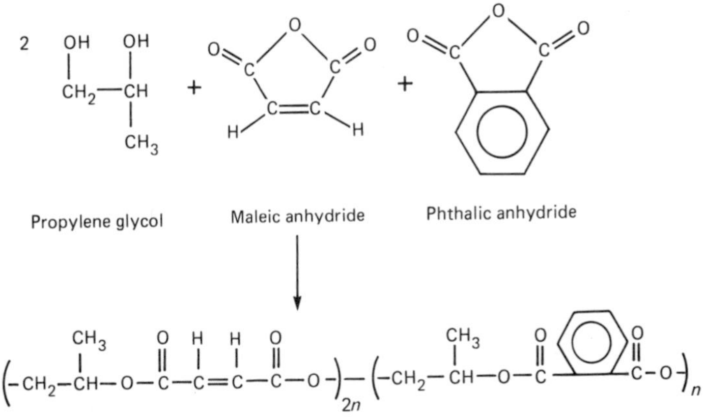

Propylene glycol Maleic anhydride Phthalic anhydride

$n \simeq 4 \quad M_r$ c. 2000

Figure 13.7 Components of a typical polyester laminating resin

dissolved in a reactive monomer, styrene, to form a liquid with a convenient viscosity. Copolymerization of the styrene with the unsaturated groups in the polyester component is initiated by adding a peroxide initiator to the resin solution, usually butanone peroxide (TLV 0.2 ppm, Section 3.2). The reaction is catalysed by an accelerator, typically cobalt naphthenate, incorporated in the initial resin solution. The accelerator and the initiator must never be mixed as they form an explosive combination. Increased concentration of accelerator (>2%) causes discoloration of the cured polymer. Polyester formulations are available which provide a range of properties in the cured polymer, e.g. increased flexibility, stability to light and fire resistance. Various types of addition can be made. Fillers, e.g. calcium carbonate or microspheres, reinforcing materials, e.g. glass fibre, or colorants, e.g. dyes and pigments, are available (Chapter 14).

The vinyl polymerization (*Figure 13.8*) results first in gellation of the liquid then hardening of the solid. Considerable heat is produced and this can lead to distortion and, in extreme cases, charring. The rate of reaction can be reduced by employing less accelerator and initiator. Polymerization also results in shrinkage, up to 8% by volume, which can be minimized by reducing the rise in temperature. The reaction probably continues for some months (Demmler, 1980). Oxygen interferes with the polymerization reaction, preventing cross-linking and leaving surfaces of the resin exposed to the air tacky. This interference can be minimized by

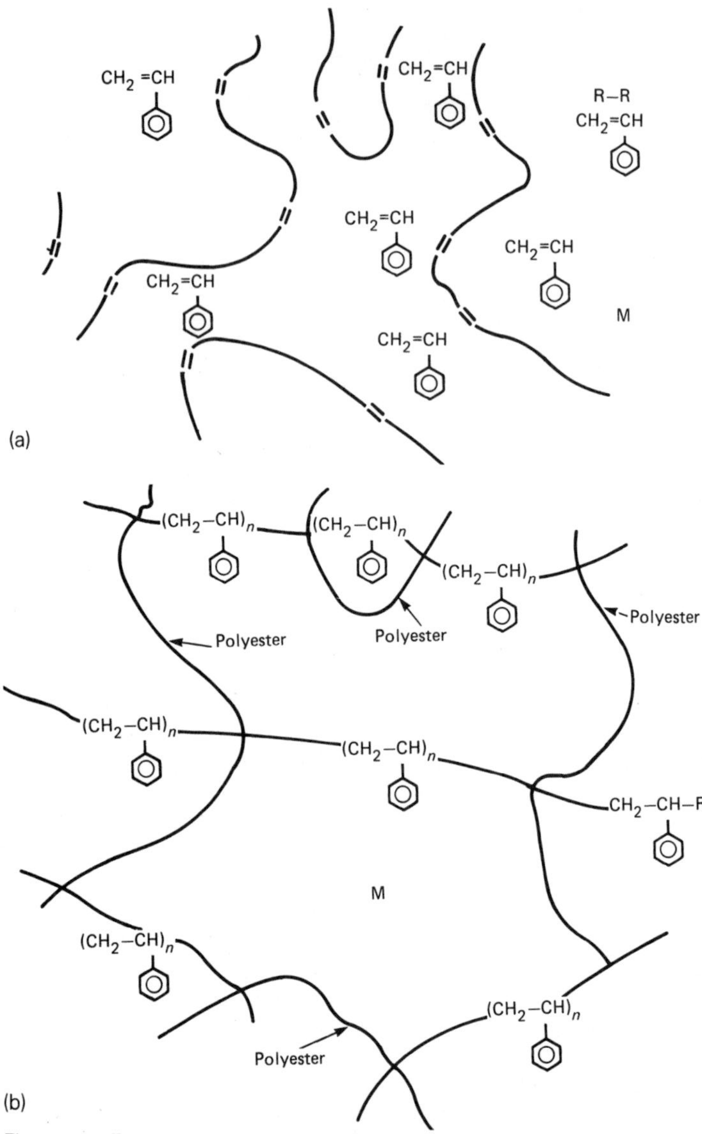

Figure 13.8 The curing of a polyester resin, adapted from Brydson (1982). (a) Components of a resin ready for application: low molecular weight unsaturated prepolymer molecules; reactive diluent molecules, usually styrene; initiator ('catalyst') molecules (R—R) which decompose to form free radicals; catalyst ('accelerator') molecules (M) which are metal compounds. (b) Structure of the cured polyester resin. The prepolymer is cross-linked by the vinyl copolymerization with the styrene. The value of *n* is 2–3 in many polymers

reducing the amount of accelerator used (Waters, 1983) or by adding wax to the resin (Brydson, 1982).

Cured polyesters yellow on exposure to light. Oxidation will also be accelerated by the oxygen absorbed into the polymer during storage and curing. Polyester resins are susceptible to swelling, hydrolysis and degradation by water and aqueous solutions (Abeysinghe *et al.*, 1982). This is worst at the defective surfaces formed during curing.

Conservation

Soon after their introduction in the 1940s, polyester resins were used for encapsulating natural history objects (Purves and Martin, 1950). This use has probably been abandoned for objects that must be preserved. One example has been published of a transparent resin that went opaque (Meurgues, 1982). The high transparencies of some embedding resins have been found useful in the restoration of glass (Husson and Wihr, 1954; Wihr, 1977 (from (*Trylon*) (EM400PA), (*Vosschemie*) (Giebharz GTS) and (*Tiranti*) (Jackson, 1983; Davison and Jackson, 1985)). They are used for the consolidation of wood (Plenderleith, 1956; Werner, 1978) and, as filled putties, for the gap-filling of wood (O'Connor, 1979) and metal (Organ, 1959a; Lane, 1974) objects. Polyester resins have frequently been used as adhesives for stone (Sintolit) (*Pisani*) (Larson, 1978) and ceramics (Larney, 1975) where high strength is required to bond strong fragments. Polyester resins have been used to consolidate stone, both as simple chemically initiated mixtures painted on to surfaces (Larson, 1980a) and as gamma-radiation-initiated monomers following vacuum impregnation (Amoroso and Fassina, 1983). Ranges of polyester resins are available from local manufacturers and agents. The cured polymers cannot be dissolved in organic solvents but may be removed from smooth surfaces after swelling (Appendix 3.29).

13.3 Polyurethane polymers

Background (Brydson, 1982)

The urethane bond is produced by reaction between an isocyanate group and an alcohol group (*Figure 13.9*). By varying the isocyanate component, R (Table 13.4), and the alcohol component, R′, the polyurethanes, from fibres to coatings, are made. Both di- and polyisocyanates and alcohols are used to build up linear and cross-linked polymers. Most polyurethane formulations

Table 13.4 Commonly used isocyanates and their uses

Name	*Abbreviation*	*Formula*	*Control limit (ppm)*[1]	*Uses*
2,4-Toluene diisocyanate	TDI	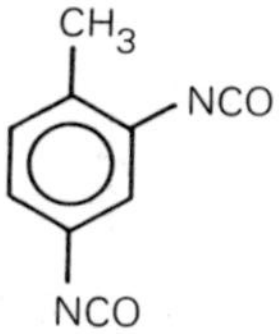 CH_3 NCO NCO —	0.005	Foams, adhesives
4,4′-diisocyanato-diphenylmethane (impure)	MDI	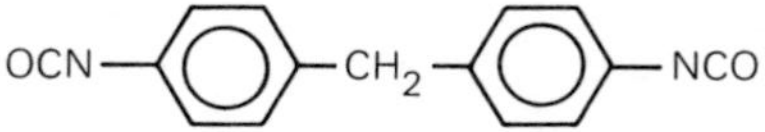 OCN—CH_2—NCO	0.02	Foams, adhesives
1,5-Naphthelene diisocyanate		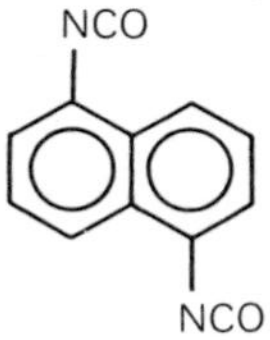 NCO NCO —	0.02	Rubbers

Hexamethylene diisocyanate	HDI	$OCN—(CH_2)_6—NCO$	0.005	Coatings
Adduct of HDI with water		$NH—(CH_2)_6—NCO$ | $C=O$ | $N—(CH_2)_6—NCO$ | $C=O$ | $NH—(CH_2)_6—NCO$		Coatings

Note
(1) Control limit (concentration of vapour in the workroom air) should not be exceeded (HSE, 1974) (section 3.2)

$$\begin{array}{lll} \text{Isocyanate} & R-N=C=O & \\ & \quad\ \vdots\quad\ \vdots & \longrightarrow \quad R-\underset{\underset{H}{|}}{N}-\overset{\overset{O}{\|}}{C}-OR' \\ \text{Alcohol} & \quad H-O-R' & \end{array}$$

Urethane bond

Figure 13.9 The formation of the urethane link

are proprietary and the ingredients undeclared. All the isocyanates are highly toxic. Less volatile di-isocyanates such as MDI or high molecular weight derivatives are preferred. Isocyanates can react with most —OH groups, so eliminating water contamination from surfaces and creating chemical links between the polymer and the surface. These reactions increase adhesion considerably. Polyurethane polymers are sensitive to thermal and photolytic-induced oxidation (Osawa, 1982) and are therefore usually compounded with stabilizers.

Foams make up a large volume of the polyurethanes used. The polyol-containing component may be based on a polyester or a polyether. The polyester-type foams frequently have better mechanical properties but are more susceptible to photolytic, hydrolytic and oxidative breakdown. The foam can yellow and disintegrate into a friable sticky mass. Where longer life is required, polyether foams are used. Polyurethane foams are not greatly affected by organic solvents but may be broken down by vigorous treatments, e.g. hot alcoholic alkali or 95% sulphuric acid (Roff and Scott, 1971). It is therefore advisable to avoid contact between the foaming materials and objects. The prepolymers may be dissolved in pyridine, dimethyl sulphoxide or formic acid.

Various forms of polyurethane coatings are available. For maximum toughness and light-stability, an acrylic polyol and a light-stable polyisocyanate, e.g. the HDI derivatives, may be applied. Polyisocyanates and derivatives are frequently added to alkyd resins to improve their properties of toughness and adhesion. They suffer from many of the instabilities of the parent alkyds.

Polyurethane adhesives are frequently applied in solution as thermoplastics made from reacting diols, such as polyesters or polyethers with hydroxyl end groups, with di-isocyanates. These materials are rubbery, tough and, because of the urethane and other polar groups, have good adhesion to textiles and leathers. In addition they are more resistant to oxidation than diene-type rubbers. However, they are still unstable. They can be cross-linked and bound to the substrate by incorporating a small quantity of di-isocyanate either free or attached to the polyol. Strength is increased and resistance to solvents is ensured.

Conservation

One-part formulations are composed of an isocyanate prepolymer in an anhydrous solvent. As the solvent evaporates, cross-links are produced to form the polymer. Isocyanate and polyol in the two-part formulation react when they are mixed. Except when applied to a smooth unreactive surface, a polyurethane treatment is irreversible.

Xylamon LX Hardening N (*Desowag*), a resin dissolved in a petroleum solvent, sets to a solid (perhaps a polyurethane) on exposure to the moisture of the air. It has been extensively used since the 1950s for the consolidation of fragile wood (Packard, 1971). Modified isocyanate solutions have been used for consolidating earth (Steen, 1971; Sawada, 1981a).

Commercial polyurethane adhesives, applied as solutions, have been adapted to the conservation of leather, both as adhesives (White, 1980) and as consolidants (Haines, 1984). The most effective, and irreversible, of these materials are composed of flexible polyurethane polymers with active isocyanate groups which cross-link on to the substrate.

A two-part polyurethane coating is applied to stained glass for protection and consolidation (Bettembourg, 1976).

80 parts by weight Viacryl SM 564 (formerly VC363) (*Vianova*) (an acrylic polymer incorporating alcohol groups), a 65% solution in 2-ethoxyethyl acetate
20 parts by weight Desmodur N75 (*Bayer*) (an HDI adduct with water, *Table 13.4*), a 75% solution in 2-ethoxyethyl acetate

The cured polymer is removed by swelling in solvents (Appendix 3.30), e.g. dichloromethane-based resin disintegrators, and scraping off the resulting gel.

Rigid polyurethane foams have been used for temporary facing supports when treating pictures with high impasto (Honig, 1974; Kottulinsky, 1982) using an appropriate isolating varnish. The bulk of the foam is removed mechanically, with the final, adhering layer being removed when the separating layer is dissolved. Rigid preformed foams have also been used as more permanent support for display (Shorer, 1969), storage and treatments (White, 1979). Foam is widely used in the lifting and temporary support of archaeological objects (Price, 1975). Foaming polyurethane generates a large amount of heat and is an excellent insulator. Damage by heating should be considered before the foam is applied. The reacting polyurethane should be kept rigorously isolated from objects while in the liquid state.

13.4 Epoxy resins

Background (Lee and Neville, 1967; Potter, 1970)

An epoxy resin system is made up of two parts – one incorporates the epoxide group, and the other is the hardener which reacts with the epoxide and cross-links the molecules (*Figure 13.10*). A wide range of polymers can be produced by changing the epoxide and cross-linking components. Further modification can be achieved using catalysts, diluents and plasticizers. Epoxy adhesives and gap-fillers have high strength and good adhesion to many substrates. Shrinkage, c. 5%, occurs in two stages about equally, in the liquid state and later in the gel state (Dannenberg and May, 1969). The force exerted by a room-temperature-setting resin was found to be 4.4 MPa (Igarashi *et al.*, 1979).

The basic epoxide resin of industry is the diglycidyl ether of bisphenol A, DGEBA, a viscous (or solid) oligomer. The benzene in the chain ensures that the resin cures to a strong rigid polymer in a short time. When the molecules are small the material is liquid. In order to be able to calculate the correct proportions of epoxy resin and amine, one must know the number of epoxide groups in a known quantity. The equivalent weight is defined as the molecular weight of the epoxy divided by the number of epoxide rings in each molecule.

The hardeners for room temperature use are the aliphatic amines and amides (*Figure 13.11*). Other materials such as acid anhydrides are used in high-temperature curing. The amount of amine required for reaction is described in the same way as for the

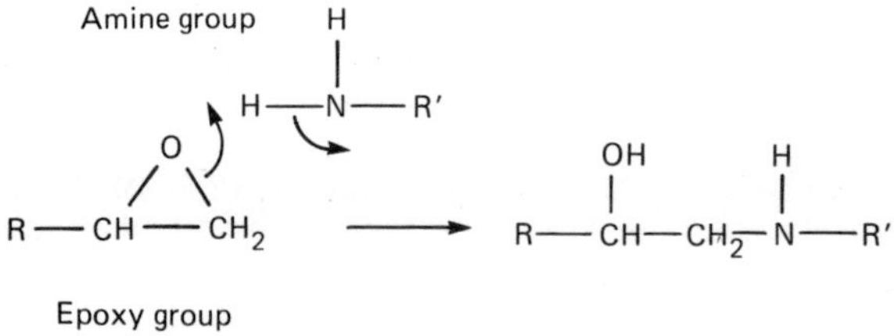

Figure 13.10 Epoxy-amine cross-linking reaction

	Comment
$H_2N(CH_2{-}CH_2{-}NH)_2{-}CH_2{-}CH_2{-}NH_2$ Triethylene tetramine (TETA)	Low viscosity, fast cure, toxic (skin)
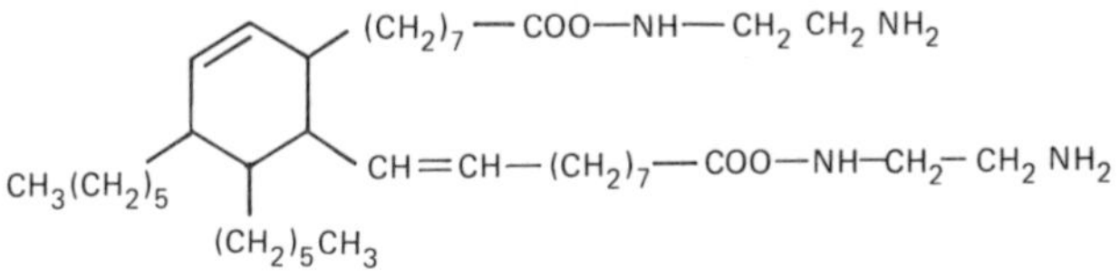 Cyclohexene ring bearing $(CH_2)_7{-}COO{-}NH{-}CH_2\,CH_2\,NH_2$, $CH{=}CH{-}(CH_2)_7{-}COO{-}NH{-}CH_2{-}CH_2\,NH_2$, $CH_3(CH_2)_5$ and $(CH_2)_5CH_3$ Polyamide	Very viscous, low toxicity
$H_2N{-}CH_2{-}CH_2{-}N(H){-}CH_2{-}CH_2{-}(OCH_2CH_2)_n{-}N(H){-}CH_2CH_2NH_2$ Poly(ethylene glycol) diethylamine adduct	Fast cure, low toxicity
$R{-}CH_2{-}CH(OH){-}CH_2{-}NH{-}CH_2{-}CH_2{-}NH_2{-}CH_2{-}CH_2{-}NH$ Glycidyldiethylamine adduct	Fast cure
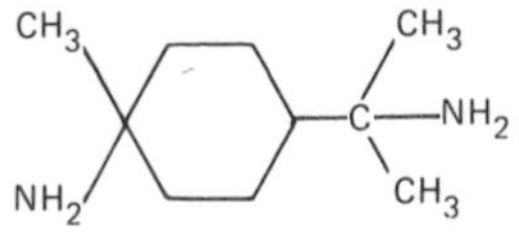 Cyclohexane ring with CH_3 and NH_2 on one carbon, and $C(CH_3)_2{-}NH_2$ on the opposite carbon 1,8-Menthane diamine	Low viscosity, very slow cure

Figure 13.11 Typical amine cross-linking agents

epoxy resin. The molecular weight is divided by the number of active hydrogen atoms. In practice, a slightly smaller proportion of amine is required to allow for the reaction of the resin with the hydroxyl groups produced during curing. All amines are toxic. For this reason less unpleasant pasty or liquid polyamides are made for domestic use. Many require a catalyst for curing (Wake, 1978) within reasonable times (days). The low-viscosity amines cause serious skin irritation, have unpleasant and toxic vapours, are hygroscopic and may cause staining on copper alloy substrates (Tuttle, 1983). These amines have small equivalent weights and small quantities of them are required. Great care has to be exercised in each aspect of their use.

DGEBA resins are frequently too viscous for easy application and form stiff polymers on curing. Low-viscosity formulations based on DGEBA resins can be made in various ways (Munnikendam, 1978). Serious damage by shrinkage can result when added solvents or plasticizers are lost. Mono- or di-epoxy diluent, e.g. butyl glycidyl ether, can be used more successfully. During consolidation, differential movement of the components will result in uneven setting. It is usually better to choose resins that are inherently more suitable, e.g. low molecular weight aliphatic epoxide resins (*Figure 13.12*), which have low viscosity.

	Viscosity mPa.s	*Comments*
$CH_3-C(CH_3)_2-O-CH_2-CH(O)CH_2$ (epoxide ring) *t*–Butyl glycidyl ether		Reactive diluent for epoxy resins
$CH_2(O)CH-CH_2-O(CH_2CH(CH_3)-O)_n-CH_2-CH(O)CH_2$ (epoxide rings) Poly(propylene glycol) diglycidyl ether	30–100	Imparts flexibility
$CH_2(O)CH-CH_2-O-(CH_2)_n-OCH_2-CH(O)CH_3$ (epoxide rings) $n > 4$ ω-Alkyl diglycidyl ether	c. 20	In Rutapox I 93/1
$CH_2(O)CH-CH-O-C_6H_4-O-CH-CH(O)CH_2$ (epoxide rings) Resorcinol diglycidyl ether	c. 30	In Rutapox I 93/2

Figure 13.12 Low-viscosity epoxy prepolymers

However, their disadvantages are slowness in setting, greater sensitivity to water action and the high cross-linking density. This last property results in a rigid polymer and can only be circumvented by attaching the epoxide groups to either end of a flexible chain, frequently of a polypropylene glycol oligomer (Salva, 1977). Filled epoxies are commonly used for structural restoration and mounting.

The cross-linked polymers are not soluble but are swelled by solvents (Appendix 3.31) which enable the gel to be removed mechanically (Daniels, 1981). The aromatic DGEBA is prone to yellowing by light and ultraviolet absorption (Allen *et al.*, 1983). Many commercial products contain reactive impurities which contribute to the yellowing (Potter, 1970; Tennent, 1979) but aliphatic epoxies are less susceptible than the aromatic epoxies to yellowing (Brydson, 1982). Deterioration of properties occurs during storage of the separate components by reaction with the air and water (Christensen and Pedersen, 1982). Cured polymers also yellow in the dark, presumably by slow oxidation of impurities in the formulation (Down, 1984). It was found that the polyamide types of hardener, often found in household packs, produced unacceptably unstable polymers. There is no reliable method of assessing the likely yellowing of commercial products which vary from batch to batch. It is to be hoped that epoxy resin formulations will be produced with known, and declared, ingredients of a purity comparable to the other polymers used in conservation. Formulations of materials that cure to form thermoplastics should also be possible, thus enabling the application of the versatile epoxies to a much wider range of problems. The use of epoxy resin formulations which cure by ultraviolet irradiation is under active investigation both for industrial purposes and in conservation (Tennent, 1983; Garnett and Major, 1982).

Conservation

Epoxy adhesives for wood (Werner, 1952), metal (Organ, 1959a) and ceramics and as consolidants for wood were developed during the 1950s (Anon, 1961). Because of their high strength and gap-filling ability, they were used for the consolidation and restoration of stone (Munnikendam, 1967b). The use of specially tailored adhesives of commercial products for specific tasks is normal in stone conservation (Amoroso and Fassina, 1983).

Epoxy adhesives have been widely used (Gedye, 1968; Wihr, 1977) and tested (Fiorentino and Vlad Borelli, 1975; Tennent,

Table 13.5 Low-viscosity expoxy formulations

Product	*Manufacturer*	*Components*[1]	*Viscosity* (mPa.s)	*Working/ setting time*[5] (h)	*Shrinkage* (linear %)	n_D[3]	*Elastic modulus* (MPa)	T_g[4] (°C)	*Relative stability*[5]	*Comments*
Ablebond 342-1	Abelstik	DGEBA/polyoxypropylene diamine	200	8/48	0.3	1.566	3280	54	2	
Rutapox I-93/1	Bakelite	Aliphatic diglycidylether menthane diamine	20	8	0.04	1.576		–10		was 1210
Rutapox I-93/2		As I-93/1 with resorcinol diglycidyl ether added	27	1.5	0.5	1.528		16		was 1200
Araldite AY103/HY951	Ciba-Geigy	DGEBA/triethylene diamine	800	1.5/24	0.2	1.576	2800		3	Discontinued
Hxtal-Nyl-1	Conservation materials			2/7 days	0.02	1.5201	2100	45	1	

Notes
(1) Resin/hardener, DGEBA = diglycidyl ether of bisphenol A.
(2) At room temperature (c.25 °C), reaction speeded with heating.
(3) Refractive index (Tennent and Townsend, 1984a,b).
(4) Glass transition temperature, measured by differential scanning calorimetry at 10 °C/min; values courtesy Perkin Elmer (UK) Ltd.
(5) Stability to yellowing with light exposure, 1 is most stable (Tennent and Townsend, 1984b).

1979) for use as adhesives for sticking glass objects that will be kept in the museum environment. Epoxies are not used for the adhesion of stained glass windows *in situ* as coupling agents would be necessary to ensure an adequate life. A small range of fluid adhesives whose refractive index may be modified has been tested (Table 13.5). No room-temperature curing epoxy material has been found to be sufficiently free of colour to be used in restoring missing portions of water-white glass objects.

Two epoxy resins were specially developed for consolidating wood (Rutapox I-93/2) and leather (Rutapox I-93/1) (Table 13.5) (Munnikendam, 1978). The low viscosities of these low molecular weight resins result in deep penetration of porous substrates. The I-93/2 forms a hard tough polymer because of the stiffening effect of the aromatic group. The I-93/1 is flexible and rubbery. Both polymers are a light yellow colour but cause considerable darkening of the material they are consolidating.

Epoxy resins have been used in canvas picture conservation. An unfortunate use as a varnish caused problems in identification and removal (Keck and Feller, 1964). Epoxy resin adhesives have been used for sticking threads across tears in canvases and also as a filler (Berger, 1975). The formulations need to be of sufficiently high viscosity to prevent absorption into the canvas, but must be flexible enough to respond to movement in the fabric.

13.5 Formaldehyde resins

Background

The formaldehyde family of resins are highly cross-linked polymers formed by condensation reactions. The group has three main members: phenol-formaldehyde (PF), urea-formaldehyde (UF), and melamine-formaldehyde (MF) resins. The process of polymerization takes place in two stages. The first stage is the creation of water-soluble oligomers of formaldehyde combined with phenol, urea or melamine (Brydson, 1982; Roff and Scott, 1971). These are used immediately to impregnate moulding materials. Stable solutions of oligomers can be produced by using appropriate grades of resin and pH conditions (*Figure 13.13*). The oligomers are then cross-linked by acid catalysts and/or heat. Initially a gel is formed which reacts further to create a polymer that is highly cross-linked. During the process of polymerization, a large amount of water is produced. The polymers can be used as coatings if the films are thin enough to allow the water to escape. The polymers are hard brittle materials. UF resins can be modified

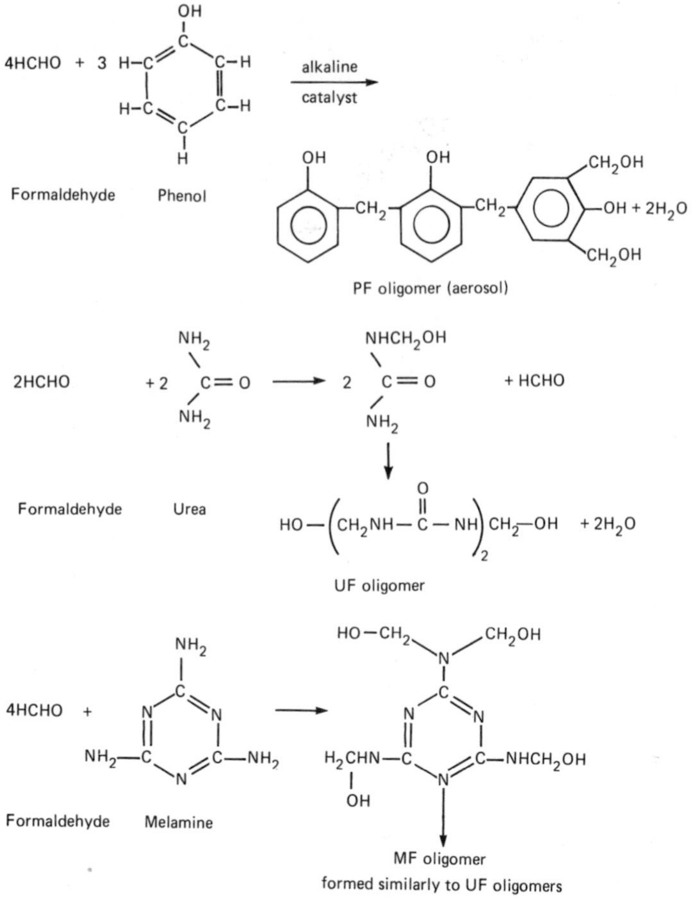

Figure 13.13 First stage in the polymerization of formaldehyde resins. The oligomers that are formed are mixtures whose composition depends on the proportion of reactants and the reaction conditions

with butanol to create oligomers that are readily applied in organic solvents. These cure to form more flexible polymers than the unmodified UF polymers.

The materials used in conservation have usually been acid-catalysed formulations. The polymers are entirely insoluble but can be decomposed by concentrated acids and alkalis or molten phenols. Water-white polymers can be produced if low-temperature acid cure is employed. The melamine resins show the greatest resistance to yellowing.

Conservation

Fossil bones were soaked in PF (*Bakelite*) varnish solutions and allowed to dry and cure at room temperature for up to six months (Case, 1925; Nichols and Orr, 1932). An alternative was to bake at 93 °C. Numerous different Bakelite solvent grades were employed up to the 1960s for fossil bone and wood (Plenderleith, 1956; Howie, 1984).

UF resins were used initially as transparent encapsulating resins for plants (Schmidt, 1939). UF resins were more widely adapted from commercial use and used as consolidants (Takakage and Tomokichi, 1952) and adhesives for wood (Rawlins and Werner, 1949; Plenderleith, 1956; Hayward, 1976).

An MF resin, Arigal C, was proposed as a consolidant for waterlogged wood (Haas, 1969; Grattan, 1982). The polymer is employed as a solution in water. It was cured in solution using an added catalyst and heat (80 °C). Butylated amino-formaldehyde resins have been used as coatings, especially for ceramics (Chinaglaze) (Tennent, 1983). The resin solution is mixed with an acid catalyst before application. Chinaglaze is a UF resin modified by the addition of an alkyd (phthalic acid polyester) which yellows badly.

14 Fillers and colorants

14.1 Fillers

Fillers are added to polymers for many reasons (Katz and Milewski, 1978) (Table 14.1). A filler reduces the volume and cost of polymer used in a formulation. Calcium carbonate is frequently added to polyester casting resins as an extender. Hollow spheres, e.g. glass or phenol micro-balloons (Nishiura, 1981a) or vermiculite (Bradley *et al.*, 1983), can be used to reduce the weight of an adhesive layer. The reduced polymer volume also restricts the possible shrinkage. The size of filler particles determines the

Table 14.1 Fillers for polymers. (All these fillers are available in various purities and sizes.)

Type	*Supplier*[1]	*Use*
Calcium carbonate	Chem	Reducing volume of polymer, as extender can provide some reinforcement
Talc	Chem	
Purified sand	Buil	
Glass fibre	Poly	Reinforcement
Carbon fibre	Poly	
Precipitated silica	*Degussa*	Flatting (matting) agent, thickening agent for liquids
Fumed silica	*Degussa*	
Micro balloons		
phenolic	*Union Carbide*	Extending, reducing weight, increasing workability of set polymer
PVCC	*Dow*	
glass	*Emmerson*	
fly ash	*Fillite*	
vermiculite	Pack	

Note
(1) Chem = chemical suppliers, e.g. (*BDH*); Buil = builders'suppliers (must be dried); Poly = suppliers of polyester resins; Pack = packaging and insulation suppliers.

amount of filler that can be incorporated into the liquid polymer. A mixture of large particles with small particles which partially fill the voids between them enables most complete filling of the polymer. Sufficient polymer must be added to fill the voids between the particles if strength retention is required.

Fillers alter the mechanical properties of the set polymer. Frequently the filler is used to increase strength and hardness. Sand and larger aggregate is used in building restoration (Amoroso and Fassina, 1983). Weak fillers are incorporated into polymers to allow the set material to be reworked by drilling or sanding. These can be solid, e.g. talc and calcium carbonate, or hollow microspheres.

Added filler will increase the viscosity and resistance to flow of a polymer. This is essential in adhesives which would drain out of the joint by gravity or be sucked out of the glue line by capillary attraction. Viscosity increase becomes larger as the particle size is reduced. Fumed (aerosol) silica, a filler that introduces a structure to the liquid, can produce a thixotropic mixture (Byrne, 1984). Ease of handling of a liquid adhesive can be improved by additions to the polymer of 3–10% of its own weight in silica. The thickening effect is greatest in non-polar solvents when the powder is well-dispersed.

14.2 Colorants

Colorants for polymers may be divided into two groups, pigments and dyes. Pigments remain as solids dispersed in polymers and increase its opacity, while dyes dissolve in polymers, producing transparent colours. Many colorants tend to fade when exposed to light (Allen and McKellar, 1980). A wide variety of inorganic and organic pigments are available which are very light-stable (Thomson, 1978). Pure pigments (*Winsor & Newton*) can be ground into the appropriate polymer liquid. Colorants may be designed for use with specific polymers: polyesters (*Ryland*), silicones (*Rhodia*) and epoxies (*Ciba-Geigy*). Some pigments react adversely with cross-linking polymers. The light-stability of many pigments is affected by the medium. Powdered metals may react with components of the polymer, e.g. amines in epoxy formulations will react with copper alloys. Powdered metals, e.g. lead, bronze and copper, can be purchased separately (*Tiranti*) or ready mixed in epoxy resins (*Devcon*).

Dyes are exposed in the full depth of the coloured polymer, so especially stable materials are needed. Unfortunately there are

Table 14.2 Light-stable dyes (Orosol (*Ciba-Geigy*)). Many dyes react with cross-linking resins and some combinations are unsuitable, indicated by 'X'. The numbers indicate the blue wool light-fastness equivalent (section 2.2). Lack of a number indicates that light-fastness is poor. Similar dyes are available from other manufacturers, e.g. *BASF*.

Dy name		*Solvent-borne acrylic*	*Polyurethane*	*Epoxy*	*Polyester acrylic resin*
Yellow	2GLN	7	8	6	6–7
	3R	–	8	–	X
Orange	G	–	8	–	X
	RLN	–	8	6	6–7
Brown	GR	–	8	–	X
	2GRL	–	7–8	–	–
	2RL	5–6	6–7	–	–
	5R	–	6–7	–	X
	6RL	–	8	–	–
Red	3GL	–	7–8	–	6–7
	GLN	–	7–8	–	–
	2BL	–	8	–	–
	G	–	7–8	X	–
	B	–	7–8	–	–
	2B	–	8	5–6	–
Violet	RN	–	8	–	X
Blue	GN	6	–	–	6–7
	2GLN	5–6	X	–	6–7
Black	BA	–	8	X	X
	CN	–	8	–	X
	RL	–	8	5–6	X

few dyes that approach pigments in light-fastness (Table 14.2). Finely ground pigments may be used to achieve coloration with some loss of transparency. Problems of incompatibility are greater with dyes than with pigments. For a critical use, preliminary tests of compatibility and fastness should be made.

Appendices

Appendix 1 Polymer properties

Chapter	Polymer			$Tg^{(3)}$ (°C)	$n_D^{(4)}$	Modulus of tensile elasticity	Solubility chart[5]	Stability[6]	Introduction	
	Name[1]	Abbreviation	IUPAC[2]						Commercial	Conservation[7]
6.1	Polyethylene	PE	Polymethylene	−20	1.49–1.52	150–340		C	1943 (1850 wax	1949 1887)
6.1	Poly(ethylene/vinyl acetate)	EVA		−24			3.3	A		1966
6.2	cis-1,4-Polyisoprene	rubber	Poly(1-methyl-cis-1-butenylene)	−75	1.53	1–3	3.4	T	1790s	1904
6.2	Chlorinated rubber				1.55–1.60		3.5	T	1918	1926
7.1	Poly(vinyl acetate)	PVAC	Poly(1-acetoxyethylene)	18–29	1.46		3.6	A	1917 (1936 emulsion	1932 1952)
7.2	Poly(vinyl alcohol)	PVAL	Poly(1-hydroxyethylene)	#75	1.15	200–800		A	1933	1951
7.3	Poly(vinyl butyral)	PVB	Poly[(2-propyl-1,3-dioxane-4,6-diyl) methylene]	45–66	1.49	2100	3.7	B(A)	1920	1956
8	Poly(methyl acrylate)	PMA	Poly[1-(methoxycarbonyl)-ethylene]	8	1.479			C	1927	1949
8	Poly(ethyl acrylate)	PEA	Poly[1-(ethyoxycarbonyl)-ethylene]	−22	1.464			C		
8	Poly(*n*-butyl acrylate)	PBA	Poly[1-(*n*-butoxycarbonyl)-ethylene]	−54	1.474			B		

8	Poly(2-ethylhexyl acrylate)	PEHA	Poly[1-(2-ethylhexoxycarbonyl)-ethylene]	−55				B		
8	Poly(methyl methacrylate)	PMMA	Poly[1-(methoxycarbonyl)-1-methyl ethylene]	105	1.489	3000	3.8	A	1932	1937
8	Poly(ethyl methacrylate)	PEMA	Poly[1-(ethoxycarbonyl)-1-methyl ethylene]	65	1.484		3.9	A		1940
8	Poly(*n*-butyl methacrylate)	PnBMA	Poly[1-(*n*-butoxycarbonyl)-1-methyl ethylene]	20	1.483			B		1932?
8	Poly(*i*-butyl methacrylate)	PiBMA	Poly[1-(*i*-butoxycarbonyl)-1-methyl ethylene]	55	1.486			B		1932?
8	Poly(methyl cyanoacrylate)		Poly[1-(methoxycarbonyl)-1-cyano ethylene]	165					1960s	1976
9.1	Poly(vinyl chloride)	PVC	Poly(1-chloroethylene)	83	1.54	2800	3.14	T	1930s	1958
9.2	Poly(vinylidene chloride)	PVCC	Poly(1,1-dichloroethylene)	−17	1.62	20–60	3.15	T	1940s	1949
9.3	Polystyrene	PS	Poly(1-phenylethylene)	80	1.59	3500	3.16	C	1930	1937
9.4	Poly(vinyl pyrrolidone)	PVP	Poly[1-(2-oxypyrrolidin-1-yl)-ethylene]	#86	1.53		3.17		1940s	1978
9.5	Poly(*p*-xylyene)	PPX	Poly(1,4-dimethylene benzene)	60–80	1.669	2400		C	1950s	1984
9.6	Cyclohexanone polymer	Ketone resin		c.100	1.515		3.18	B	1930s	1952
9.7	Poly(ethylene glycol)	PEG	Polyoxyethylene	−55	1.47		3.19	B	1930s	1957
9.7	Perfluoropolyether				1.304			A	1970s	1982
9.8	*N*-methoxymethyl nylon	Soluble nylon			c.1.53	15 (nylon 66 210)		T	1948	1958
10.1	Methyl cellulose	MC		140	1.49			B	1930s	1924

Appendix 1 Continued

Chapter	Polymer: Name[1]	Polymer: Abbreviation	Polymer: IUPAC[2]	Tg[3] (°C)	n_D[4]	Modulus of tensile elasticity	Solubility chart[5]	Stability[6]	Introduction: Commercial	Introduction: Conservation[7]
10.1	Ethyl cellulose	EC			1.49			B		1961
10.1	Hydroxyethyl cellulose	HEC			1.51			B	1930s	1968
10.1	Hydroxypropyl cellulose	HPC			1.56	414	3.20	B		1976
10.1	Methyl hydroxyethyl cellulose	MHEC								
10.1	Ethyl hydroxyethyl cellulose	EHEC								
10.1	Sodium carboxy-methyl cellulose	CMC			1.515			B	1930s	1966
10.2	Cellulose diacetate	CA		180?	1.47	2000	3.21	B	1910s	1923
10.2	Cellulose nitrate	CN		56?	1.51	2500	3.22	C	1877	1899
11.1	Starch			#	1.53	?3.5		B	traditional	
11.1	Gum arabic							B	traditional	
11.1	Agar–agar							B	traditional	
11.1	Funoran	funori						B	traditional	
11.2	Glue			#210		3700 (65% RH)		B	traditional	
11.3	Casein				1.53					
12.1	Dammar			100	1.53		3.23	B	1826	1842

12.2	Mastic			72	1.547		3.24	B	traditional	
12.3	Rosin							C	traditional	
12.4	Shellac			40	1.52	1340	3.25	C		1868
12.5	Polymerized linseed oil	linoxyn			1.48–1.57		3.26	C	traditional	
13.1	Silane							A	1920s	1923
13.1	Siloxane	silicone rubber		−125	1.41	3	3.27	A	1940s	1950s
13.2	Polyester resin				1.55	5000	3.28	C-B	1946	1950
13.3	Polyurethane resin						3.29		1930s	
13.4	Epoxy resin [(8)]				1.56	2000–4500	3.30	T-B	1940s	1952
13.5	Phenol-formaldehyde	PF	Phenol methanal polymer			3400			1910	1925
13.5	Urea-formaldehyde	UF	Urea methanal polymer		1.55	7000–10 000			1920s	1939
13.5	Melamine-formaldehyde	MF	Melamine methanal polymer		1.65	7000–10 000			1930s	1960s

Notes

These data are derived from many diverse sources and refer to the set polymer without modifications. The values given may be only approximate but should enable qualitative comparisons of properties. The values will vary with the molecular weight, grade, etc. Good manufacturers will provide information about properties and test methods for their products.

(1) Commonly used trivial name derived from international standards (section 2.1) and current commercial practice.
(2) Name derived from chemical structure according to IUPAC rules (section 2.1).
(3) Glass transition temperature; # in this and the following two columns indicates that the values are significantly lowered by increasing water content at higher relative humidities.
(4) Refractive index at room temperature (20 or 25°C).
(5) Solubility behaviour is indicated in the chart in appendix 3.
(6) A very approximate indication of the stability of the polymer, using Feller's classification of useful life (section 2.6): A > 100 years, 100 years > B > 20 years, 20 years > C > 6 months, T < 6 months. Lack of a classification usually indicates that there are types of the polymer available with significantly different stabilities.
(7) The earliest date for use of the polymer, usually the date of publication of an article describing the application. Many of these dates are much later than the first use in conservation.
(8) Values refer to polymers derived from DGEBA (section 14.4).

Appendix 2.1 Solvent properties

No.[1]	Name[2]	Synonym[3]	Chemical structure	Boiling point (°C)	Evaporation rate[4]	Viscosity at 20°C (mPa.s)	TLV (ppm)[5]	Flash point (°C)	Fractional solubility parameters[7]			Comments[8]
									$100f_d$	$100f_p$	$100f_h$	
1	Odourless mineral spirits								98	1	1	Appendix 2.2
2	Hexane		$CH_3(CH_2)_4CH_3$	69	8.1	0.38	50	−21	100	0	0	KB no. 30
3	Heptane		$CH_3(CH_2)_5CH_3$	98	2.8	0.42	400	−5.5	100	0	0	
4	Mineral spirits								90	4	6	Appendix 2.2
5	Cyclohexane		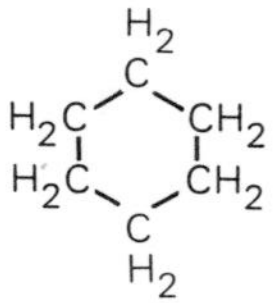	81	4.5	1.0	100	−18	94	2	4	
6	Benzene		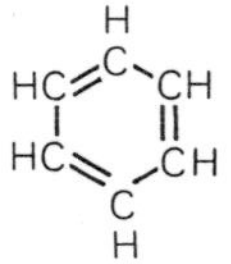	80	5.4	0.65	10(C)	−11	78	8	14	KB no. 100
7	Toluene	Methyl benzene	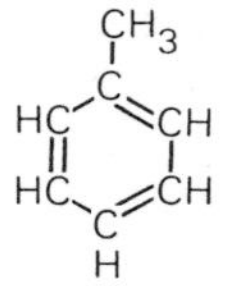	110	2.3	0.58	100(N,S)	4	80	7	13	

8	Xylene	Dimethyl benzene	(o-xylene)	138	0.75	0.63	100(S)	30	83	5	12	KB no. 94 (mixture of isomers)
9	Ethyl benzene			136		0.68	100	15	87	3	10	
10	Styrene	Vinyl benzene		146		0.75	50	31	78	4	17	
	Tetrahydro naphthalene	(Tetralin)		207		2.2		77	80	8	12	Rapidly oxidizes
	Turpentine			150–180			100	>32	77	18	5	Rapidly oxidizes
11	Dichloromethane	Methylene chloride	CCl_2H_2	40	6.4	0.43	100(N)	–	59	21	20	KB no. 136
12	Chloroform	Trichloromethane	CCl_3H	61		0.57	10(N,C)	–	67	12	21	
13	Tetrachloromethane	Carbon tetrachloride	CCl_4	77		0.97	5(N,C,S)	–	85	2	13	KB no. 114
14	Trichloroethylene		$CCl_2{=}CClH$	87	4.9	0.57	50(N,C)	–	68	12	20	KB no. 132
	Tetrachloroethylene	(Perchloroethylene)	$CCl_2{=}CCl_2$	122	(1.29)	0.9	50	–	67	23	10	KB no. 90

Appendix 2.1 Continued

No.[1]	Name[2]	Synonym[3]	Chemical structure	Boiling point (°C)	Evaporation rate[4]	Viscosity at 20°C (mPa.s)	TLV (ppm)[5]	Flash point (°C)	Fractional solubility parameters[7] 100f_d	100f_p	100f_h	Comments[8]
15	1,1,1-trichloroethane	(Methyl chloroform)	CCl_3CH_3	74	4.7	1.1	350(N)	–	70	19	11	KB no. 124
	1,1,2-Trichlorotrifluorethane		CCl_2FCClF_2	48		0.69	1000	–				KB no. 31
16	Diethyl ether	Oxydiethane	$O(CH_2CH_3)_2$	35	(11)	0.25	400(N)	−40	64	13	23	Forms peroxides on storage
17	Tetrahydrofuran		$H_2C—CH_2$ / H_2C–O–CH_2 (ring)	65	(4.9)	0.48	200(N,C)	−22	55	19	26	ditto
18	1,4-Dioxacyclohexane	(Dioxane)	H_2C–O–CH_2 / H_2C–O–CH_2 (ring)	101	(1,7)	1.52	25(S)	11	67	7	26	ditto
19	2-Ethoxyethanol	(Cellosolve)	$C_2H_5OC_2H_4OH$	135	0.35	2.1	50(S)	42	42	20	38	ditto
20	2-Methoxyethanol	(Methyl cellosolve)	CH_3OC_2HOH	125	0.51	1.7	5(C)	37	39	22	39	ditto
21	2-Butoxyethanol	(Butyl cellosolve)	$C_4H_9OC_2H_4OH$	171	0.076	3.2	25(S)	60	46	18	36	ditto
22	2-Ethoxyethyl acetate	(Cellosolve acetate)	$C_2H_5OC_2H_4OCOCH_3$	156	0.19		50(S)	51	51	15	34	ditto
23	Methyl acetate		CH_3OCOCH_3	57	6.9	0.38	200	−10	45	36	19	
24	Ethyl acetate		$C_2H_5OCOCH_3$	77	4.3	0.45	400(N,C)	−4	51	18	31	
25	Isopropyl acetate		$(CH_3)_2CH_2OCOH_3$	89	3.3	0.52	250(N,C)	12	54	16	30	
26	*n*-Butyl acetate		$CH_3(CH_2)_3OCOCH_3$	126	1	0.73	150	25	60	13	17	
	Methyl methacrylate	Methyl-(2-propeonate)	$CH_2=C(CH_3)–C(=O)–OCH_3$	101			100	10				

27	Propane-1,2-diol carbonate	(Propylene carbonate)	$O=C(O-)(O-)$ ring: H_2C—CH—CH_3	242		2.8 (25 °C)	–	–	48	38	14	
28	Butyrolactone	4-Butanolide	H_2C—CH_2, H_2C, $C=O$, O (ring)	204		2.0	–	94	44	39	17	
29	Acetone	Propanone	CH_3COCH_3	56	7,8	0.32	750(N)	−17	47	32	21	
30	Butan-2-one	Ethyl methyl ketone (Methyl ethyl ketone, MEK)	$CH_3COC_2H_5$	80	4.6	0.42	200(N)	−1	53	30	17	
31	Cyclohexanone		$O=C$, H_2C, CH_2, H_2C, CH_2, CH_2 (ring)	157	0.25	2.2	25(N)	43	55	28	17	
32	4-Methyl pentan-2-one	Isobutyl methyl ketone	$(CH_3)_2CHCH_2COCH_3$	117	1.4	0.59	50(N)	14	58	22	20	
33	2,6-Dimethyl heptan-4-one	Di-isobutyl ketone	$((CH_3)_2CHCH_2)_2CO$	168	(0.2)		25	49	67	16	17	
34	Ethane-1,2-diol	(Ethylene glycol)	HOC_2H_4OH	197		21	50	119	30	18	52	
35	Methanol	Methyl alcohol	$HOCH_3$	65	4.1	0.61	200(N,C,S)	11	30	22	48	
36	Ethanol	Ethyl alcohol	HOC_2H_5	78	(2.4)	12	1000(N)	12	36	18	46	Pure ethanol
37	Propan-2-ol	Isopropyl alcohol	$CH_3—CH(OH)—CH_3$	82	2.2	2.4	400(N,S)	12	(38	17	45	extrapolated)
38	Butanol	*n*-Butyl alcohol	$CH_3(CH_2)_3OH$	118	0.46	3.0	50(S)	35	43	15	42	
39	Nitromethane		CH_3NO_2	101		0.66	100	36	40	47	13	
40	Nitroethane		$C_2H_5NO_2$	115			100(C)	28	44	43	13	
41	Ethane nitrile	(Acetonitrile)	CH_3CN	82		0.36	40(S)	2	39	45	16	

Appendix 2.1 Continued

No.[1]	Name[2]	Synonym[3]	Chemical structure	Boiling point (°C)	Evaporation rate[4]	Viscosity at 20°C (mPa.s)	TLV (ppm)[5]	Flash point (°C)	Fractional solubility parameters[7]			Comments[8]
									$100f_d$	$100f_p$	$100f_h$	
42	*N*-Methyl-2-pyrrolidone		H_2C–CH_2–CH_2–N(CH_3)–CH_2–CH_2 (ring)	202		c.1.7			48	32	20	
43	*N,N*-Dimethyl formamide	Dimethyl methanamide	$H-CO-N(CH_3)_2$	155		0.92	10(C,S)	58	41	32	27	
44	Pyridine		HC=CH–CH=N–CH=CH (ring)	115		0.96	5(C)	23	56	26	18	
45	Carbon disulphide		CS_2	46		0.36	10(N,C,S)	−30	88	8	4	
46	Dimethyl sulphoxide		$(CH_3)_2SO$	189		2.3	(?0.1)	95	41	36	23	
47	Water		H_2O	100	0.27	1.0	–	–	18	28	54	

Notes

(1) Number used to identify solvents used for the solubility charts in appendix 3.
(2) Follows British Standards Institution (1983) or IUPAC (1979b) for naming of solvents. Manner of writing substituents varies from country to country, but different ways are equivalent, e.g. propan-2-ol (UK), 2-propanol (USA), propanol-2 (Germany).
(3) Systematic names are given for trivial equivalents. Obsolete names in brackets.
(4) Evaporation rate, measured by evaporating the solvent from a 10% solution of tritolyl phosphate (Shell Chemicals Ltd, 1977a; ASTM D 3539-76) relative to *n*-butyl acetate (=1). Values in brackets were measured by evaporation of the solvent from filter paper.
(5) Threshold limit value, time weighted average (section 3.4). The letters in brackets indicate the type of toxic hazard which is of particular importance. The absence of a value does not indicate lack of risk – only a lack of knowledge of the risk. N = narcotic; C = chronic (including carcinogenic); S = skin absorption.
(6) Closed cup flash point, e.g. ISO 1516-1981. 'A' indicates that the vapour will not explode. Chlorinated solvents will be altered by burning or heating to produce highly toxic fumes, e.g. phosgene. Indicates the maximum temperature that the solvent can be used without much risk of spontaneous ignition and explosion. Flash points of mixtures can be roughly estimated by the method in Shell Chemicals Ltd. (1977b).
(7) Tess fractional solubility parameters (Barton, 1983) (section 3.2).
(8)

Appendix 2.2 Some representative hydrocarbon solvents derived from petroleum by distillation etc. (Reynolds, 1967)[1]

Name	*Manufacturer*	*Boiling range* (°C)	*Evaporation rate*[(2)]	*Flash point*[(3)] (°C)	*Composition %*			*KB no.*[(4)]	*Comment*
					Paraffin	*Naphthenic*	*Aromatic*		
n-Pentane	BP	32–37	18	−51	99.8	0.1	0.12	29	TLV of pure pentane 600 ppm
SBP62/68 Hexane	BP	63–69	8.5	−51	88.3	11.7	<0.05	29	TLV of gasoline c. 300 ppm
SBP2	Shell	71–90	5.9	−34			0.1	33	
Exsol heptane	Esso	94–99	5.5	−8			0.02	34	
Solvesso toluene	Esso	110–111	2.4	4			99.6	105	
Solvent xylene	BP	114–139	(0.75)	(26)			99.7	97	
VM&P spirit	Shell	119–129		13	48	42	10	38	f_d 94, f_p 3, f_h 3[(5)], TLV 300 ppm similar to Stoddard's solvent
Odourless mineral spirits D70	Shell	92–127		21				29	f_d 98, f_p 1, f_h 1[(5)]
White spirit	Shell	152–196	0.19	41			17	37	Commonly available in the UK
Shellsol A	Shell	165–185	0.25	43	0.9		99.1	90	Mostly trimethyl benzenes
Shellsol E	Shell	163–200	0.16	43	15.1		84.3	75	

Notes

(1) Manufacturer's information, TLV values are not available.
(2) Different methods of assessing evaporation rates may have been used. Comparisons between solvents may be only qualitative.
(3) Measured by various closed cup methods depending on the flash point.
(4) Kauri-butanol gum number (ASTM D 1133-83).
(5) Teas partial solubility parameters (Barton, 1983) (Section 3.2).

Appendix 2.3 Hazards and warnings
(see also section 3.4)

Toxicity

Toxic

Harmful

The toxicity may be apparent through various routes: swallowing, contact with skin, or by inhalation. Precautions must be taken to prevent exposure by all of these routes to the worker directly involved and to those in the area or who might later come into contact with contaminated materials and facilities.

Corrosiveness

Corrosive

Corrosive materials usually cause damage and rapid pain to skin, eyes etc. Precautions against all possible contact with the material should be made.

Irritant

Irritant substances cause damage more insidiously by damaging or irritating the skin.

Flammability

The grading of the flammability of liquids is made in terms of the flash point. The dividing lines vary from country to country. For example, in the UK, the grades are:

Extremely flammable

Extremely flammable–flash point 0 °C and boiling point 35 °C or less.

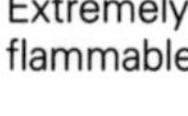

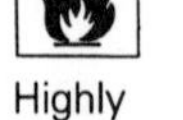

Highly flammable

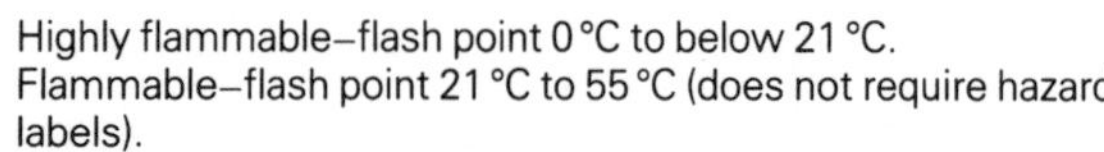

Highly flammable–flash point 0 °C to below 21 °C.
Flammable–flash point 21 °C to 55 °C (does not require hazard labels).
The value of the flash point is usually indicated on the label.

Oxidizing agent

Oxidizing agents are those that can cause fire in combustible materials.

Appendix 3 Solubility charts of polymers

The following charts are based on the reduced solubility parameters of Teas (Gardon and Teas, 1976) as given by Barton (1983) (section 3.2). The solvent numbers refer to those listed in appendix 2, Table A2.1. Unless otherwise stated the solubility properties were assessed using ASTM D3132-72.

Teas partial solubility parameters of solvents

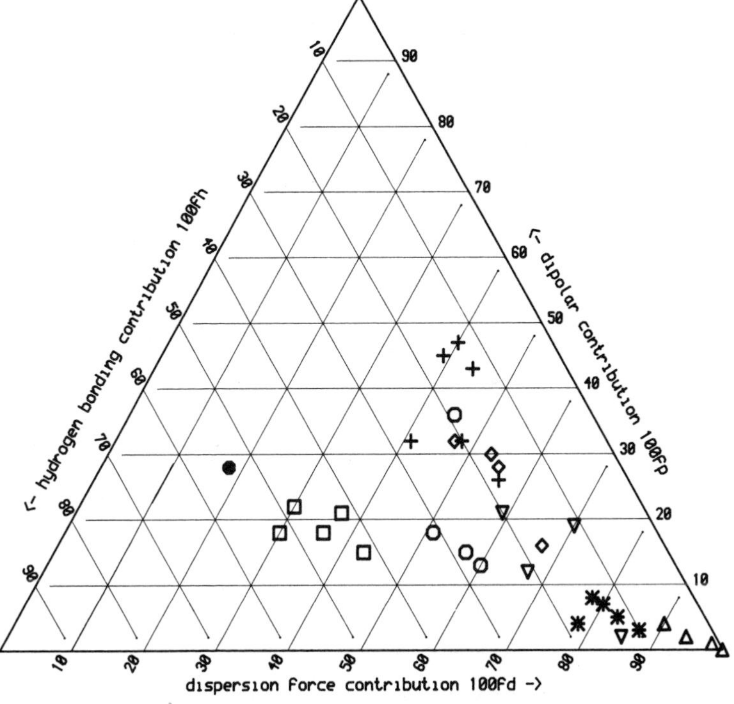

△ = aliphatic hydrocarbons ✱ = aromatic hydrocarbons
○ = esters ◇ = ketones □ = alcohols + = nitrogen solvents
▽ = chlorinated hydrocarbons ● = water

Figure A3.1 Major classes of solvents and their position on the Teas chart

Teas partial solubility parameters of solvents

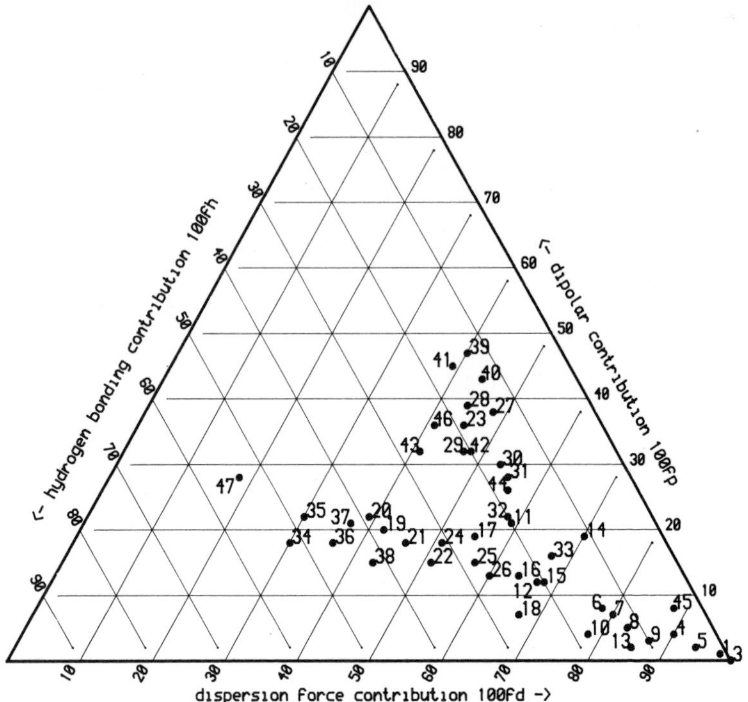

Figure A3.2 Location of solvents listed in Table A2.1

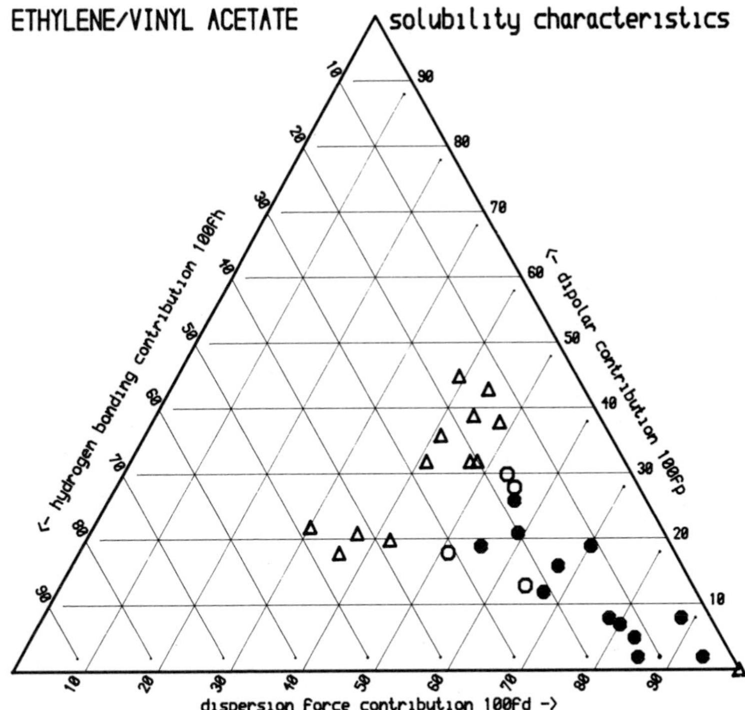

● = soluble O = borderline Δ = insoluble

solvents 5 6 7 8 11 12 13 14 17 33 44 45

borderline 16 24 30 31

non-solvents 3 19 27 28 29 35 36 37 40 41 42 43 46

Figure A3.3 Solubility of a medium molecular weight ethylene/vinyl acetate copolymer with a 40% vinyl acetate content (Elvax 40W (DuPont))

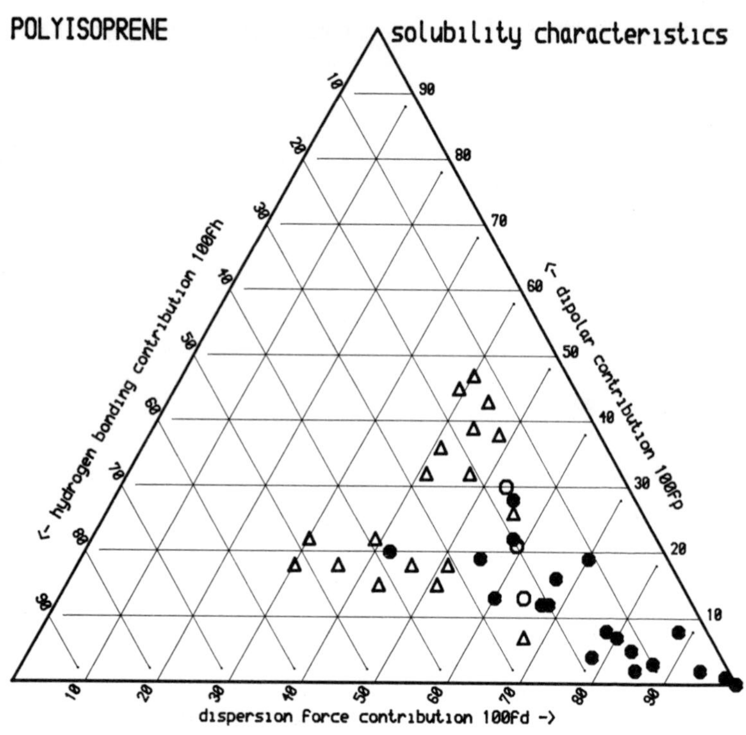

● = soluble O = borderline Δ = insoluble

solvents 1 2 3 5 6 7 8 9 10 12 13 14 15 17 19 26 31 32 33 45

borderline 11 16 30

non-solvents 18 20 21 22 24 27 28 29 34 35 36 38 39 40 41 43 44 46

Figure A3.4 Solubility of cis-1,4-polyisoprene (Cariflex IR305 (Shell)), data from Hansen (1967)

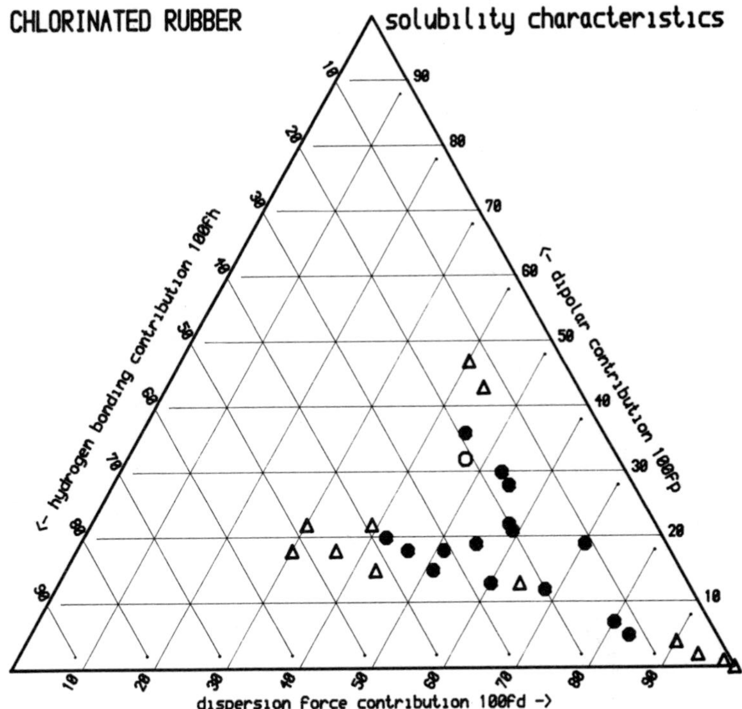

● = soluble ○ = borderline △ = insoluble

solvents 7 8 11 14 15 17 19 21 22 23 24 26 30 31 32

borderline 29

non-solvents 1 2 4 5 16 20 34 35 36 38 39 40

Figure A3.5 Solubility of chlorinated rubber, data from Parker (1967)

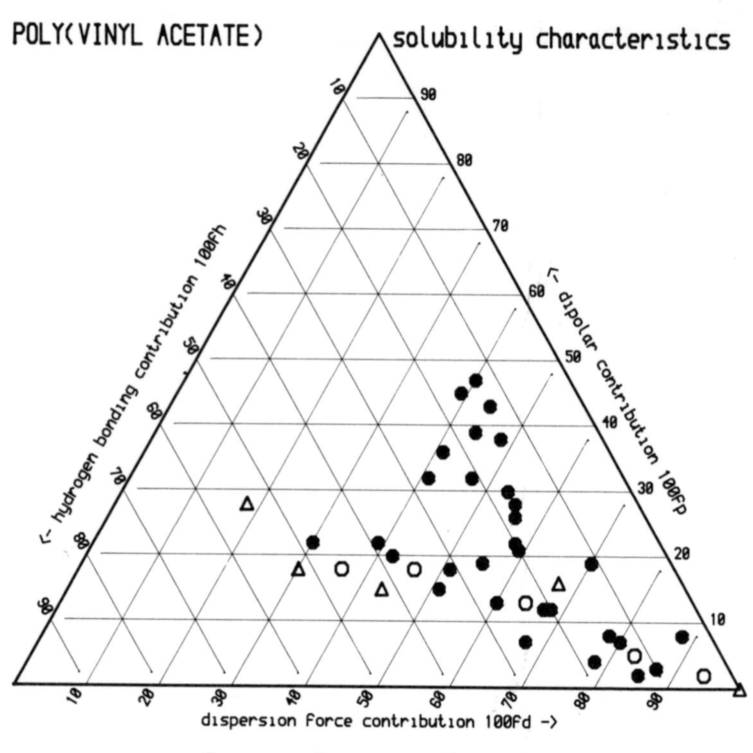

solvents 6 7 9 10 11 12 13 14 15 17 18 19 20 22 24 26 27 28 29 30 31 32 35 39 40 41 43 44 45 46

borderline 5 8 16 21 36

non-solvents 2 33 34 38 47

Figure A3.6 Solubility of a medium molecular weight poly(vinyl acetate) (Mowilith 50 (*Hoechst*)), data from Hansen (1967)

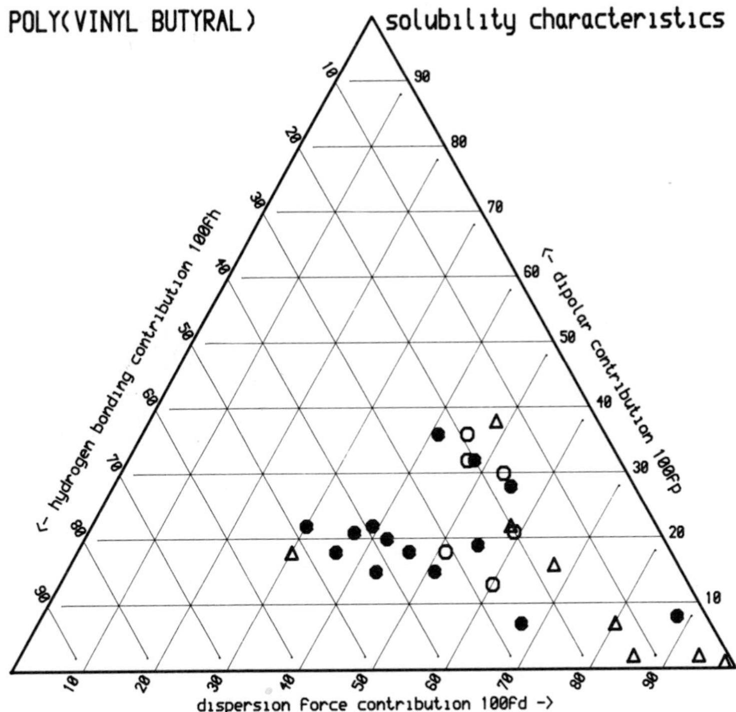

● = soluble ○ = borderline △ = insoluble

solvents 17 18 19 20 21 22 31 35 36 37 38 42 45 46

borderline 11 23 24 26 29 30

non-solvents 1 5 7 13 27 32 33 34

Figure A3.7 Solubility of a poly(vinyl butyral) with a high vinyl alcohol content (20%) (Mowital B60H (*Hoechst*)), manufacturer's data

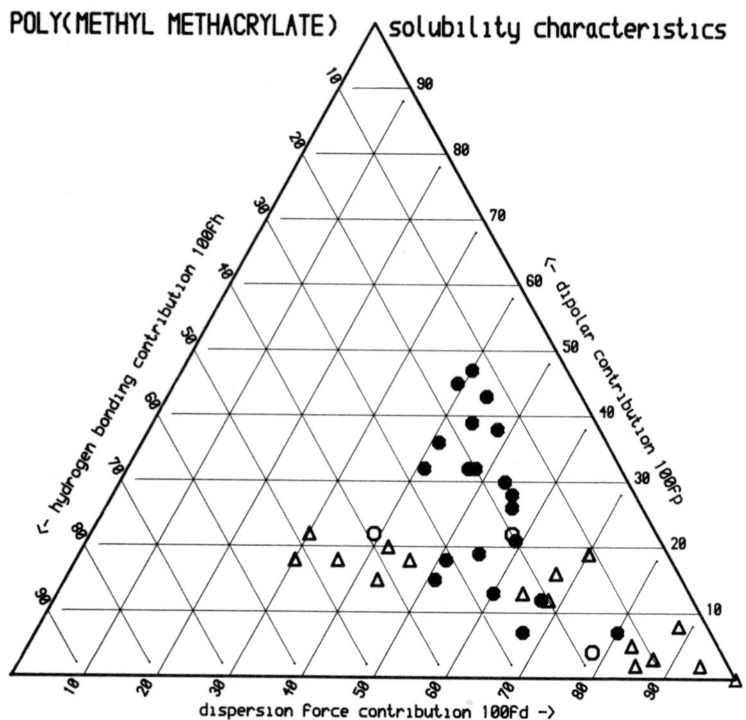

● = soluble O = borderline Δ = insoluble

solvents 7 11 12 17 18 22 24 26 27 28 29 30 31 39 40 41 42 43 44 46

borderline 10 20 32

non-solvents 2 5 8 9 13 14 15 16 19 21 33 34 35 36 38 45

Figure A3.8 Solubility of a medium molecular weight poly(methyl methacrylate) (Elvacite 2010 (*Du Pont*)), manufacturer's data

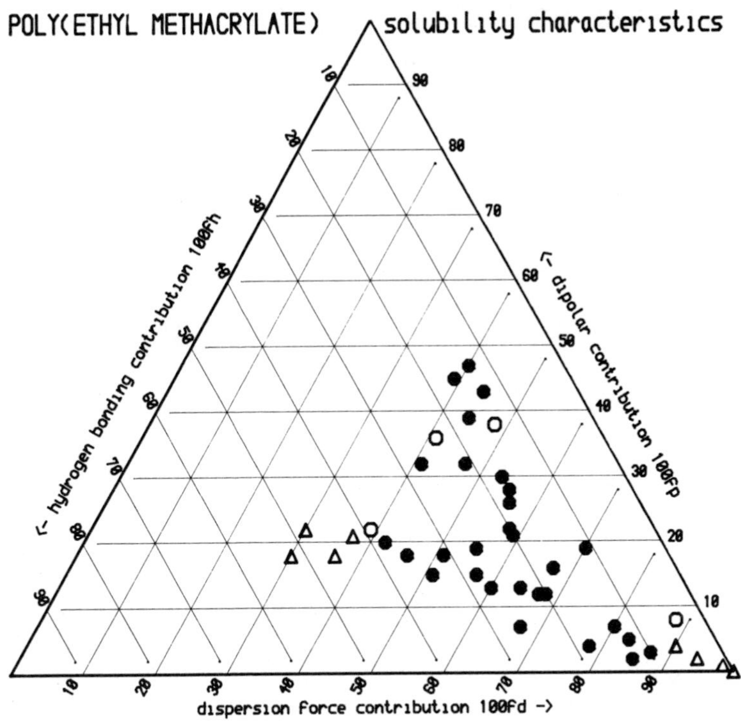

● = soluble ○ = borderline Δ = insoluble

solvents 7 8 9 10 11 12 13 14 15 16 17 18 19 21 22 24 25 26 28 29 30 31 32 33 39 40 41 43 44

borderline 20 27 45 46

non-solvents 1 2 4 5 34 35 36 37

Figure A3.9 Solubility of a low molecular weight poly(ethyl methacrylate) modified for improved adhesion (Elvacite 2043 (*Du Pont*)), manufacturer's data

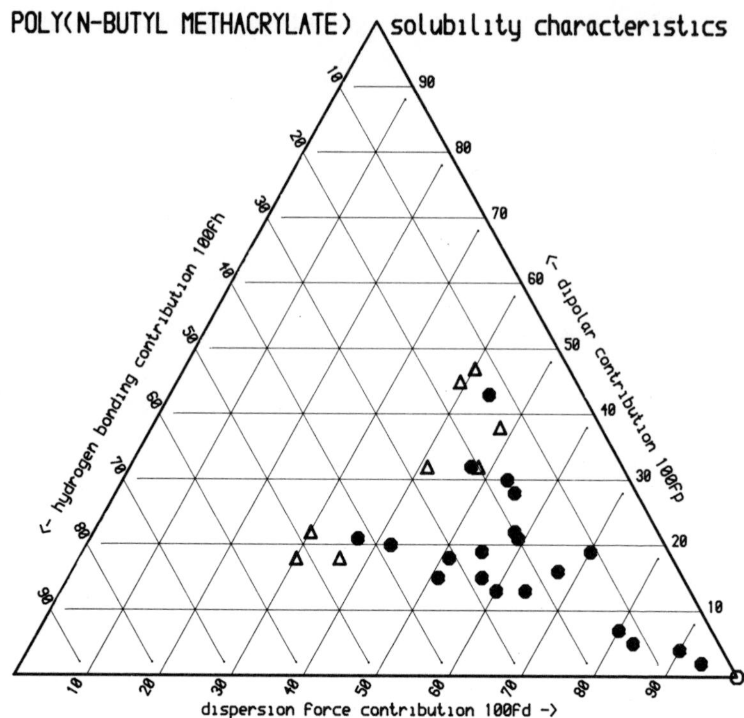

● = soluble O = borderline Δ = insoluble

solvents 4 5 7 8 11 14 16 17 19 22 24 25 26 29 30 31 32 33 37 40

borderline 2

non-solvents 27 34 35 36 39 41 42 43

Figure A3.10 Solubility of a high molecular weight poly (*n*-butyl methacrylate) (Elvacite 2044 (*Du Pont*)), manufacturer's data. Solubility of poly(isobutyl methacrylate) is similar

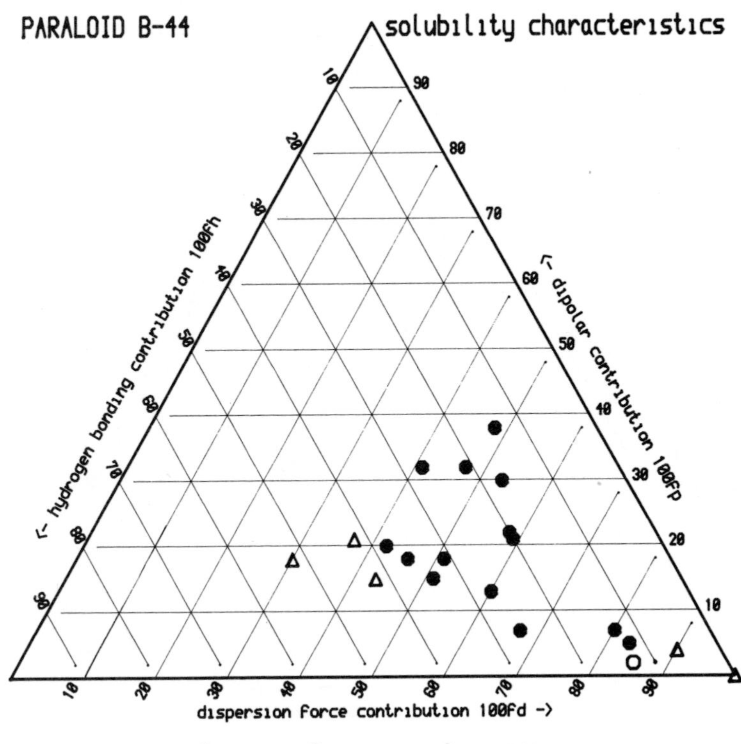

solvents 7 8 11 18 19 21 22 24 26 27 29 30 32 43

borderline 13

non-solvents 3 4 34 37 38

Figure A3.11 Solubility of Paraloid B-44 (*Rohm & Hass*), manufacturer's data

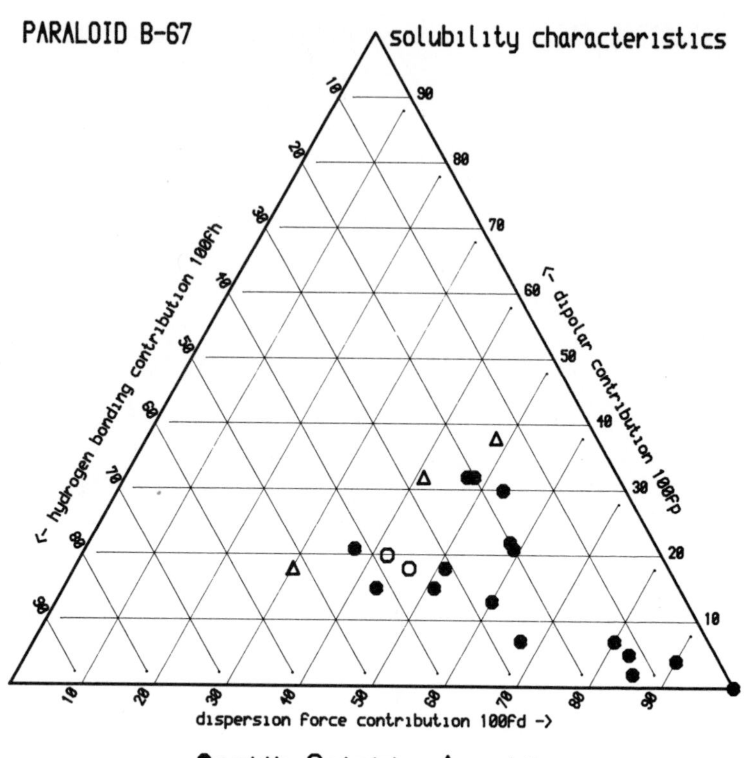

solvents 3 4 7 8 11 13 18 22 24 26 29 30 32 37 38 42

borderline 19 21

non-solvents 27 34 43

Figure A3.12 Solubility of Paraloid B-67 (*Rohm & Hass*), manufacturer's data

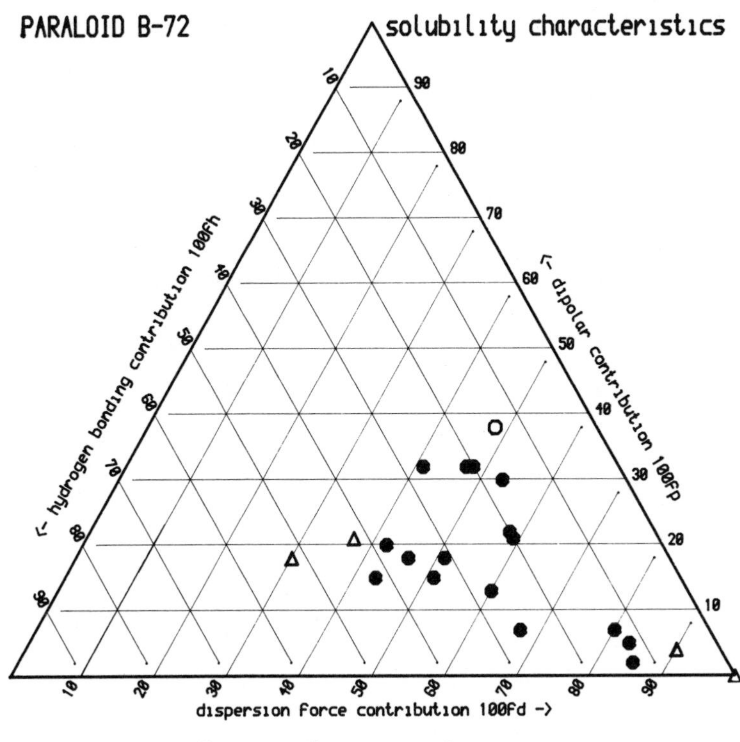

● = soluble ○ = borderline △ = insoluble

solvents 7 8 11 13 18 19 21 22 24 26 29 30 32 38 42 43

borderline 27

non-solvents 3 4 34 37

Figure A3.13 Solubility of Paraloid B-72 (*Rohm & Hass*), manufacturer's data

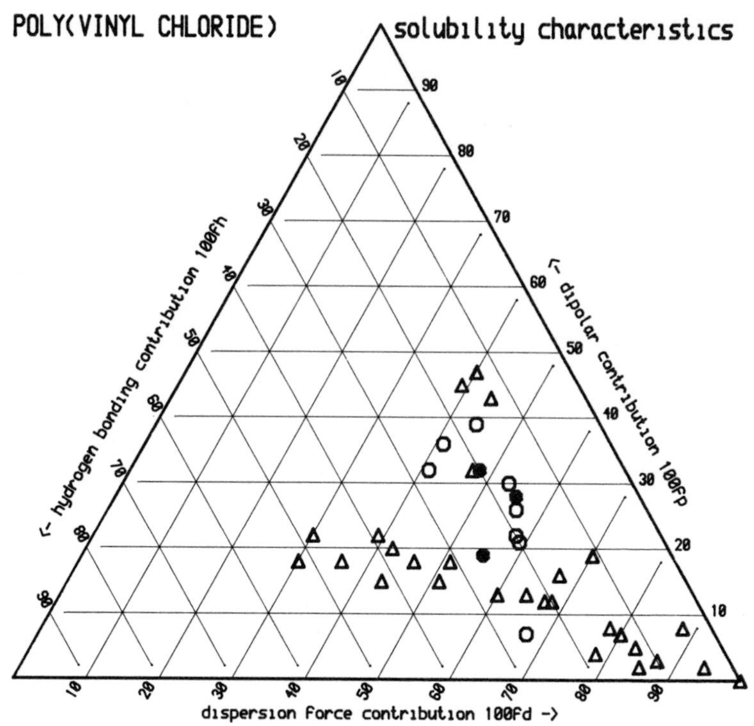

● = soluble ○ = borderline △ = insoluble

solvents 17 31 42

borderline 11 18 28 30 32 43 44 46

non-solvents 2 5 6 7 8 9 10 12 13 14 15 16 19 20 21 22 24 26 29 33 34 35 36 38 39 40 41 45

Figure A3.14 Solubility of poly(vinyl chloride) (Vipa KR (*Montecatini*)), data from Hansen (1967)

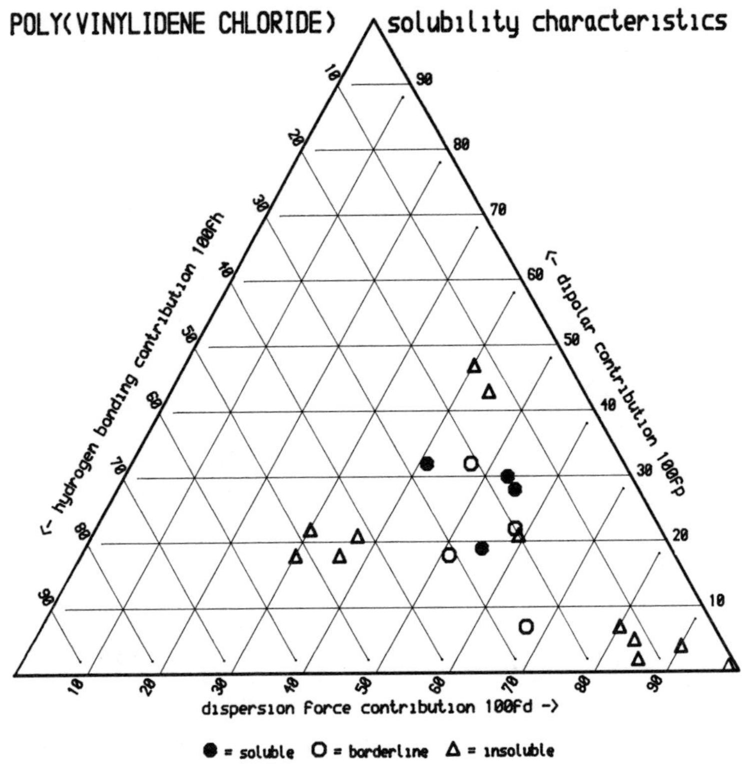

solvents 17 30 31 43

borderline 18 24 29 32

non-solvents 1 4 7 8 11 13 34 35 36 37 39 40

Figure A3.15 Solubility of a vinylidene chloride/acrylonitrile copolymer (Saran F310 (*Dow Chemical*)), manufacturer's data

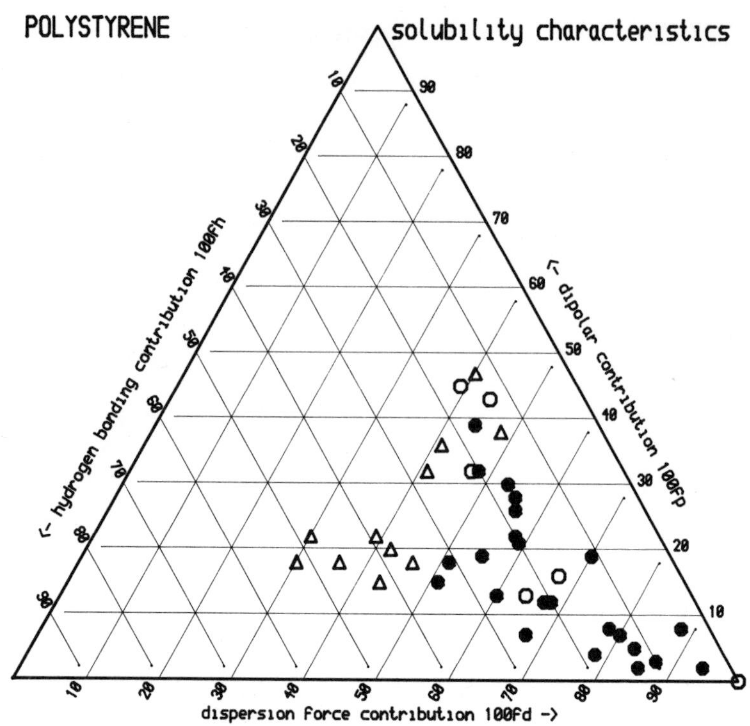

● = soluble ○ = borderline △ = insoluble

solvents 5 6 7 8 9 10 11 12 13 14 15 17 18 22 24 26 28 30 31 32 42 44 45

borderline 2 16 29 33 40 41

non-solvents 19 20 21 27 34 35 36 38 39 43 46

Figure A3.16 Solubility of polystyrene (Polystyrene LG (*BASF*)), data from Hansen (1967)

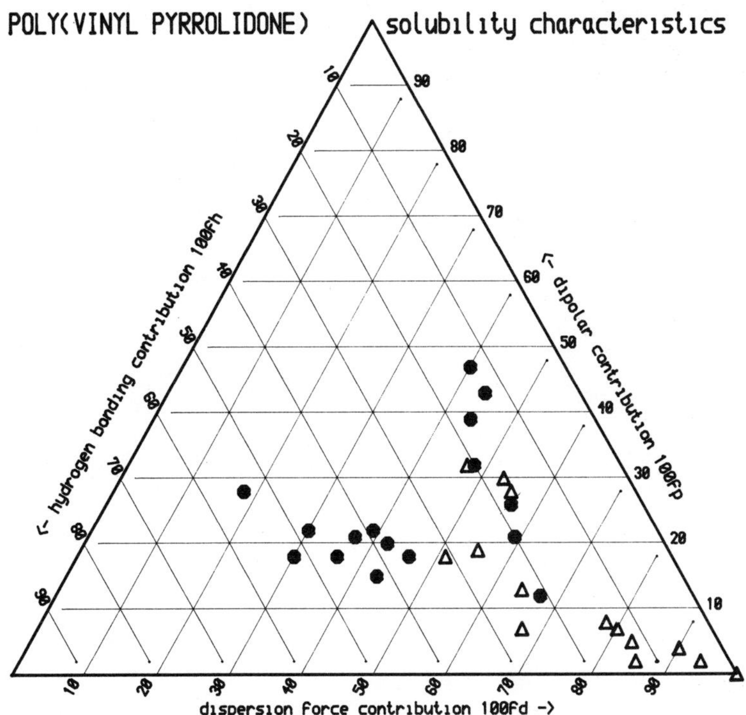

● = soluble ○ = borderline Δ = insoluble

solvents 11 12 19 20 21 28 34 35 36 37 38 39 40 42 44 47

borderline

non-solvents 2 3 4 5 6 7 8 13 16 17 18 24 29 30 31

Figure A3.17 Solubility of poly(vinyl pyrrolidone) (*GAF*), data from Blecher *et al.* (1980)

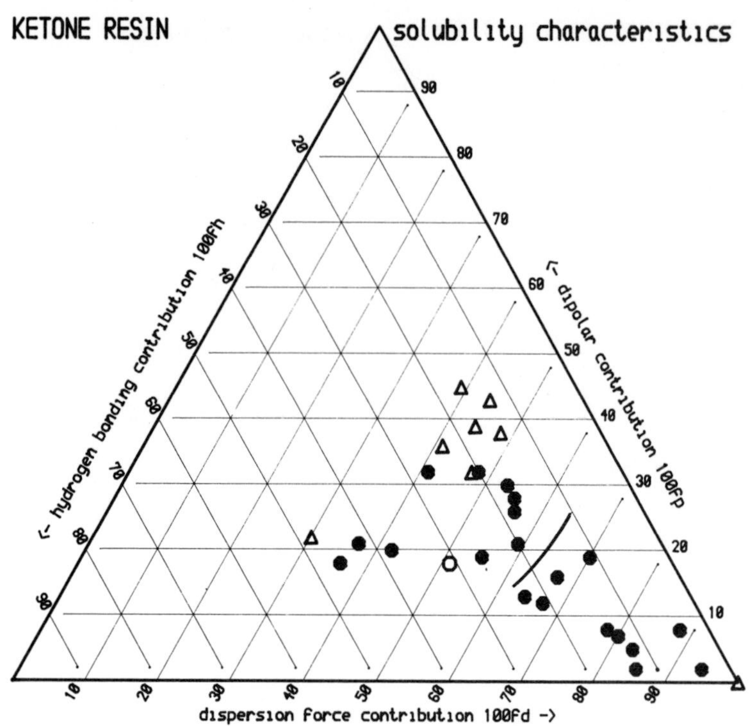

● = soluble ○ = borderline △ = insoluble

solvents 5 6 7 8 11 12 13 14 16 17 19 30 31 33 36 37 42 43 44 45

borderline 24

non-solvents 3 27 28 29 35 40 41 48

Figure A3.18 Solubility of a cyclohexanone resin (Ketone Resin N (*BASF*)). ——— indicates the approximate limit of solubility when exposed to light and oxidation equivalent to 100 years on a gallery wall (Feller and Curran, 1975)

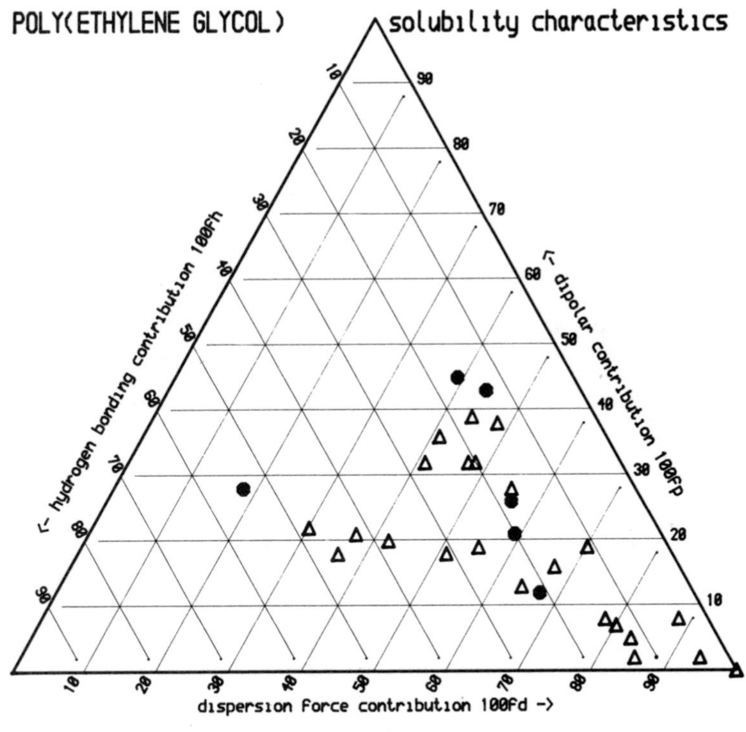

● = soluble ○ = borderline Δ = insoluble

solvents 11 12 40 41 44 47

borderline

non-solvents 3 5 6 7 8 13 14 16 17 19 24 27 28 29 31 33 35 36 37 42 43 45 46

Figure A3.19 Solubility of poly(ethylene glycol) (Carbowax PEG 3350 (*Union Carbide*))

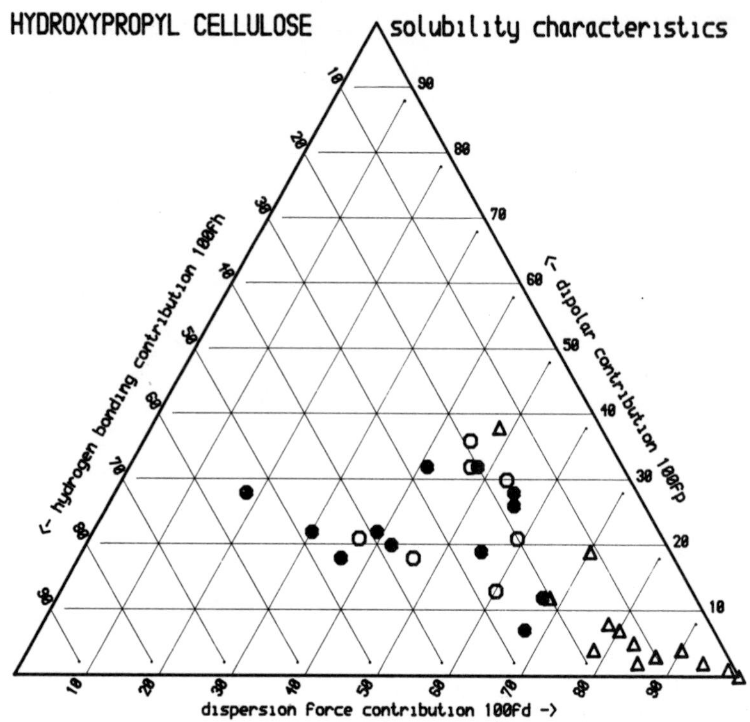

● = soluble O = borderline Δ = insoluble

solvents 12 17 18 19 20 31 35 36 42 43 44 47

borderline 11 21 23 26 29 30 37

non-solvents 1 2 4 5 6 7 8 9 10 13 14 15 27

Figure A3.20 Solubility of hydroxypropyl cellulose (Klucel G (*Hercules*)), manufacturer's data

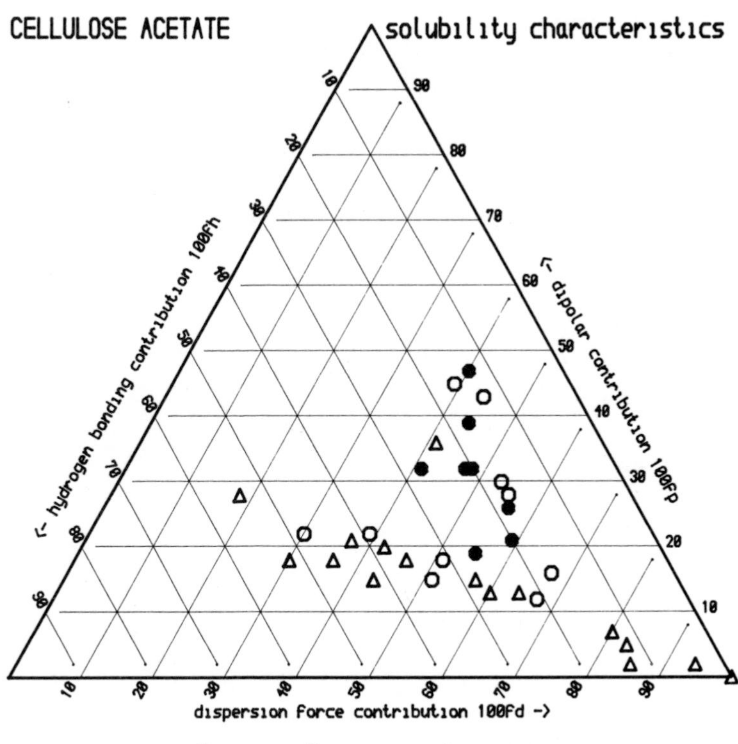

● = soluble ○ = borderline △ = insoluble

solvents 11 17 28 29 39 42 43 44

borderline 12 20 22 24 30 31 33 35 40 41

non-solvents 3 5 7 8 13 16 19 21 25 26 34 36 37 38 46 47

Figure A3.21 Solubility of a medium molecular weight cellulose acetate, degree of substitution 2.4 (*Hercules*), manufacturer's data

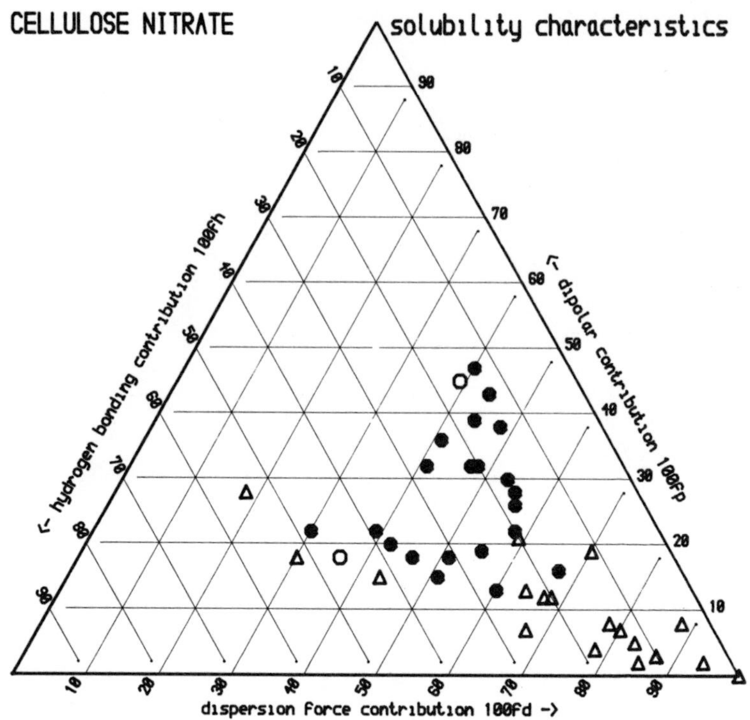

● = soluble ○ = borderline Δ = insoluble

solvents 17 19 20 21 22 24 26 27 28 29 30 31 32 33 35 39 40 42 43 44 46

borderline 36 41

non-solvents 2 5 6 7 8 9 10 11 12 13 14 15 16 18 34 38 45 47

Figure A3.22 Solubility of cellulose nitrate, '1/2 second' grade, data from Hansen (1967)

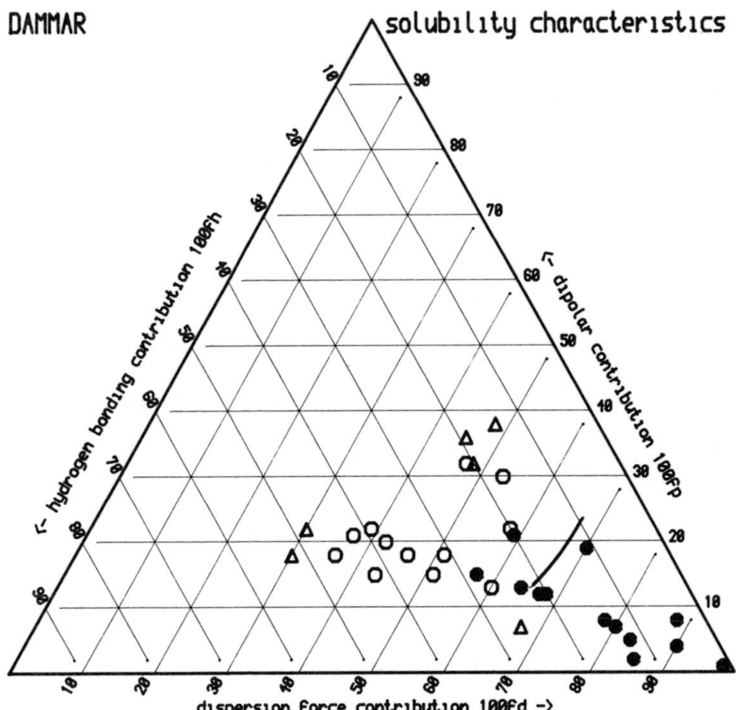

● = soluble O = borderline Δ = insoluble

solvents 1 4 6 7 8 11 12 13 14 15 16 25 45

borderline 19 20 21 22 24 26 29 30 32 36 37 38

non-solvents 18 23 27 34 35 42

Figure A3.23 Solubility of dammar resin, data from Mantell *et al.* (1942) ——— indicates the approximate limit of solubility when exposed to light and oxidation equivalent to 100 years on a gallery wall (Feller and Curran, 1975)

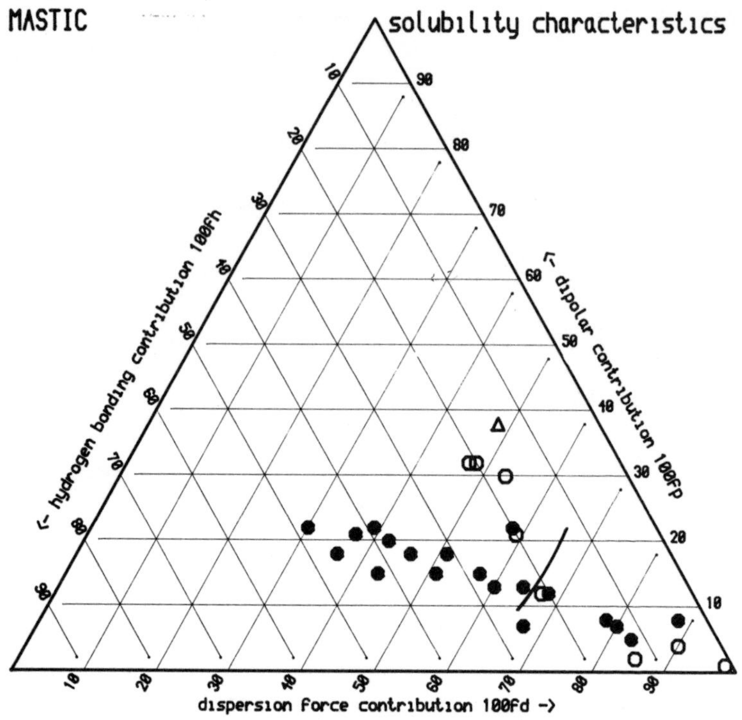

● = soluble ○ = borderline Δ = insoluble

solvents 6 7 8 15 16 18 19 20 21 22 24 25 26 32 35 36 37 38 45

borderline 1 4 11 12 13 29 30 42

non-solvents 27

Figure A3.24 Solubility of mastic resin, data from Mantell *et al.* (1942) ——— indicates the approximate limit of solubility when exposed to light and oxidation equivalent to 100 years on a gallery wall (Feller and Curran, 1975)

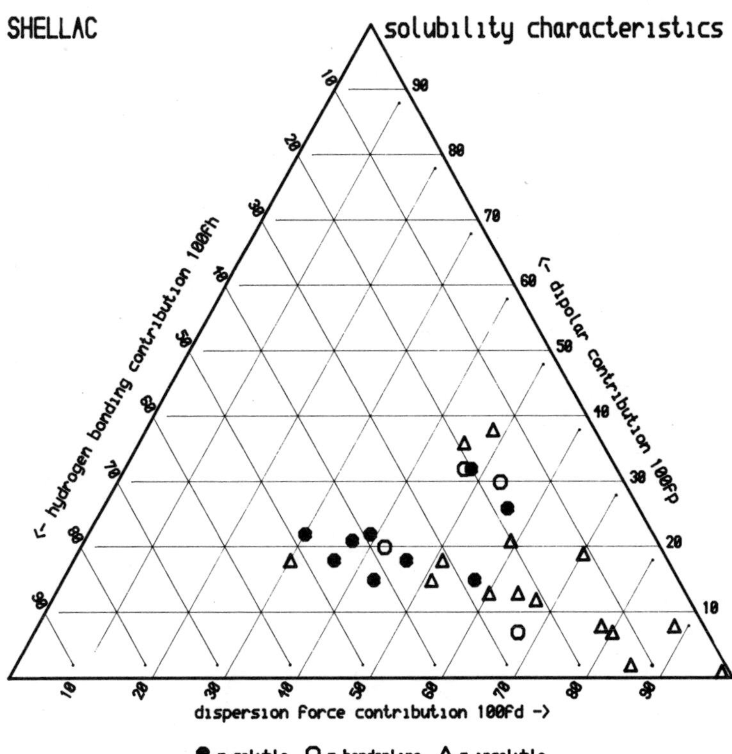

solvents 20 21 25 35 36 37 38 42 44

borderline 18 19 29 30

non-solvents 1 6 7 11 12 13 14 16 22 23 24 26 27 34 45

Figure A3.25 Solubility of shellac, data from Gardner and Whitmore (1929)

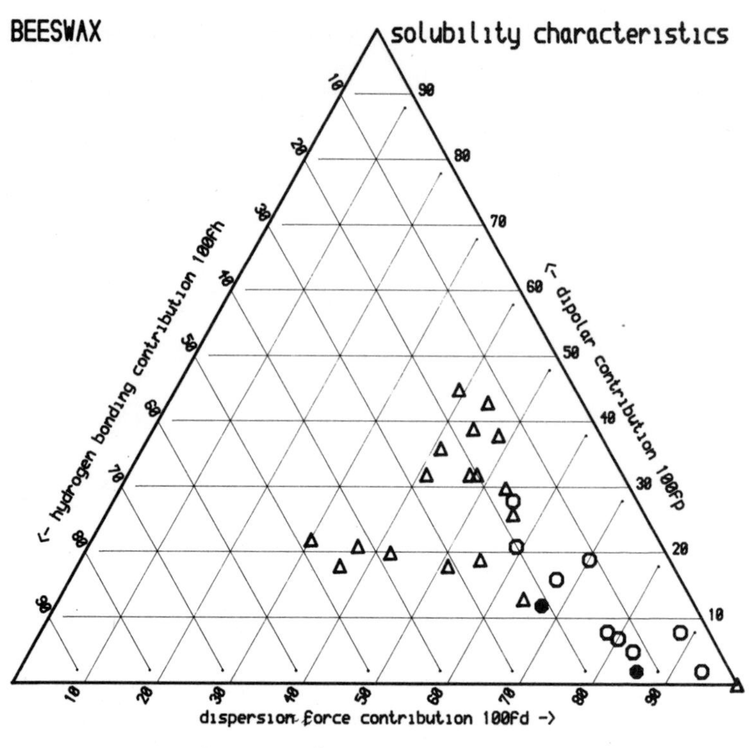

● = soluble ○ = borderline △ = insoluble

solvents 12 13

borderline 5 6 7 8 11 14 31 33 45

non-solvents 3 16 17 19 24 27 28 29 30 35 36 37 40 41 42 43 44 48

Figure A3.26 Solubility of beeswax

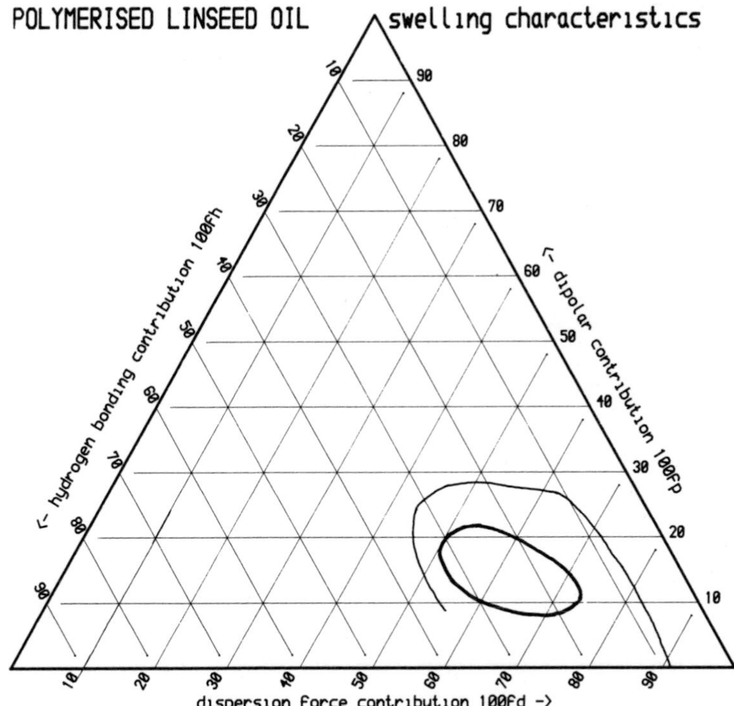

Figure A3.27 Swelling behaviour of polymerized linseed oil films. Contours at 60% swelling are shown for a film aged 27 weeks (———) and a film aged 14 years (———). The older film is obviously more resistant to swelling and is less affected than the younger film by low-polarity solvents. Data from Stolow (1971)

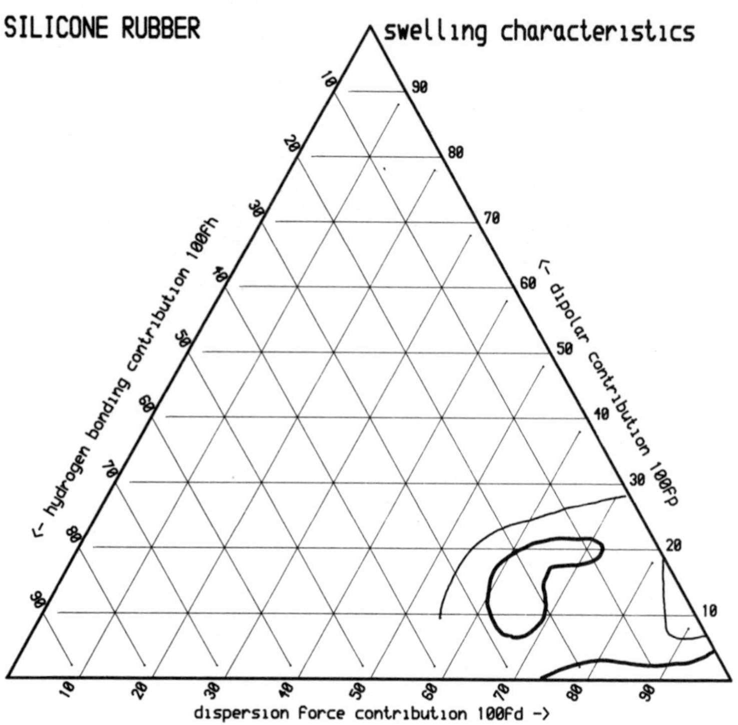

Figure A3.28 Swelling behaviour of a silicone rubber (GAF 3 (*Rhône-Poulenc*)). Contours are shown at 150% (———) and 300% (———) swelling in solvent

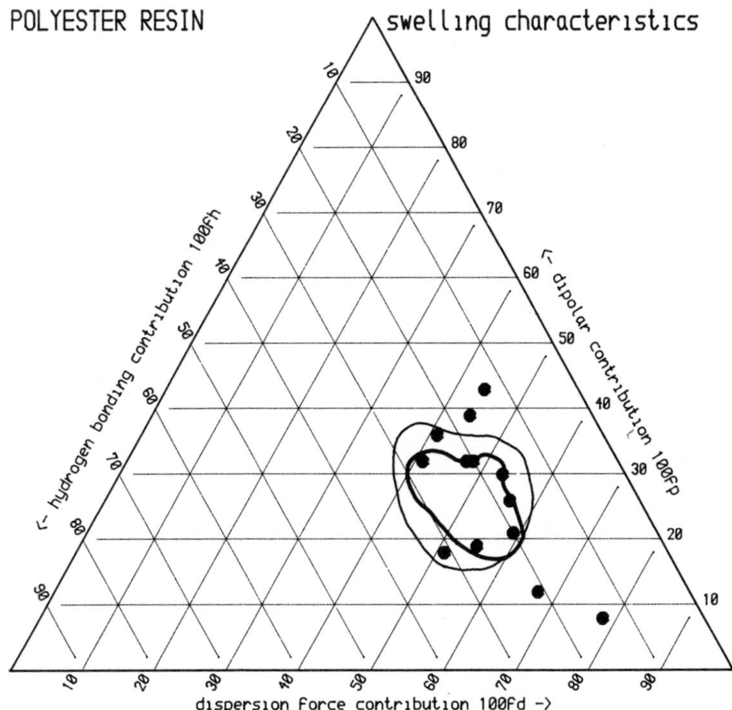

Figure A3.29 Swelling behaviour of a polyester embedding resin (Polymaster 1209AC (*Warwick*)). Contours are shown at 50% (——) and 100% (——) swelling in solvent

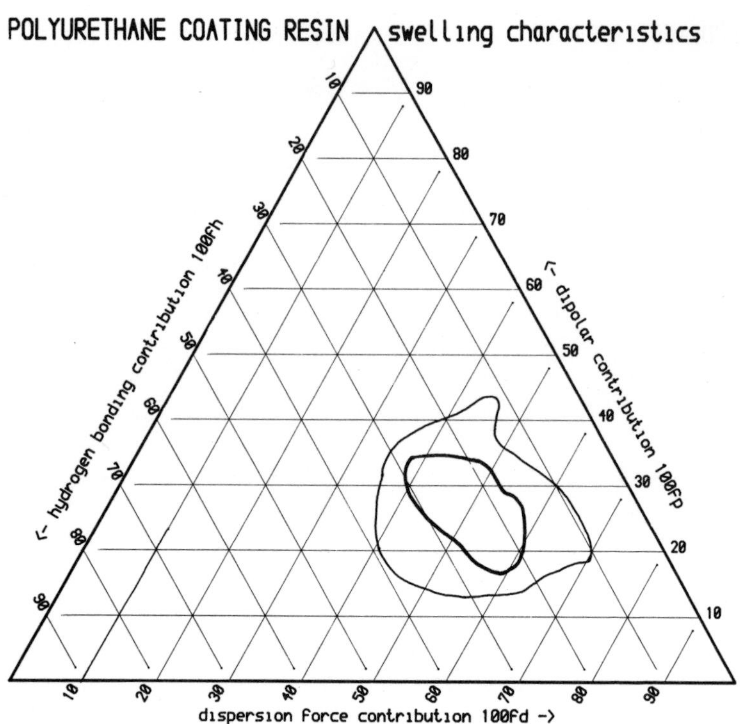

Figure A3.30 Swelling behaviour of a polyurethane (Viacryl/Desmodur, see section 13.3). Contours are shown at 100% (———) and 200% (———) swelling in solvent

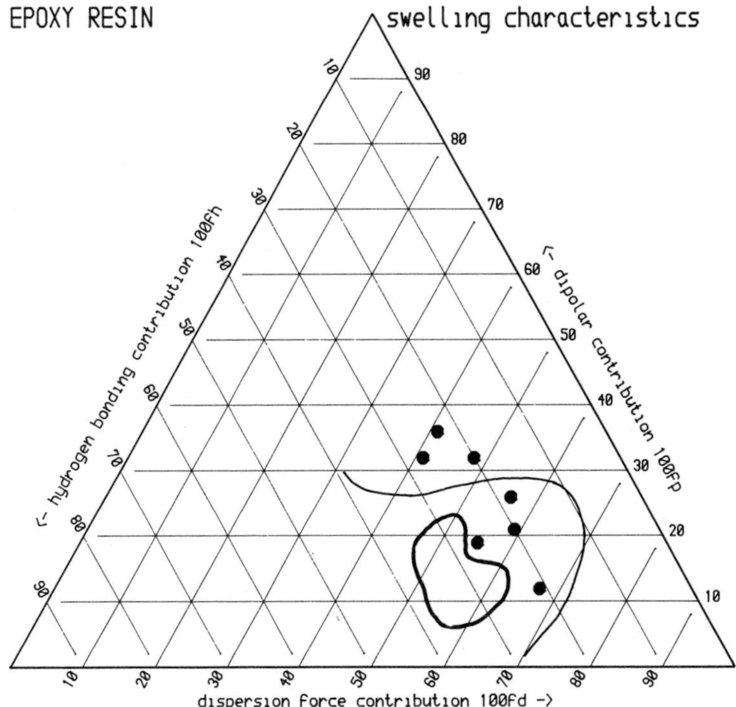

● = causes disintegration

solvents causing disintegration 11 12 17 42 43 44 46

Figure A3.31 Swelling behaviour of an epoxy resin (Araldite AY103/HY951 (*Ciba-Geigy*)). Contours are shown at 20% (———) and 40% (———) swelling in solvent

Appendix 4 International system of units (SI) and some conversion factors

Quantity (SI unit, abbreviation)	*Unit*	*Symbol*[1]	*Multiplication factor*[2]
Factor	mega	M	10^6
	kilo	k	10^3
	deci	d	10^{-1}
	centi	c	10^{-2}
	milli	m	10^{-3}
	micro	μ	10^{-6}
	nano	n	10^{-9}
Length (metre, m)	kilometre	km	10^3
	decimetre	dm	10^{-1}
	centimetre	cm	10^{-2}
	millimetre	mm	10^{-3}
	micrometre	μm	10^{-6}
	nanometre	nm	10^{-9}
	yard	yd	0.914
	foot	ft	0.3048
	inch	in	0.0254
Area (square metre, m^2)	square centimetre	cm^2	10^{-4}
	square millimetre	mm^2	10^{-6}
	square foot	ft^2	9.29×10^{-2}
	square inch	in^2	0.645×10^{-3}
Volume (cubic metre, m^3)	cubic decimetre	dm^3	10^{-3}
	cubic centimetre	cm^3	10^{-6}
	litre	l	10^{-3}
	deciliter	dl	10^{-4}
	millilitre	ml	10^{-6}
	cubic inch	in^3	1.639×10^{-5}
Time (second, s)	year	a	3.16×10^7
	month	month	2.63×10^8
	day	d	8.64×10^4
	hour	h	3.6×10^3
	minute	min	
Mass (kilogram, kg)	gram	g	10^{-3}
	milligram	mg	10^{-6}
	pound	lb	0.4536
	ounce	oz	2.83×10^{-2}

Appendix 4 (*Continued*)

Quantity (SI unit, abbreviation)	*Unit*	*Symbol*[(1)]	*Multiplication factor*[(2)]
Density (kilogram per cubic metre, kg/m^3)	gram per cubic centimetre	g/cm^3	10^3
	pound per cubic foot	lb/ft^3	16.02
	pound per cubic inch	lb/in^3	2.768×10^4
Force or weight (newton, N = $kg.m/s^2$	dyne	dyn(=$g.cm/s^2$)	10^{-5}
	gram-force	gf	9.81×10^{-3}
	kilogram-force	kgf	9.81
	pound-force	lbf	4.448
Force per unit area (pascal, Pa = N/m^2)	dyne per sq. centimetre	dyn/cm^2	10^{-1}
	kilogram-force per m^2	kgf/m^2	9.81
	kilogram-force per mm^2	kgf/mm^2	9.81×10^6
	pound-force per ft^2	lbf/ft^2	47.88
	pound-force per in^2	lbf/in^2 (psi)	6.89×10^3
	atmosphere (pressure)	atm.	1.013×10^5
	millimetre of mercury	mmHg	133.3
	inch of mercury	inHg	3.386×10^3
	bar (=10^6 dyn/cm^2)	bar	10^5
Surface tension (newton per m, N/m)	dyne per centimetre	dyne/cm	10^{-3}
Viscosity (dynamic) (pascal second Pa.s)	poise	P(=$dyn.s/cm^2$)	10^{-1}
	centipoise	cP	10^{-3}
Viscosity (kinetic) (square metre per second, m^2/s)	stokes	cm^2/s	10^{-4}
	centistokes	$cm^2/(100\,s)$	10^{-6}

Notes

Derived from Van Krevelen (1976) and IUPAC (1979a)

(1) The use of units which are combined can be expressed in two ways. For example, density can be expressed as kg/m^3 or as kgm^{-3}.

(2) To convert the value of a property into SI units multiply the original value by the multiplication factor. For example, the tensile strength of Parylene N (Union Carbide) is given as 6500 psi. The appropriate factor is 6.89×10^3. The tensile strength is therefore $(6.5 \times 10^3) \times (6.89 \times 10^3) = 4.5 \times 10^7$ Pa or 45 MPa.

Appendix 5 Manufacturers mentioned in text

Aabbitt Adhesives Inc., 2403 N.Oakley Avenue, Chicago, Illinois 60647, USA.

Adam Chemical Co. Inc., 18 Spring Hill Terrace, Spring Valley, NY 10977, USA.

Air Products and Chemicals, Five Executive Mall, Swedesford Road, Wayne, Pa 19087, USA.

Akemi Erich Höntsch GmbH, P.O.B 130163, Lechstrasse 28, D8500 Nürnberg 13, FDR.

Allied Corporation, P. O. Box 2332R, Morristown, NJ 07960, USA.

Archival Aids, P. O. Box 5, Spondon, Derby, DE2 7BP, UK.

Astor Chemical Ltd, Tavistock Road, West Drayton, Middlesex, UB7 7RA, UK.

Bakelite Gesellschaft GmbH, 4100 Duisberg 12, Varziner Str. 149, Postfach 76, FDR.

BASF Aktiengesellschaft, D6700 Ludwigshafen, FDR.

BDH Chemicals Ltd, Broom Road, Parkstone, Poole, BH12 4NN, UK.

Berol Kemi AB, Box 851, S44401 Stenungsund, Sweden.

BP Chemicals International Ltd, 76 Buckingham Palace Road, London, SW1 0SU, UK.

Cairn Chemicals Ltd, 60 High Street, Chesham, Buckingham, HD5 1EG, UK.

Ciba-Geigy AC, CH-4002 Basel, Switzerland.

Colebrand Ltd, 20 Warwick Street, Regent Street, London, WR1 6BE, UK.

Conservation Materials Ltd, 240 Freeport Blvd, Box 2884, Sparks, NV 89431, USA.

Cray Valley Products Ltd, Farnborough, Kent, BR6 7EA, UK.

Degussa AG, Postfach 110533, D6000 Frankfurt 11, FDR.

Desowag Bayer Holzschutz GmbH, P. O. Box 320 220, D-4000 Düsseldorf 30 FDR.

Devcon Corp., Danvers, Mass. 01923, USA.

Dow Chemical Co., Midland, Michigan 48640, USA.

Dow Corning Corp., Midland, Michigan 48640, USA.

Drägerwerk ag Lübeck, Postfach 1339, Moisliger Allee 53/55, D2400 Lübeck 1, FDR.

Du Pont Co., Wilmington, De. 19898, USA.

Dynamit Nobel (UK) Ltd, Gateway House, 302/308 High St, Slough, SL1 1MF, UK.

Emerson and Cuming Inc., Canton, Mass. 02021, USA.

Fillite (Runcorn) Ltd, Goddard Road, Astmoor Industrial Estate, Runcorn, Cheshire, UK.

Chemsiche Ind. Filoform B. V., Postbus 4001, 3502 HA Utrecht, Postbus 4001, Utrecht, Holland.

GAF Corp., 140 West 51 Street, New York, NY 10020, USA.

H. M. Guest, Riverside Works, Collyhurst Road, Manchester 10, UK.

Heraeus-Vötsch GmbH, D7460 Balingen, FDR.

Hercules Inc., Hercules Plaza, Wilmington, DE 19894, USA.

Hoechst Aktiengellschaft, D6230 Frankfurt (Main) 80. FDR.

Chemische Werke Hüls AG, Postfach 1320, D-4370 Marl, FDR.

ICI, Imperial Chemical House, Millbank, London, SW1P 3JF, UK.

Kulzer & Co. GmbH, Postfach 1320, D6382 Friedrichsdorf 1, FDR.

Laporte Industries Ltd, P. O. Box 26, Grimsby, Lincolnshire, UK.

Linger & Fischer GmbH, Postfach 1440, D7580 Buhl (Baden), FDR.

Mander-Domolac Ltd, Ruabon, Wrexham, Clwyd, LL14 6HU, UK.

Microscal Ltd, 79 Southern Road, London, W10 5AL, UK.

Monsanto Polymers & Petrochemicals Co., 800 N. Lindergh Blvd, St. Louis, MO 63166, USA.

Montecatini, via F. Turati 18, Milan, Italy.

Montedison, via Principe Eugenio 1/5, 20155, Milano, Italy.

Petrolite Corp., 6910 East 14th Street, Tulsa, Oklahoma 74112, USA.

Picreator Enterprise Ltd, 44 Park View Gardens, London, NW4 2PN, UK.

C. A. Pisani & Co. Ltd, Transport Avenue, Great West Road, Brentford, Middlesex, UK.

Ard Filli Raccanello S. P. A., 350100 Padova, Zona Industriale, 1A Strada No13, Italy.

Randolph Products Co., Carstadt, New Jersey, USA.

The Rawlplug Co. Ltd, London Road, Kingston, Surrey, UK.

R. A. Reed Inc., 167 Pleasant Street, P. O. Box 508, Reading, Mass. 01867-0690, USA.

Rhône-Poulenc Industries, 22 Avenue Montaigne F, 75008 Paris, France.

Röhm GmbH, Postfach 4242, Kirschenallee, D6100 Darmstadt 1, FDR.

Rohm and Haas Company, Philadelphia, PA 19105, USA.

Llewellyn Ryland Ltd, Haden Street, Birmingham, B12 9DB, UK.

A. Schmidt, St. German-Str. 14, Speyer, FDR.

Scott Bader Co. Ltd, Wollaston, Wellingborough, Northamptonshire, NN9 7RL, UK.

Sheen Instruments Ltd, Sheendale Road, Richmond, Surrey, TW4 2JL, UK.

Shell Chemicals (UK) Ltd, Halifax House, 51–55 Strand, London, UK.

J. G. Shelley Co. Inc., Fine Arts Division, 16 Mica Lane, Wellesley Hills, MA 02181-0101, USA.

A. F. Suter & Co. Ltd, Victory Works, 83–84 Eastway, Hackney Wick, London E9 5JA, UK.

A. Tiranti, Ltd, 21 Goodge Place, London, W1, UK.

Trylon Ltd, Thrift Stret, Wollaston, Northamptonshire, NN9 7QJ, UK.

Union Carbide Corp., Old Ridgeway Road, Danbury, CT 06817, USA.

Vianova Kunstharz, A 1120 Wien, Altsmannsdorfer St. 104, Austria.

Vinyl Products Ltd, Mill Lane, Carshalton, Surrey, SM5 2JU, UK.

Vosschemie, D2082 Vetersen, FDR.

Wacker-Chemie GmbH, Sparte E, Postfach D800, München 22, FDR.

Warwick International Ltd, 54 Willow Lane, Mitcham, Surrey, CR4 4NA, UK.

Winsor & Newton Ltd, Wealdstone, Harrow, Middlesex, HA3 5RH, UK.

References

ABEYSINGHE, H. P., EDWARDS, W., PRITCHARD, G. and SWAMPLILLAI, G. J. (1982) Degradation of cross-linked resins in water and electrolyte solutions. *Polymer,* **23,** 1785–1790

ACCARDO, G., CASSANO, R., ROSSI-DORIA, P., SAMMURI, P. and TABASSO, M. (1981) Screening of products and methods for the consolidation of marble. In Rossi-Manaresi (ed) (1981)

ACGIH (1983) *TLV's. Threshold limit values for chemical substances and physical agents in the workroom environment with intended changes for 1983–4.* American Conference of Governmental Industrial Hygienists, Ohio

AFIFI-EFFAT, A. M. and HAY, J. N. (1972) Thermal stabilization of PEO. *European Polymer Journal,* **8,** 289–297

AGEEVA, E. N., GRASSIMOVA, N. G., LEBEL, M. N. and MEL'NIKOVA (1978) Changes of limestone properties as a result of treatment with polybutyl methacrylate and copolymer BMK-5. In ICOM (1978) 78/10/5

AGRAWAL, O. P. (1975) Conservation of Asian cultural objects: Asian materials and techniques. *Museum,* **27,** 166–211

ALFREY, T., GURNEE, E. F. and LLOYD, W. C. (1966) Diffusion in glassy polymers. *Journal of Polymer Science,* **(C) 12,** 249–261

ALLEN, K. W. (1984) Adhesion and adhesives – some fundamentals. In Brommelle *et al.* (eds) (1984), pp. 5–12

ALLEN, N. S. and McKELLAR, J. F. (1980) *Photochemistry of Dyed and Pigmented Polymers.* Applied Science

ALLEN, N. S., BINKLEY, J. P., PARSONS, B. J., PHILLIPS, G. O. and TENNENT, N. H. (1983) Spectroscopic properties and photosensitivity of epoxy resins. *Polymer Photochemistry,* **2,** 97–107

AMOROSO, G. G. and FASSINA, V. (1983) *Stone Decay and Conservation.* Elsevier

ANDRÉ, J.-M. (1976) *The Restorer's Handbook on Ceramics and Glass.* Van Nostrand

ANGST, W. (1979) Problems with objects of historic significance. *American Institute for Conservation Preprints,* 1–9

ANON (1852) Nimrod antiquities. *Illustrated London News*

ANON (1931) Duroprene. *Museums Journal,* **31,** 379

ANON (1942) Durofix. *Museums Journal,* **44,** 169

ANON (1950) Acryloid helps preserve art treasures. *The Rohm and Hass Reporter,* **8,** no. 3, 14

ANON (1961) 'Araldite' as an aid to archaeology. *CIBA Technical Notes,* **281,** 2–10

ANON (1968) Synthetic materials used in the conservation of cultural property. In UNESCO (1968), pp. 303–335

ANON (1973) Paste for mending paper currently in use by the Conservation Laboratory, Smithsonian Institution, 'Florence Paste (modified)'. *Bulletin of the American Institute for Conservation,* **14, no. 1,** 23

ASHER, C. G. (1981) Conservation of a large collection of architectural drawings. *American Institute of Conservation Preprints,* 20–27

ASHLEY-SMITH, J. (1978) Why conserve collections? *Museum Assistants Group, Transactions,* **15,** 18–25

ASTM (1984) *Annual Book of ASTM Standards.* American Society for Testing and Materials, Philadelphia

ASTM D 523-80 Test method for specular gloss. (In ASTM, 1984)

ASTM D 624-81 Rubbery properties–tear resistance. (In ASTM, 1984)

ASTM D 1133-83 Test method for kauri-butanol value of hydrocarbon solvents. (In ASTM, 1984)

ASTM D 1925-70 Test method for the yellowness index of plastics. (In ASTM, 1984)

ASTM D 2134-66 Test method for softening of organic coatings by plastic compositions. (In ASTM, 1984)

ASTM D 3132-72 Solubility range of resins and polymers. (In ASTM, 1984)

ASTM D 3539-76 Test method for evaporation rates of volatile liquids. (In ASTM, 1984)

AUGUSTI, S. (1959) Traitement de conservation de quelques object de fouille en bois. *Studies in Conservation,* **4,** 146–157

AUTENRIETH, J. S. (1977) Resins for rubber based adhesives. In Skeist (ed.) (1977), pp. 222–241

BAER, N. S., INDICTOR, N. and JOEL, A. (1972) The aging behaviour of impregnating agent-paper systems as used in paper conservation. *Restaurator,* **2,** 5–23

BAER, N. S., INDICTOR, N. and JOEL, A. (1976) An evaluation of glues for use in paper conservation. In Brommelle and Smith (eds) (1976), pp. 182–190

BAILEY, B. A. DE V. (1938) Preservation of gesso surfaces. *Museum News,* Sept.

BAKER, C. A. (1984) Methylcellulose and sodium carboxymethyl cellulose: an evaluation for use in paper conservation through accelerated ageing. In Bromelle *et al.* (eds) (1984), pp. 55–59

BAKKEN, A. and AARMO, K. (1981) A report on the treatment of barkcloth. In ICOM (1981) 81/3/4

BAMFORD, C. H. and TIPPER, C. F. H. (eds) (1975) *Comprehensive Chemical Kinetics, Vol. 14, Degradation of Polymers.* Elsevier

BARCLAY, R. (1981) Wood consolidation on an eighteenth century English fire engine. *Studies in Conservation,* **26,** 133–139

BARKER, H. (1975) Early work on the conservation of waterlogged wood in the UK. In Oddy (ed.) (1975), pp. 61–63

BARKER, S. J. and PRICE, S. B. (1970) *Polyacetals.* Iliffe

BARKMAN, L. (1975) The preservation of the warship Wasa. In Oddy (ed.) (1975), pp. 65–105

BARROW, W. J. (1964) *Permanence/Durability of the Book-II.* W. J. Barrow Research Laboratory

BARROW, W. J. (1965) *Permanence/Durability of the Book-IV, Polyvinyl acetate (PVA) Adhesives for Use in Library Bookbinding.* W. J. Barrow Research Laboratory

BARTON, A. F. M. (1983) CRC Handbook of Solubility Parameters and other Cohesion Parameters. CRC Press

BARTON, K. J. (1960) Conservation at Bristol. *Museums Journal,* **59,** 262–265

BAUMGARTNER, H. and LANOOY, R. (1982) Eine Methode zur Wassersältigung trochener, fossiler Knocken, Zähne und Hölzer für die Konservierung mit PEG 6000-12000. *Präparator,* **28,** 269–274

BAYNES-COPE, A. D. (1972a) The dismounting of 'Dry Mounted' photographic prints. *Restaurator,* **2,** 1–3

BAYNES-COPE, A. D. (1972b) An organic solvent for dissolving old flour paste. *Restaurator,* **2,** 25–27

BAYNES-COPE, A. D. (1975) Science, chemistry and conservation. *3 Internationaler Graphischer Restauratorentag 1975* (1977) 11–24

BEECHER, E. R. (1959) Treatment of weakened fabrics. *Museums Journal,* **58,** 234–235

BEECHER, E. R. (1963) Reinforcing weakened textiles with synthetic fibre net. In Thomson (ed.) (1963), pp. 195–196

BEECHER, E. R. (1968) The conservation of textiles. In UNESCO (1968), pp. 251–264

BEERS, M. D. (1977) Silicone adhesive sealants. In Skeist (ed.) (1977), pp. 628–639

BELAYA, I. K. (1958) Glues for the restoration of leather bindings. In Belyakova and Kozulina (eds) (1958), pp. 168–178

BELEN'KAYA, N. G., GORSENINA, W. F. and KUZENETSOVA, E. N. (1965) The use of methylcellulose for the restoration of archival and library material. *Štareniye bumagi, USSR Academy of Sciences,* 94–111

BELEN'KAYA, N. G. Methods of restoration of books and documents. In Solechnik (ed.), pp. 24–49

BELEN'KAYA, N. G. and STREL'TSOVA, T. N. Restoration and preservation of books and documents by thermoplastic film coating. In Solechnik (ed.), pp. 50–61

BELYAKOVA, L. A. and KOZULINA, O. V. (eds) (1958) *Collection of Materials on the Preservation of Library Resources, Documents and Books.* Israel Program for Scientific Translations (1964)

BENGTSSON, S. (1975) Preservation of the 'Wasa' sails. In Leigh *et al.* (eds) (1975), pp. 33–35

BERGEON, S., LEPAVEC, Y., SOTTON, M. and CHEVALIER, M. (1978) La rentoilage Francais a' la colle. In ICOM (1978) 78/2/3

BERGER, G. A. (1974) Beva lining of torn paintings – three films. *Bulletin of the American Institute for Conservation,* **14,** no. 2, 22–27

BERGER, G. A. (1975) Heat sealing of a torn painting with Beva 371. *Studies in Conservation,* **20,** 126–151

BERGER, G. A. (1976) Formulating adhesives for the conservation of paintings. In Brommelle and Smith (eds) (1976), pp. 169–181

BERGER, G. A. and RUSSELL, W. H. (1986) Investigations in the reactions of plastic materials to environmental changes, Part I. *Studies in Conservation,* **31,** 49–64

BERGER, G. A. and ZELINGER, H. I. (1975) Detrimental and irreversible effects of wax impregnation on easel paintings. In ICOM (1975) 75/11/2

BERGER, G. A. and ZELINGER, H. I. (1984) The procedure of developing an adhesive for paintings: the importance of valid tests. In Brommelle *et al.* (eds) (1984), pp. 13–17

BETTEMBOURG, J.-M. (1975) Études de mastics elastomeres – Le masticage des panneaux de vitraux anciens. In Leigh *et al.* (eds) (1975), pp. 137–138

BETTEMBOURG, J.-M. (1976) Protection des verres de vitraux contre les agents atmospériques. Étude de films de résins synthétiques. *Verres Réfract,* **30,** 87–91

BHOWMIK, S. K. (1967) A non-aqueous method for the restoration of Indian miniature paintings. *Studies in Conservation,* **12,** 116–123

BIEK, L. (1952) Protective coatings for silver. *Museums Journal,* **52,** 60–61

BILLMEYER, F. W. (1971) *Textbook of Polymer Science,* 2nd edn. Wiley

BILLMEYER, F. W. and SALTZMAN, M. (1981) *Principles of Color Technology.* Wiley

BLACKSHAW, S. M. (1974) The conservation of wooden writing-tablets from Vindolanda Roman Fort, Northumberland. *Studies in Conservation,* **19,** 244–246

BLACKSHAW, S. M. (1975) Comparison of different makes of PEG and results on corrosion testing of metals in PEG solutions. In Oddy (ed) (1975), pp. 51–58

BLACKSHAW, S. M. and WARD, S. E. (1983) Simple tests for assessing materials for use in conservation. Tate *et al.* (eds) (1983), chapter 2

BLANK, M. G. (1978) The effect of polymer additions on the strength of paper of different compositions. *Restaurator,* **2,** 155–162

BLECHER, L., LORENZ, D. H., LOWD, H. L., WOOD, A. S. and WYMAN, D. P. (1980) Polyvinylpyrrolidone. In Davidson (ed) (1980), chapter 21

BLUM, D. (1983) An evaluation of some uses of synthetic resins in textile conservation. In Tate *et al.* (eds) (1983), chapter 8

BOCKOFF, F. J., GUO, K. M., RICHARDS, G. E. and BOCKOFF, E. (1984) Infra-red studies of the kinetics of insolubilization of soluble nylon. In Brommelle *et al.* (eds) (1984), pp. 81–86

BRADLEY, S. M. (1984) Strength testing of adhesives and consolidants for conservation purposes. In Brommelle *et al.* (eds) (1984), pp. 22–25

BRADLEY, S. M., BOFF, R. M. and SHORER, P. H. T. (1983) A modified technique for the lightweight backing of mosaics. *Studies in Conservation,* **28,** 161–170

BRAUN, D. (1982) *Simple Methods for the Identification of Plastics.* Hanser

BRENNER, A. (1974) High polymers for forming an invisible, soil-resistant, coating on canvas. In Carmean, E. A. (ed) *The Great Decade of American Abstraction Modernist Art 1960–1970,* pp. 130–138. The Museum of Fine Arts (Houston, Texas)

BRETHERICK, L. (1981) *Hazards in the Chemical Laboratory,* 3rd edn. Royal Society of Chemistry.

BRISCOE, B. and SMITH, A. C. (1983) Rheology of solvent-cast polymer films. *Journal of Applied Polymer Science,* **28,** 3827–3834

BRITISH STANDARDS INSTITUTION (1973) Recommendations for repair and allied processes for the conservation of documents. BS 4971:1. British Standards Institution

BRITISH STANDARDS INSTITUTION (1983) Chemical nomenclature for industry. BS 2474. British Standards Institution

BROMMELLE, N. S. (1956) Material for a history of conservation. *Studies in Conservation,* **2,** 176–188

BROMMELLE, N. S. and SMITH, P. (eds) (1976) *Conservation and Restoration of Pictorial Art.* Butterworths

BROMMELLE, N. S., MONCRIEFF, A. and SMITH, P. (eds) (1978) *Conservation of Wood in Painting and the Applied Arts.* IIC

BROMMELLE, N. S., THOMSON, G. and SMITH, P. (eds) (1980) *Conservation Within Historic Buildings.* IIC

BROMMELLE, N. S., PYE, E. M., SMITH, P. and THOMSON, G. (eds) (1984) *Adhesives and Consolidants.* IIC

BROWN, R. P. (ed) (1981) *Handbook of Plastics Test Methods.* Godwin (with Plastics and Rubber Institute)

BROWN, W. and STILBS, P. (1982) On the solution conformation of poly(ethylene oxide). An FT pulsed field gradient nmr self diffusion study. *Polymer,* **23,** 1780–1784

BROWNING, B. L. and WINK, W. A. (1968) Studies on the permanence and durability of paper I. *TAPPI,* **51,** no. 4, 156–163

BRUINS, P. F. (1976) *Unsaturated Polyester Technology.* Gordon & Breach

BRYCE, T., McKERELL, H. and VARSANYI, A. (1975) The acetone-rosin method for the conservation of waterlogged wood and some thoughts on the penetration of PEG into oak. In Oddy (ed) (1975), pp. 35–43

BRYDSON, J. A. (1982) *Plastics Materials,* 4th edn. Butterworths

BURSTALL, M. L., MOLLETT, C. C. and BUTLER, C. E. (1984) Graft polymerisation as a method of preserving papers: problems and potentialities. In Brommelle *et al.* (eds) (1984), pp. 60–63

BUTLER, R. W. and KLUG, E. D. (1980) Hydroxypropylcellulose. In Davidson (ed) (1980), chapter 13

BYRNE, G. S. (1984) Adhesive formulations manipulated by the addition of fumed colloidal silica. In Brommelle *et al.* (eds) (1984), pp. 78–80

CASE, E. L. (1925) The use of Bakelite in the preservation of fossil material. *Science,* **61,** 543–544

ČEJKA, J. (1975) A simple method for the conservation of zinc and copper printing blocks. In ICOM (1975) 75/25/1

CHAN, M. G. and ALLARA, D. L. (1972) Infra-red reflection studies of metal–polymer interfaces. *Polymer Engineering and Science,* **14,** 12–15

CHANDOK, Y. M. and GUPTA, A. L. (1964) Yellowing in white films, part 1, a review. *Paintindia Annual,* 83–87

CHARLESBY, A. (1960) *Atomic Radiation and Polymers.* Pergamon

CHEMICAL SECTION & SECTION FOR REPAIRING TECHNIQUES (1968) Conservative treatment of colors on sliding-door paintings at Zuigan-ji. *Science for Conservation,* **4,** 17–26

CHEUNG, H. T. (1968) Constituents of dipterocarpaceae resins part II. *Journal of the Chemical Society,* **C,** 2682–2689

CHRISTENSEN, B. B. (1970) *The Conservation of Waterlogged Wood in the National Museum of Denmark.* National Museum, Copenhagen

CHRISTENSEN, B. B. (1975) Discussion. In Oddy (ed) (1975), 27

CHRISTENSEN, G. and PEDERSEN, C. M. (1982) The storage instability of some oxygenated raw materials. *XVI Fatipec Congress,* **4,** 15–40

CIABACH, J. (1983) Investigation of the cross-linking of thermoplastic resins effected by ultra-violet radiation. In Tate *et al.* (1983), chapter 5

CLAPP, A. F. (1978) *Curatorial Care Works of Art on Paper,* 3rd edn. Intermuseum Conservation Association, Oberlin

CLARKE, C. D. (1936) Moulding and casting formulas for wax reproductions. *Technical Studies in the Field of Fine Arts,* **4,** 187–206

COHEN, S. M., KASS, R. E. and LAVIN, E. (1958) Chemical interactions in the poly(vinyl formal)-phenolic resin system. *Industrial and Engineering Chemistry,* **50,** 229–232

COLE, F. (1977) Discoloration of a silicone sealant. *Corpus Vitrearum,* **25,** para. 1.5

COLLINS, T. J. (1983) Modern materials in the preservation of works of art on paper. In Tate *et al.* (eds) (1983), chapter 7

COMYN, J. (ed.) (1985) *Polymer Permeability.* Elsevier Applied Science

COOPER, F. J. (1939) Ivory discoloured by proximity to rubber. *Museums Journal,* **39,** 23

COOPER, H. W. and WICKER, T. H. (1964) 2-cyanoacrylate ester polymers. In Mark *et al.* (eds) Vol. 6, pp. 337–342

CORCORAN, E. M. (1972) Adhesion. In Sward (ed) (1972), pp. 314–322

COREMANS, P. (1941) Transfer of mural paintings, discovered in 1940, at Tournai and Nivelles. *Bulletin des Musées Royaux d'Art et d'Histoire,* **6,** 125–132

COREY, A. E., DRAGHETTI, P. M. and FANTL, J. (1977) Polyvinyl acetate emulsions and polyvinyl alcohol for adhesives. In Skeist (ed) (1977), pp. 465–483

COUNCIL OF EUROPE (1977) supplement (1980) *Dangerous Chemical Substances and Proposals Concerning Their Labelling, (The Yellow Book),* 4th edn. Also supplement no. 1 to the 4th edn. Council of Europe, Strasbourg

CRAFTS COUNCIL (1983) *Science for Conservation, Book 3, Adhesives for Conservation.* Crafts Council, London

CROLL, S. G. (1979) Internal strain in solvent cast coatings. *Journal of Coatings Technology,* **51,** no. 648, 64–88

CROLL, S. G. (1980a) An overhanging beam method for measuring the internal stress in coatings. *Journal of the Oil and Colour Chemists Association,* **63,** 271–275

CROLL, S. G. (1980b) Adhesion loss due to internal strain. *Journal of Coatings Technology,* **52,** no. 665, 35–43

CROLL, S. G. (1981) Residual stress due to solvent loss from a crosslinked coating. *Journal of Coatings Technology,* **53,** no. 672, 85–92

CRONYN, J. M. and HORIE, C. V. (1985) *St. Cuthbert's Coffin.* Dean and Chapter of Durham Cathedral

CUNHA, G. M. and CUHNA, D. G. (1971) *Conservation of Library Materials,* 2nd edn. Scarecrow Press, New Jersey

CURISTER, S. and DE WILD, A. M. (1939) Picture relining. *Technical Studies in the Field of Fine Arts,* **7,** 191–195

DADIC, V. and RIBKIN, T. (1970) Techniques of delaminating polyethylene laminates. *Restaurator,* **1,** 141–148

DANIELS, V. (1981) Removal of epoxy resins from antiquities. *Conservation News,* no. 16, 11

DANIELS, V. (1984) The Russell Effect – a review of its possible uses in conservation and the scientific examination of materials. *Studies in Conservation,* **29,** 57–62

DANIELS, V. D., PASCOE, M. W. and HOLLAND, L. (1978) Plasma reactions in the conservation of antiquities. In ICOM (1978) 78/23/1

DANNENBERG, H. and MAY, C. A. (1969) Epoxide adhesives. In Patrick, R. L. (ed) *Treatise on Adhesion and Adhesives,* Vol. 2, pp. 3–76. Arnold

DAS GUPTA, R. and WHITEFIELD, B. D. *Documentation Preservation – Archival Permanence of Texicryl Laminations.* HMSO Technical Services Report no. 95. HMSO

DAUCHOT-DEHON, M. and DE WITTE, E. (1978) Étude du temps de sechage du vernis Paraloid B-72 sur les peintures. In ICOM (1978) 78/16/2

DAVID, C. (1975) Thermal degradation of polymers. In Bamford and Tipper (eds) (1975), pp. 1–174

DAVID, C., BORSU, M. and GEUSKENS, G. (1970) Photolysis and radiolysis of poly(vinyl acetate). *European Polymer Journal,* **6,** 959–963

DAVIDSON, R. L. (ed.) (1980) *Handbook of Watersoluble Gums and Resins.* McGraw-Hill

DAVISON, S. (1978) The problems of restoring glass vessels. *The Conservator,* **2,** 3–8

DAVISON, S. and JACKSON, P. R. (1985) The restoration of decorative flat glass: four case histories. *The Conservator,* **9,** 3–13

DEMMLER, K. (1980) The determination of residual active oxygen in parts of unsaturated polyester resins and its influence on post curing and yellowing by light. *Kunstoffe,* **70,** 786–792

DEUTSCHE FORSCHUNGSGEMEINSCHAFT (1982) *Maximum Concentrations at the Workplace and Biological Tolerance Values for Working Materials 1982.* Commission for Investigation of Health Hazards of Chemical Compounds in the Work Area, Report 18, Verlag Chemie

DE WITTE, E. (1973/4) The protection of silverware with varnishes. *Bulletin Institute Royal du Patrimonie Artistique,* **14,** 140–151

DE WITTE, E. (1975a) Soluble nylon as consolidation agent for stone. *Studies in Conservation,* **20,** 30–34

DE WITTE, E. (1975b) The influence of light on the gloss of matt varnishes. In ICOM (1975) 75/22/6

DE WITTE, E. (1976/7) Polyvinyl alcohol. *Bulletin Institute Royal du Patrimonie Artistique,* **16,** 120–129

DE WITTE, E., HUGET, P. and VAN DEN BROECK, P. (1977) Comparative study of three consolidation methods on limestone. *Studies in Conservation,* **22,** 190–196

DE WITTE, E., GOESSENS-LANDRIE, M., GOETHALS, E. J. and SIMONDS, R. (1978) The structure of 'old' and 'new' Paraloid B-72. In ICOM (1978) 78/16/3

DE WITTE, E., GOESSENS-LANDRIE, M., GOETHALS, E. J., VAN LERBERGHE, K. and VAN SPRINGEL, C. (1981) Synthesis of an acrylic varnish with high refractive index. In ICOM (1981) 81/16/4

DE WITTE, E., FLORQUIN, S. and GOESSENS-LANDRIE, M. (1984) Influence of the modification of dispersions on film properties. In Brommelle *et al.* (eds) (1984), pp. 32–35

DOMASLOWSKI, W. (1958) Problems in the conservation of wood. *Materialz Zachodnio-Pormoskii,* **4,** 398–424

DOMASLOWSKI, W. and LEHMAN, J. (1971) Recherches sur l'affermissment structural des pierres en moyen des solutions des resines thermoplastiques. In Rossi-Manaresi and Torraca (eds) (1971), pp. 225–272

DOWN, J. L. (1984) The yellowing of epoxy resins adhesives, report on natural dark ageing. *Studies in Conservation,* **29,** 63–76

DROOP, J. P. (1915) *Archaeological Excavation.* Cambridge

DUNN, A. S., COLEY, R. L. and DUNCALF, B. (1968) Thermal decomposition of poly(vinyl alcohol). In Finch, C. A. (ed) *Properties and Applications of Poly(vinyl alcohol),* pp. 208–221. Monograph no. 30, Society of Chemical Industry, London

DU PONT *Solvent Formulating Maps for Elvacite Acrylic Resins.* Du Pont Company, Wilmington, DE 19898, USA

DURRANS, T. H. (1971) *Solvents.* Chapman & Hall

DUVE, G., FUCHS, O. and OVERBECK, H. (1975) *Hoechst Solvents,* 5th edn. Hoechst

DUVE, G., FUCHS, O. and OVERBECK, H. (1976) *Lösemittel Hoechst,* 6th edn. Hoechst, Frankfurt

EASTHAUGH, N. (1984) Gloss. *The Conservator,* **8,** 10–14

ELIAS, H.-G. (1977) *New Commercial Polymers 1969–1975.* Gordon and Breach

EMMENEGGER, O. (1975) The cemetery chapel of Santa Maria, Pontresina. In ICOM (1975) 75/1/0

ERHARDT, D. (1983) Removal of silicone adhesives. *Journal American Institute for Conservation,* **22,** 100

ERRETT, R. F., LYNN, M. and BRILL, R. H. (1984) The use of silanes in glass conservation. In Brommelle *et al.* (eds) (1984), pp. 185–190

EVERS, G. (1968) Restaurierungs – und Rekonstruktionsprobleme am Biespiel des Kalottenhelms von Niederealta. *Arbeitsblätter* Heft **1,** Gruppe **1,** Seite **1**

FALWEY, D. (1981) The advantages of Mowiol (polyvinyl alcohol): comparative studies of organic and synthetic binding media for fillers for paintings in canvas. In ICOM (1981) 81/2/13

FEAST, A. A. J. (1982) Synthetic laticies. In Calvert, K. O. (ed) *Polymer Laticies and their Applications,* pp. 24–46. Applied Science

FELLER, R. L. (1957) Factors affecting the appearance of picture varnishes. *Science,* **125,** 1143–1144

FELLER, R. L. (1958) Dammar and mastic varnishes – hardness, brittleness and change in weight upon drying. *Studies in Conservation,* **3,** 162–174

FELLER, R. L. (1959) Resins and the properties of varnishes. In Feller *et al.* (eds) (1959), pp. 94–165

FELLER, R. L. (1963) New solvent-type varnishes. In Thomson (ed) (1963), pp. 171–175

FELLER, R. L. (1966) First description of dammar picture varnish translated. *Bulletin American Group-International Institute for Conservation,* **7,** no. 1, 8, 20

FELLER, R. L. (1971a) Resins and the properties of varnishes. In Feller *et al.* (eds) (1971), pp. 117–168

FELLER, R. L. (1971b) Early studies on the cross-linking of polymers. In Feller *et al.* (eds) (1971), pp. 195–201

FELLER, R. L. (1971c) Solubility and removability of aged polymeric films. In Feller *et al.* (eds) (1971), pp. 202–210

FELLER, R. L. (1971d) Grades of poly(vinyl acetate) resins with respect to their viscosity in solution. In Feller *et al.* (eds) (1971), pp. 226–229

FELLER, R. L. (1971e) Polymer emulsions. In Feller *et al.* (eds) (1971), pp. 218–225

FELLER, R. L. (1976a) Problems in the investigation of picture varnishes. In Brommelle and Smith (eds) (1976), pp. 137–144

FELLER, R. L. (1976b) Relative solvent power needed to remove various aged solvent-type coatings. In Brommelle and Smith (eds) (1976), pp. 158–161

FELLER, R. L. (1977) Stages in the deterioration of organic materials. In Williams, J. C. (ed.) *Preservation of Paper and Textiles of Historic and Artistic Value,* pp. 314–335. American Chemical Society

FELLER, R. L. (1978) Standards in the evaluation of thermoplastic resins. In ICOM (1978) 78/16/4

FELLER, R. L. (1981) Developments in the testing and application of protective coatings. In ICOM (1981) 81/16/7

FELLER, R. L. (1983) Thermoplastic polymers currently in use as protective coatings and potential directions for further research. In *Conservation: The Art, the Craft and the Science,* pp. 5–18. ICCM, Brisbane

FELLER, R. L. and BAILIE, C. W. (1966) Studies on the effect of light on protective coatings using aluminium as a support: determination of ratio of chain breaking to cross-linking. *Bulletin American Group-International Institute for Conservation,* **6,** no. 1

FELLER, R. L. and BAILIE, C. W. (1972) Solubility of aged coatings based on dammar, mastic and Resin AW-2. *Bulletin American Group-International Institute for Conservation,* **12,** no. 2, 72–81

FELLER, R. L. and CURRAN, M. (1970) Solubility and cross-linking characteristics of ethylene/vinyl acetate copolymers. *Bulletin American Group-International Institute for Conservation,* **11,** no. 1, 42–45

FELLER, R. L. and CURRAN, M. (1975) Changes in solubility and removability of varnish resins with age. *Bulletin American Institute for Conservation,* **15,** no. 2, 17–26

FELLER, R. L., STOLOW, N. and JONES, E. H. (1959, 1971) *On Picture Varnishes and Their Solvents,* 1st and 2nd edns. Case Western University

FELLER, R. L., CURRAN, M. and BAILIE, C. (1981) Photochemical studies of methacrylate coatings for the conservation of museum objects. In Pappas, S. P. and Winslow, F. H. (eds) *Photodegradation and Photostabilisation of Coatings.* American Chemical Society Symposium Series, no. 151, 183–196

FENN, J. (1984) Some practical aspects in the choice of synthetic resins for the repair of ethnographical skin and gut. In Brommelle *et al.* (eds) (1984), pp. 138–140

FERRAGNI, D., FORTI, M., MALLIET, J., MORA, P., TEUTONICO, J. M. and TORRACA, G. (1984) Injection grouting of mural paintings and mosaics. In Brommelle *et al.* (eds) (1984), pp. 110–116

FERRANZZINNI, J. C. (1976) Advantages and techniques of applying cyano-acrylate monomer adhesives to protect paint on stained glass (in German). *Glastech. Ber.,* **49,** 264 (abstract in Corpus Vitrearum Newsletter 24 ref 255)

FERRY, J. D. (1982) *Viscoelastic Properties of Polymers,* 3rd edn. Wiley

FETTES, E. M. (ed.) (1964) *Chemical Reactions of Polymers.* Interscience

FIEUX, R. E. (1984) Silicone polymers for relining of paintings. In Brommelle *et al.* (eds) (1984), pp. 46–49

FILATOV, V. V. (1975) Principal stages of the restoration of monumental painting in archaeological monuments of the RSFSR. In ICOM (1975) 75/12/11

FINCH, C. A. (ed.) (1973) *Polyvinyl Alcohol.* Wiley

FINK, C. G. (1933) Care and treatment of outdoor bronze statues. *Technical Studies in the Field of Fine Arts,* **2,** 34

FIORENTINO, P. and VLAD BORRELLI, L. (1975) A preliminary note on the use of adhesives and fillers in the restoration of ancient materials with special reference to glass. *Studies in Conservation,* **20,** 201–205

FLIEDER, F. (1981) Étude experimentale sur les fixatifs des traces pulverulents. In ICOM (1981) 81/14/8

FRANKLIN-EWING, J. S. I. (1950) A new technique for removing bones from limestone brecia. *Antiquity,* **24,** 102–105

FRANTIŠ, P. (1957) Restoration of murals. *Zprävy Pamätkové Péce,* **17,** 105–107

FREDANI, P., MANGANELLI, DEL FÁ, MATTEOLI, U. and TIANO, P. (1982) Use of perfluoropolyethers as water repellants: study of their behaviour on pietra serena, a Florentine building stone. *Studies in Conservation,* **27,** 31–37

FREEMAN, N. T. and WHITEHEAD, I. (1982) *Introduction to Safety in the Chemical Laboratory.* Academic Press

FRERE, S. (1958) Lifting mosaics. *Antiquity,* **32,** 116–119

GABBAY, S. M. and STIVALA, S. S. (1976) Kinetics of the thermal oxidation of poly(4-methyl-1-pentene). *Polymer,* **17,** 137–141

GAIROLA, T. R. (1958–1960) Preservation of parchment. *Journal of Indian Museums,* **14–16,** 43–45

GAIROLA, T. R. (1958–1960) A note on the preservation of paintings by Rabinbranath Tagore. *Journal of Indian Museums,* **14–16,** 40–42

GAMBLE, D. L. and STUTZ, G. F. A. (1929) Ultraviolet transmission characteristics of some synthetic resins. *Industrial and Engineering Chemistry,* **21,** 330–333

GANIARIS, H., KEENE, S. and STARLING, K. (1982) A comparison of some treatments for excavated leather. *The Conservator,* **6,** 12–23

GARDNER, W. H. and WHITMORE, W. F. (1929) Nature and constitution of shellac I. *Industrial and Engineering Chemistry,* **21,** 226–229

GARDON, J. L. and TEAS, J. P. (1976) Solubility parameters. In Myers, R. R. and Long, J. S. (eds) *Treatise on Coatings,* Vol. 2, part 2, pp. 414–471. Dekker

GARNETT, J. L. and MAJOR, G. (1982) The technique of radiation polymerisation in fine art conservation – a potentially new method of restoration and preservation. *Journal of Radiation Curing,* **9,** no. 1, 4–10

GAYNES, N. I. (1967) *Formulation of Organic Coatings.* Van Nostrand

GEDYE, I. (1968) Pottery and glass. In UNESCO (1968), pp. 109–114

GEIJER, A. (1961) Dangerous materials for the conservation of textiles. *Bulletin de liason du Centre Internationale d'études des Textiles Anciens,* **13**

GEIJER, A. and FRANZÉN, A. M. (1975) Textile conservation in Sweden: problems and practice. In Leigh *et al.* (eds) (1975), pp. 7–13

GERASSIMOVA, N. G. and MEL'NIKOVA, E. P. (1978) The effect of the treatment with polybutyl methacrylate solutions on physical and mechanical properties of loess plaster. In ICOM (1978) 78/15/13

GETTENS, R. J. (1935) Polymerised vinyl acetate and related compounds in the restoration of object of art. *Technical Studies in the Field of Fine Arts,* **4,** 15–27

GETTENS, R. J. and STOUT, G. L. (1965) *Painting Materials.* Dover

GEUSKINS, G., BORSU, M. and DAVID, C. (1972) Photolysis and radiolysis of polyvinyl acetate – III. *European Polymer Journal,* **8,** 1347–1352

GEYER, A. and FRANZÉN, A. M. (1956) Textiles found in excavations at the cathedral of Trondheim, Norway. *Nordenfjellske Kunstindustrimuseums Arbok,* 1–42

GLICKSMAN, M. and SANDS, R. E. (1973) Gum Arabic. In Whistler and BeMiller (eds) (1973), pp. 197–264

GRASSIE, N. (1982) Structural information from degradation studies. *Pure and Applied Chemistry,* **54,** 337–349

GRASSIE, N. and SCOTT, G. (1985) *Polymer Degradation and Stabilisation.* Cambridge University Press

GRASSIE, N. and WEIR, N. A. (1965) Photooxidation of polymers IV. *Journal of Applied Polymer Science,* **9,** 999–1003

GRATTAN, D. W. (1982) A practical comparative study of several treatments for waterlogged wood. *Studies in Conservation,* **27,** 124–136

GRATTAN, D. W. (ed.) (1982) *Proceedings of the ICOM Waterlogged Wood Conference, Ottawa September 1981*. ICOM Committee for Conservation, Waterlogged Wood Working Group

GRAY, A. A. (1969) An accelerated ageing study comparing kinetic rates vs Tappi Standard 453. *TAPPI,* **52,** no. 2, 325–334

GREMINGER, G. K. and KRUMEL, K. L. (1980) Alkyl and hydroxyalkyl cellulose. In Davidson (ed.) (1980), chapter 3

GRIEBENOW, W. *et al.* (1982) Wasserlöscliche Polyvinylalkohol – Folie die Konservierung brüchiger und tintenfrassgeschädigter Papiere. *Maltechnik,* 280–282

GRISSOM, C. A. and WEISS, N. R. (1981) Alkoxysilanes in the conservation of art and architecture 1861–1981. *Art and Archaeology Technical Abstracts,* **18,** no. 1, 149–202

GYERMEK, S. A. (1964) Conservation of ethnographical materials. *Museum News,* **43,** 49–56

HAAS, A. (1969) Weitere Fortschritte bei der Konservierung von Feuchthölzern mit Arigal C. *Arbeitsblätter* Heft 2 Gruppe 2 Seite 16–20

HACKFORTH-JONES, L. (1981) Conservation and restoration of 'A Roman Triumph', a drawing by Rubens. *The Conservator,* **5,** 23–26

HAINES, B. M. (1984) The conservation of leather bookbindings. In Brommelle *et al.* (eds) (1984), pp. 50–54

HALMAGYI, E. (1958) A statue saved from ruin. *Bulletin Mus. Nat. Hongrois des Beaux Arts,* **12,** 40–44

HAMM, P. and HAMM, J. (1981) The removal and conservation treatment of a scenic wallpaper. *Journal of the American Institute for Conservation,* **20,** 116–125

HANSEN, C. M. (1967) Three dimensional solubility parameters – key to paint component affinities. *Journal of Paint Technology,* **39,** 104–117

HANSEN, C. M. and BEERBOWER, A. (1971) Solvent parameters. In *Kirk-Othmers Encyclopedia of Chemical Technology,* supplementary volume, pp. 889–910. Interscience

HARRIS, F. W. and SEYMOUR, R. B. (eds) (1977) *Structure–Solubility Relationships in Polymers.* Academic Press

HARRIS, J. E. and WENTE, E. F. (1980) *An X-Ray Atlas of the Royal Mummies.* University of Chicago Press

HATTON, M. (1977) Enzymes in a viscous medium. *Paper Conservator,* **2,** 9–10

HAWKINS, W. L. and WINSLOW, F. H. (1964) Oxidative reactions. In Fettes (ed.) (1964), pp. 1055–1084

HAYWARD, C. H. (1960) *Staining and Polishing.* Evans, London

HAYWARD, C. H. (1976) *Antique Furniture Repairs.* Evans, London

HEATON, N. (1921) The preservation of stone. *Journal of the Royal Society of Arts,* **70,** 123–139

HEDLEY, G. (1980) Solubility parameters and varnish removal: a survey. *The Conservator,* **4,** 12–18

HEDVAL, J. A., JAGITSCH, R. and OLSON, G. (1951) *The Problem of Restoring Antique Glass Part II. Covering the Glass Surface with Protective Film.* Official Technical Service Reports PB 105977. US Department of Commerce

HEIJBOER, J. (1965) Mechanical properties and molecular structure of organic polymers. In Prins, J. A. (ed.) *Physics of Non-Crystalline Solids,* pp. 231–254. North-Holland, Amsterdam

HELLWIG, F. (1981) Reversibilität – ein restaurotorisches Ideal. In Ankner, D. and Wihr, R. (eds) *Der Restaurator – Heute, Arbeitsgemeinschaft des technischen Museumspersonals,* 25–27

HEMPEL, K. (1976) An improved method for the vacuum impregnation of stone. *Studies in Conservation,* **21,** 40–43

HENDY, P. H. (1947) *An Exhibition of Cleaned Pictures.* National Gallery, London

HEY, M. (1970) The use of the scanning electron microscope in document restoration problems. *Restaurator,* **1,** 233–244

HEY, M., ALTHÖFER, H. and ORGAN, R. (1960) The limitations of polyethylene glycols: some advice and warnings. *Studies in Conservation,* **5,** 159–162

HIBBEN, J. H. (1937) Preservation of biological specimens by means of transparent plastics. *Science,* **86,** 247–248

HIGUCHI, S. (1980) Treatment of painting of sliding screens and wall panels to prevent exfoliation in Japan. In Organising Committee (1980) *Conservation of Far Eastern Art Objects,* pp. 69–77. National Research Institute of Cultural Properties, Tokyo

HILDITCH, T. P. and WILLIAMS, P. N. (1964) *The Chemical Composition of Natural Fats,* 4th edn. Chapman & Hall, London

HILL, A. (1948) Manufacture and use of AW-2 Resin. *Modern Plastics,* **25,** 119–120

HOERNSCHEMEYER, D. (1974) The influence of solvent type on the viscosity of concentrated polymer solutions. *Journal of Applied Polymer Science,* **18,** 61–75

HOFENK-DE GRAAFF, J. (1981) Hydroxylpropyl cellulose, a multipurpose conservation material. In ICOM (1981) 81/14/9

HOFFMANN, E. and SARACZ, A. (1972) Weathering of paint films V: Chalking in emulsion paint films caused by silicone-coated anatase titanium dioxide and zinc oxide. *Journal of the Oil and Colour Chemists Association,* **55,** 1079–1085

HOFFMANN, P. (1983) A rapid method for the detection of polyethylene glycol in wood. *Studies in Conservation,* **28,** 189–193

HOFFMANN, P. (1984) On the stabilization of waterlogged oak with PEG: Molecular size versus degree of degradation. In Ramiére, R. and Colardelle, M. (eds) *Waterlogged Wood, Proceedings of the 2nd ICOM Waterlogged Wood Working Group, Grenoble 1984,* pp. 95–115. Centre d'Etude et de Traitemente des Boise Gorgés d'Eau, Grenoble

HONIG, M. (1974) Two further applications of polyurethane foam in the process of transfer. *Bulletin of the American Institute for Conservation,* **14,** no. 2, 53–64

HORIE, C. V. (1983a) Reversibility of polymer treatments. In Tate *et al.* (eds) (1983), chapter 3

HORIE, C. V. (1983b) Sealing of museum jars. *Conservation News,* no. 20, 13–14

HORSLEY, L. H. (1973) *Azeotropic data III. Advances in Chemistry Series,* no. 116. American Chemical Society

HOUSE OF COMMONS (1852–3) *Parliamentary Papers 135 754.* In Chadwick Healey Microfiche 57–227, pp. 802–803

HOWELLS, R., BURNSTOCK, A., HEDLEY, G. and HACKNEY, S. (1984) Polymer dispersions artificially aged. In Brommelle *et al.* (eds) (1984), pp. 36–43

HOWIE, F. M. P. (1984) Materials used for conserving fossil specimens since 1930: a review. In Brommelle *et al.* (eds) (1984), pp. 92–97

HSE (1984) *Occupational exposure limits 1984.* Health & Safety Executive (UK) Guidance Note EH10

HUBBARD, J. R. (1977) Animal glues. In Skeist (ed.) (1977), pp. 139–151

HÜBNER, P. H. (1934) La décomposition des Objects en Ambre et leur reconstitution moleculaire. *Mouseion,* **XXVII–XXVIII,** 248–253

HULMER, E. C. (1976) Notes on the formulation and application of acrylic coatings. In Brommelle and Smith (eds) (1976), pp. 145–147

HUMMEL, D. O. and SCHOLL, F. (1978, 1981, 1982) *Atlas of Polymer and Plastics Analysis.* Carl Hanser Verlag/Verlag Chemie 2nd and 3rd (1984) edns

HUMPHREY, B. J. (1984) The application of Parylene conformal coating technology to archival and artifact conservation. *Studies in Conservation,* **29,** 117–123

HUNTER, R. S. (1975) *The Measurement of Appearance,* 3rd edn. Wiley

HUSSON, L. and WIHR, R. (1954) An important improvement in the reproduction and reconstruction of antique glasses. *Triere Zeitschrift,* **23,** 213–238

ICOM (1975) *4th Triennial Meeting, Venice, October 1975, Preprints.* ICOM Committee for Conservation

ICOM (1978) *5th Triennial Meeting, Zagreb, October 1978, Preprints.* ICOM Committee for Conservation

ICOM (1981) *6th Triennial Meeting, Ottawa, September 1981, Preprints.* ICOM Committee for Conservation

ICOM (1984) *7th Triennial Meeting, Copenhagen, September 1984, Preprints.* ICOM Committee for Conservation

IGARASHI, T., KONDO, S. and KUROKAWA, M. (1979) Contractive stress of epoxy resin during isothermal curing. *Polymer,* **20,** 301–304

IRICK, G. (1972) Determination of the photocatalytic activities of titanium dioxide and other white pigments. *Journal of Applied Polymer Science,* **16,** 2387–2395

ISO (1982) *Catalogue 1982.* International Organization for Standardization (Geneva)

ISO 105-1978 Textiles–Tests for colour fastness. (In ISO, 1982)

ISO/R 527-1966 Plastics – Determination of tensile properties. (In ISO, 1982)

ISO/R 1043-1975 Abbreviations (symbols) for plastics. (In ISO, 1982)

ISO 1516-1981 Paints, varnishes, petroleum and related products – flash/no flash test, closed cup equilibrium method. (In ISO, 1982)

ISO/R 1628-1970 Plastics – directives for the standardization of methods for the determination of the dilute solution viscosity of polymers. (In ISO, 1982)

ISO 2409-1972 Paints and varnishes. Cross-cut test. (In ISO, 1982)

ISO 2813-1978 Paints and varnishes – measurement of specular gloss of non-metallic paint film at 20 degrees, 60 degrees and 85 degrees. (In ISO, 1982)

IUPAC (1974) List of standard abbreviations (symbols) for synthetic polymers and polymer materials. *Pure and Applied Chemistry,* **30,** 475–476

IUPAC (1976) Nomenclature of regular single-strand organic polymers. *Pure and Applied Chemistry,* **48,** 373–385

IUPAC (1979a) Manual of symbols and terminology for physicochemical quantities and units. *Pure and Applied Chemistry,* **51,** 1–41

IUPAC (1979b) *Nomenclature of Organic Chemistry.* Pergamon Press

IWASAKI, T. (1974) Preservation treatment on paint layers of screen- and wall-paintings. *Science for Conservation,* **12,** 55–58

JACKSON, F. K. and GHOSE, R. L. M. (1932) Protection of herbarium specimens. *Nature,* **129,** 402

JACKSON, L. C. (1979) Contamination detection, characterization and removal based on solubility parameters. In Mittal, K. L. (ed.) *Surface Contamination: Genesis, Detection and Control,* pp. 527–540. Plenum

JACKSON, P. R. (1983) Resins used in glass conservation. In Tate *et al.* (eds) (1983), chapter 10

JACOBS, H. and STEELE, R. (1960) Ultra-violet irradiation of poly(ethyl acrylate) in vacuum, I and II. *Journal of Applied Polymer Science,* **3,** 239–244, 245–250

JAROWENKO, W. (1977) Starch based adhesives. In Skeist (ed.) (1977), pp. 192–211

JELLINEK, H. H. G. and FLAJSMAN, F. (1969) Reaction of nitrogen dioxide with polystyrene. *Journal of Polymer Science,* **A1, 7,** 1153–1168

JENKINSON, H. (1924) Some notes on the preservation, moulding and casting of seals. *Antiquaries Journal,* **4,** 388–403

JESPERSEN, K. (1982) Some problems of using tetraethoxysilane (tetraethyl orthosilicate: TEOS) for conservation of waterlogged wood. In Grattan (ed.) (1982), pp. 203–207

JOHNSON, M. (1976) Nitrocellulose as a conservation hazard. *American Institute for Conservation Preprints,* 68–75

JOHNSON, R. (1984) Removal of microcrystalline wax from archaeological ironwork. In Brommelle *et al.* (eds) (1984), pp. 107–109

JOYE, N. M. and LAWRENCE, R. V. (1967) Resin acid composition of pine oleoresins. *Journal of Chemical and Engineering Data,* **12,** 279–282

JUDD, D. B. and WYSZECKI, G. (1975) *Color in Business, Science and Industry,* 3rd edn. Wiley

KAMAL, M. R. and SAXON, R. (1967) Analysis and predictability of weathering. In Kamal, M. R. (ed.) *Weatherability of Plastics.* Journal of Applied Polymer Science Applied Polymer Symposium no. 4, 1–28

KATHPALIA, Y. P. (1966) Solvent lamination and India-7. *Indian Pulp and Paper,* **21,** no. 4, 1–3

KATZ, H. S. and MILEWSKI, J. V. (eds) (1978) *Handbook of Fillers and Reinforcements for Plastics.* Van Nostrand Reinhold

KECK, S. and FELLER, R. L. (1964) Detection of an epoxy resin coating on a seventeenth century painting. *Studies in Conservation,* **9,** 1–8

KEENE, S. (1984) The performance of coatings and consolidants used for archaeological iron. In Brommelle *et al.* (eds) (1984), pp. 104–106

KETNATH, A. (1978) The treatment of a fire-damaged picture painted on masonite board. *Studies in Conservation,* **23,** 168–173

KIMBERLY, A. E. and SCRIBNER, B. W. (1934) *Summary Report of Bureau of Standards Research on Preservation of Records.* US Bureau of Standards Misc. Publ. 144

KING, A. G. (1976) Conservation of the Collage 'Roses' by Juan Gris. In Brommelle and Smith (eds) (1976), pp. 234–238

KINMONTH, R. A. and NORTON, J. E. (1977) Effect of spectral energy distribution on degradation of organic coatings. *Journal of Coatings Technology,* **49,** no. 633, 37–44

KISHORE, R. (1952) Preservation of pencil writing. *Indian Archives,* **6,** 34–38

KOLLER, M., HAMMER, I., PASCHINGER, H. and RANACHER, M. (1980) The Abbey Church at Melk: examination and conservation. In Brommelle *et al.* (eds) (1980), pp. 101–112

KOOB, S. P. (1979) The removal of aged shellac adhesive from ceramics. *Studies in Conservation,* **24,** 134–135

KOOB, S. P. (1982) The instability of cellulose nitrate adhesives. *The Conservator,* **6,** 30–34

KOOB, S. P. (1984) The consolidation of archaeological bone. In Brommelle *et al.* (eds) (1984), pp. 98–102

KOSTROV, P. (1956) The restoration of two Fayum portraits. *Soobshchenija Gosudartviennogo Ermitagea,* 58–61

KOTLIK, P., IGNAS, J. and ZELINGER, J. (1980) Some ways of polymerizing methyl methacrylate in sandstone. *Studies in Conservation,* **25,** 1–13

KOTTULINSKY, L. (1982) Bericht über Restaurierung eines römischen Deckenfreskos in Ennes/Österreich. *Maltechnik,* 91–97

KOZIMINA, O. P. (1968) On the mechanism of the thermo oxidative degradation of cellulose ethers. *Journal of Polymer Science,* **C16,** 4225–4240

KOZLOV, P. V. and BURDYGINA, G. I. (1983) The structure and properties of solid gelatin and principles of their modification. *Polymer,* **24,** 651–666

KRAFT, W. M., JANUSZ, E. G. and SUGHRUE, D. J. (1967) Alkyd resins. In Myers and Long (eds) (1967), pp. 71–98

KRAUSE, S. (1978) Polymer–polymer compatibility. In Paul, D. R. and Newman, S. (eds) *Polymer Blends,* Vol. 1, pp. 16–113. Academic Press

KUHN, H. (1981) *Erhaltung und Pflege von Kunstwerken und Antiquitaten 2.* Keysersche Verlagsbuch-handlung, Munich

LAFONTAINE, R. H. (1979a) Decreasing the yellowing rate of dammar varnish using antioxidants. *Studies in Conservation,* **24,** 14–22

LAFONTAINE, R. H. (1979b) Effect of Iragnox 565 on the removability of dammar films. *Studies in Conservation,* **24,** 179–181

LAFONTAINE, R. H. (1981) Uses of stabilizers in varnish formulations. In ICOM (1981) 81/16/5

LAFONTAINE, R. H. and WOOD, P. A. (1982) The stabilization of ivory against relative humidity fluctuations. *Studies in Conservation,* **27,** 109–117

LANDI, S. (1981) Practice of dry cleaning in the UK. In ICOM (1981) 81/9/2

LANE, H. (1974) The restoration of thin metal vessels using glass-fibre and polyester resin. *Studies in Conservation,* **19,** 227–232

LANK, H. (1976) Picture varnishes formulated with resin MS2A. In Brommelle and Smith (eds) (1976), pp. 148–149

LARNEY, J. (1975) Restoration of ceramics. In Leigh *et al.* (eds) (1975), pp. 39–43

LARSON, J. (1978) The conservation of marble monuments in churches. *The Conservator,* **2,** 20–25

LARSON, J. (1979) The conservation of alabaster monuments in churches. *The Conservator,* **3,** 28–33

LARSON, J. (1980a) The conservation of stone sculpture in historic buildings. In Brommelle *et al.* (eds) (1980), pp. 132–138

LARSON, J. (1980b) The conservation of terracotta sculpture. *The Conservator,* **4,** 38–45

LAVIN, E. and SNELGROVE, J. A. (1977) Polyvinyl acetal adhesives. In Skeist (ed.) (1977), pp. 507–527

LEE, H. and NEVILLE, K. (1967) *Handbook of Epoxy Resins.* McGraw-Hill

LEECHMAN, D. (1931) Technical methods in the preservation of anthropological museum specimens. *Annual Report of the National Museums of Canada 1929,* Bull. 67, 127–158

LEENE, J. E. (1963) Restoration and preservation of ancient textiles, and natural science. In Thomson (ed.) (1963), pp. 181–190

LEENE, J. E. (1972) Textiles. In Leene (ed.) (1972), pp. 4–22

LEENE, J. E. (ed.) (1972) *Textile Conservation.* Butterworths

LEIGH, D., MONCRIEFF, A., ODDY, W. A. and PRATT, P. (eds) (1975). *Conservation in Archaeology and the Applied Arts.* International Institute for Conservation

LEONARD, F., KULKARNI, R. K., BRANDES, G., NELSON, J. and CAMERON, J. J. (1966) Synthesis and degradation of poly(alkyl-cyanoacrylate)s. *Journal of Applied Polymer Science,* **10,** 259–272

LEWIN, S. Z. and PAPADIMITRIOU, A. D. (1981) Investigation of polymer impregnation of stone. II. Solvent transport of prepolymerised methyl methacrylate. In Rossi-Manaresi (ed.) (1981), pp. 605–623

LEWIS, H. L. (1946) Substitutes for gum tragacanth. *Entomological Monthly Magazine,* 202

LINDENFORS, S. and JULLANDER, I. (1973) Ethylhydroxyethylcellulose. In Whistler and BeMiller (eds) (1973), pp. 673–684

LODEWIJKS, J. and LEENE, J. E. (1972) Restoration and conservation. In Leene (ed.) (1972), pp. 137–152

LOWE, E. E. (1910) Preservation of fossil ivory. *Museums Journal,* **10,** 155–156

LUCAS, A. (1932) *Antiques, Their Restoration and Preservation,* 2nd edn. Arnold, London

LUCAS, A. and BROMMELLE, N. (1953) Failure of synthetic materials in picture conservation. *Museum Journal,* **53,** 149–155

LUSKIN, L. S. (1970) Acrylic acid, methacrylic acid and the related esters. In Leonard, E. C. (ed.) *Vinyl and Diene Monomers,* part I, pp. 105–204. Wiley Interscience

MAGNELLI, F. (1982) Careless use of adhesive tape. *Museum,* **34,** 61–62

MAJEWSKI, L. (1973) On conservation. *Museum News,* **51,** no. 8, 10–11

MANDIK, L. (1977) Applications of gel permeation chromatography in the paint industry. *Progress in Organic Coatings,* **5,** 131–198

MANTELL, C. I., KOPF, C. W., CURTIS, J. L. and ROGERS, E. M. (1942) *The Technology of Natural Resins.* Wiley

MARIJNISSEN, R. H. (1967) *Dégradation, conservation et restauration de l'oeuvre d'art.* Arcade

MARK, H. F., GAYLORD, N. G. and BIKALES, N. M. (1964 ff.) *Encyclopedia of Polymer Science and Technology.* Interscience (19 volumes)

MARSDEN, O. (1963) *Solvents Guide.* Cleaver Hulme

MARTIN, F. R. (1977) Acrylic adhesives. In Wake, W. A. C. (ed.) *Developments in adhesives-1,* 157–180. Applied Science

MARTIN, M. B. (1978) The removal of linseed oil and rejuvenation of finishes on wooden objects. In Brommelle *et al.* (eds) (1978), pp. 59–61

MASSCHELEIN-KLEINER, L. (1978) *Liant, vernis et adhésifs anciens.* Institute Royal du Patrimonie Artistique, Brusselles

MASSCHELEIN-KLEINER, L. and BERGIERS, F. (1984) Influence of adhesives on the conservation of textiles. In Brommelle *et al.* (eds) (1984), pp. 70–73

MAVROV, G. (1983) Aging of silicone resins. *Studies in Conservation,* **28,** 171–178

MAXIM, L. D., KUIST, C. H. and MEYER, M. E. (1968) UV degradation of terpolymer scissioning systems. *Macromolecules,* **1,** 86–93

McGARY, C. W. (1960) Degradation of polyethylene oxide. *Journal of Polymer Science,* **46,** 51–57

McMULLEN, O. (1978) Paper repair in older printed books. *Paper Conservator,* **3,** 18–27

MEALS, R. (1969) Silicon compounds (silicones). In *Kirk-Othmer Encyclopedia of Chemical Technology,* 2nd edn, Vol. 18, pp. 221–260. Interscience

MEER, W. (1980a) Gum agar. In Davidson (ed.) (1980), chapter 7

MEER, W. (1980b) Gum arabic. In Davidson (ed.) (1980), chapter 8

MEHRA, V. R. (1984) Dispersion as lining adhesive and its scope. In Brommelle *et al.* (eds) (1984), pp. 44–45

MELLAN, I. (1970) *Industrial Solvents Guide.* Noyes Data Corp.

MEURGUES, G. (1982) Synthetic resins can be dangerous. *Museum,* **34,** 60–61

MIBACK, E. T. G. (1975) Restoration of coarse archaeological ceramics. In Leigh *et al.* (eds) (1975), pp. 55–61

MILES, F. D. (1955) *Cellulose Nitrate.* Oliver & Boyd

MILLS, J. S. (1956) The constitution of the neutral, tetracyclic triterpenes of dammar resin. *Journal of the Chemical Society,* 2196–2202

MILLS, J. S. and WHITE, R. (1976) The gas chromatographic examination of paint media. Some examples of medium identification in paintings by fatty acid analysis. In Brommelle and Smith (eds) (1976), pp. 72–77

MILLS, J. S. and WHITE, R. (1987) *The Organic Chemistry of Museum Objects.* Butterworths

MINOGUE, A. (1956) The use of transparent plastics for the protection of manuscripts. *Manuscripts (New York),* **8,** 207–209

MISRA, G. S. and SENGUPTAL, S. C. (1970) Shellac. In Mark *et al.* (eds) Vol. 12, pp. 419–440

MITANOV, P. and KABAIVANOV, V. (1975) Obtention de polymères acryliques. ICOM (1975) 75/18/7

MODI, T. W. (1980) Polyvinyl alcohol. In Davidson (ed.) (1980), chapter 20

MOLYNEUX, P. (1983) *Water-soluble Synthetic Polymers,* Vol. 1. CRC Press

MONCRIEFF, A. (1968) Review of recent literature on wood. *Studies in Conservation,* **13,** 186–212

MONCRIEFF, A. (1975) Problems and potentialities in the conservation of vitreous materials. In Leigh *et al.* (eds) (1975), pp. 99–104

MONCRIEFF, A. (1976) The treatment of deteriorating stone with silicone resins: interim report. *Studies in Conservation,* **21,** 179–191

MONCRIEFF, A. and HEMPEL, K. F. B. (1977) Conservation of sculptural stonework: Virgin and Child on S. Maria dei Miracoli and the logetta of the Campanile, Venice. *Studies in Conservation,* **22,** 1–11

MORA, P., MORA, L. and PHILIPOTT, P. (1984) *The Conservation of Wall Paintings.* Butterworths

MORIMOTO, K. and SUZUKI, S. (1972) Ultra-violet irradiation of poly(alkyl acrylates) and poly(alkyl methacrylates). *Journal of Applied Polymer Science,* **16,** 2947–2961

MORITA, T. (1984) 'Nikawa' – traditional production of animal glue in Japan. In Brommelle *et al.* (eds) (1984), pp. 121–122

MOZES, G. Y. (ed.) (1982) *Paraffin Products.* Elsevier

MUNNIKENDAM, R. A. (1967a) Conservation of waterlogged wood using radiation polymerisation. *Studies in Conservation,* **12,** 70–75

MUNNIKENDAM, R. A. (1967b) Preliminary notes on the conservation of porous building materials by impregnation with monomers. *Studies in Conservation,* **12,** 158–162

MUNNIKENDAM, R. A. (1971) Acrylic monomer systems for stone impregnation. In Thomson (ed.) (1971a), pp. 15–18

MUNNIKENDAM, R. A. (1973) A new system for the consolidation of fragile stone. *Studies in Conservation,* **18,** 95–97

MUNNIKENDAM, R. (1978) Consolidation of fragile wood with low viscosity aliphatic epoxy resin. In Brommelle *et al.* (eds) (1978), pp. 71–73

MURRAY, B. D., HAUSER, M. and ELLIOTT, J. R. (1977) Anaerobic adhesives. In Skeist (ed.) (1977), pp. 560–568

MURRAY, R. M. and STOREY, P. R. (1964) Ozonisation. In Fettes (ed.) (1964), pp. 565–703

MYERS, C. S. (1954) Solubility characteristics of polyethylene resin. *Journal of Polymer Science,* **13,** 549–564

MYERS, R. R. and LONG, J. S. (eds) (1967) *Film Forming Compositions,* Vol. 1, part 1. Dekker

NATCHINKINA, J. and CHEININA, E. (1981) Conservation d'objets de l'Egypte ancienne en bois polychrome au musée de l'Ermitage d'Etat. In ICOM (1981) 81/5/1

NATIONAL RESEARCH COUNCIL (1983) *Prudent Practices For Disposal of Chemicals from Laboratories.* National Academy Press, Washington

NELSON, G. M. and WICKS, Z. M. (1983) Polymers of *n*-butyl methacrylate with covalently bound UV stabilizer. In Tate *et al.* (eds) (1983), chapter 4

NEWELL, L. C. (1933) Chemistry in the science of Egyptology. *Journal of Chemical Education,* **10,** 259–266

NEWMAN, D. J., NUNN, C. J. and OLIVER, J. K. (1975) Release of individual solvents and binary solvent blends from thermoplastic coatings. *Journal of Paint Technology,* **47,** no. 609, 70–88

NICHOLS, H. W. and ORR, P. C. (1932) Bakelite impregnation of fossil bones. *Museums Journal,* **32,** 47–53

NIELSEN, L. E. (1974) *Mechanical Properties of Polymers and Composites.* Dekker

NIKITINA, K. F. (1981) Conservation of archaeological leather in the State Hermitage Museum. In ICOM (1981) 81/19/2

NIMMO, B. A. F. and PRESCOTT, A. G. (1968) Moulding, casting and electrotyping. In UNESCO (1968), pp. 95–108

NISBETH, A. (1980) Deterioration and restoration of some Swedish mural paintings. In Brommelle *et al.* (eds) (1980), pp. 126–129

NISHIURA, T. (1981a) Study on the conservation of rooftiles [II]. Practical study on the consolidation of the old rooftiles of historic buildings. *Science in Conservation,* **20,** 67–75

NISHIURA, T. (1981b) Conservation of old rooftiles for reuse. In Rossi-Manaresi (ed.) (1981b), pp. 699–709

NOBLE, G. K. and JAECKLE, M. E. (1926) Mounting by paraffin infiltration. *American Museums Novitiates,* no. 233

NORLAND, R. E. (1977) Fish glue. In Skeist (ed.) (1977), pp. 152–157

NOTMAN, J. H. and TENNENT, N. H. (1980) The conservation and restoration of a seventeenth century stained glass roundel. *Studies in Conservation,* **25,** 165–175

NYUKSHA, JU. P., BLANK, M. G. and SALTYKOV-SHCHEDRIN, M. E. (1975) Restoration of paper with paper pulp containing polyvinyl alcohol fibres. In ICOM (1975) 75/15/13

O'CONNOR, S. A. (1979) The conservation of the Giggleswick Tarn boat. *The Conservator,* **3,** 36–38

ODDY, W. A. (1975a) The corrosion of metals on display. In Leigh *et al.* (eds) (1975), pp. 235–237

ODDY, W. A. (1975b) Comparison of different methods of treating waterlogged wood as revealed by stereoscan examination and thoughts on the future of the conservation of waterlogged boats. In Oddy (ed.) (1975), pp. 45–49

ODDY, W. A. (ed.) (1975) *Problems in the Conservation of Waterlogged Wood.* National Maritime Museum, Greenwich

OECD (1982) *Chemicals Control Legislation.* Organisation for Economic Cooperation and Development, Paris, 59 82 02 1

OLSON, G. and THORDEMAN, B. (1951) The cleaning of silver objects. *Museums Journal,* **50,** 250–252

ORGAN, R. M. (1959a) The treatment of the St Ninian's hanging bowl complex. *Studies in Conservation,* **4,** 41–50

ORGAN, R. M. (1959b) Carbowax and other materials in the treatment of waterlogged paleolithic wood. *Studies in Conservation,* **4,** 96–105

ORGAN, R. M. (1963) The consolidation of fragile metallic objects. In Thomson (ed.) (1963), pp. 128–134

ORGAN, R. M. and SHORER, P. (1962) An improved method of consolidating fragile iron objects. *Museums Journal,* **62,** 109–113

OSAWA, Z. (1982) Photodegradation and stabilization of polyurethanes. In Allen, N. S. (ed.) *Developments in Polymer Photochemistry 3,* pp. 209–236. Applied Science

OUANO, A. C., TU, Y. O. and CAROTHERS, J. A. (1977) Dynamics of polymer dissolution. In Harris, F. W. and Seymour, R. B. (eds) (1977), pp. 11–20

PACKARD, E. (1971) Consolidation of decayed wood sculpture. In Thomson (ed.) (1971b), pp. 13–17

PAIST, W. D. (1977) Cellulosics. In Skeist (ed.) (1977), pp. 212–221

PALEOS, C. M., MAVROYANNAKIS, E. E. and CYPRIOTAKI, I. (1981) Preservation of aged paper by alkoxysilanes. In ICOM (1981) 81/16/6

PARKER, H. E. (1967) Chlorinated rubber. In Myers and Long (ed.) (1967), pp. 129–210

PASCOE, M. W. (1985) Parylene coatings, some considerations on the reversibility of vapour formed coatings. *Studies in Conservation,* **30,** 100

PATTERSON, C. (1978) An approach to the conservation of ethnographical musical instruments. *The Conservator,* **2,** 45–48

PAUZAUREK, G. E. (1904) *Kranke Gläser.* Reichenberg

PECHOVÁ, O. and LOSOS, L. (1957) Funeral flags of Peter Vok of Rosenberg and their conservation. *Zprävy Pamätkové Pecé,* **17,** 79–87

PETRIE, W. M. F. (1888) The treatment of small antiquities. *Archaeological Journal,* **45,** 85–89

PETRIE, W. M. F. (1904) *Methods and Aims in Archaeology.* Macmillan

PETROVA, L. G. (1953) *Collection of Materials on the Preservation of Library Resources no.2. Restoration and Preservation of Library Resources, Documents and Books.* Israel Program for Scientific Translations (1964)

PHILIPOTT, P. and MORA, P. (1968) The conservation of wall paintings. In UNESCO (1968), pp. 169–190

PHILLIPS, G. O. (1980) The effects of radiation on carbohydrates. In Pigman, W. and Horton, D. (eds) *The Carbohydrates,* 2nd edn., Vol. IIB, pp. 1101–1166. Academic Press

PIPTONE, D. A. (1984) *Safe Storage of Laboratory Chemicals.* Wiley

PLENDERLEITH, H. J. (1934) *The Preservation of Antiquities.* Museum Association

PLENDERLEITH, H. J. (1955) The restoration of the Mithras Head. *Museums Journal,* **55,** 15–16

PLENDERLEITH, H. J. (1956) *The Conservation of Antiquities and Works of Art.* Oxford University Press

PLENDERLEITH, H. J. and WERNER, A. E. A. (1958) Technical notes on the conservation of documents. *Journal Society of Archivists,* **1,** 195–201

PLENDERLEITH, H. J. and WERNER, A. E. A. (1971) *The Conservation of Antiquities and Works of Art,* 2nd edn. Oxford University Press

PLOSSI, M. Z. and SANTUCCI, L. (1969) Resistance and stability of paper, VIII. An investigation on sizing. *Bull. Dell'Istituto di Patologia del Libro,* **28,** 97–117

POSSE, O. (1899) *Handschriften-Konservirung,* Dresden, reprinted in *Restaurator* Suppl. no.1 (1969)

POTTER, W. G. (1970) *Epoxide Resins.* Illiffe

POWELL, G. M. (1980) Polyethylene glycol. In Davidson (ed.) (1980), chapter 18

PRICE, C. A. (1981) *Brethane Stone Preservative.* Building Research Establishment (UK) CP1/81

PRICE, J. G. (1975) Some field experiments in the removal of larger fragile archaeological remains. In Leigh *et al.* (eds) (1975), pp. 153–164

PUCKETT, W. O. (1940) Ethyl methacrylate as mounting medium for embryological specimens. *Science,* **91,** 625–626

PURVES, P. E. and MARTIN, R. S. J. (1950) Some developments in the use of plastics in museum technology. *Museums Journal,* **49,** 293–296

RABEK, J. F. (1975) Oxidative degradation of polymers. In Bamford and Tipper (eds) (1975), pp. 425–538

RADLEY, J. A. (ed.) (1976) *Industrial Uses of Starch.* Applied Science.

RAFF, R. A. V., ZIEGLER, R. D. and ADAMS, M. F . (1967) Archives document preservation. *Northwest Science,* **41,** 184–195

RAFT, K. (1985) A preliminary report on the possibility of using bleached beeswax to improve the resolubility of picture varnishes based on polycyclohexanones. *Studies in Conservation,* **30,** 143–144

RANACHER, M. (1980) Painted lenten veils and wall coverings in Austria: technique and conservation. In Brommelle *et al.* (eds) (1980), pp. 142–148

RANBY, B. and RABEK, J. F. (1975) *Photodegradation, Photooxidation and Photostabilization of Polymers.* Wiley

RASTI, F. and SCOTT, G. (1980) The effects of some common pigments on the photo-oxidation of linseed oil-based paint media. *Studies in Conservation,* **25,** 145–156

RATHGEN, F. (1905) *The Preservation of Antiquities.* (Translated Auden, G. A. and H. A.). Cambridge University Press

RATHGEN, F. (1926) *Die Konservierung von Altertmsfunden, I Teil, Stein und steinartige Stoffe.* W. de Gruyter, Berlin

RAWLINS, F. I. G. and WERNER, A. E. A. (1949) The scientific department of the National Gallery. *Nature,* **164,** 601–603

RAZDAN, B. C. (1969) Performance of thin paste prepared with 'Sarcel MV' (sodium salt of carboxymethyl cellulose) for repair with tissue paper. *Conservation of Cultural Property in India. Proceedings of 4th Seminar,* **4,** 36

REYNOLDS, W. W. (1967) Hydrocarbon solvents. In Myers and Long (eds.) (1967)

RICE, J. W. (1972) Principles of fragile textile cleaning. In Leene (ed.) (1972), pp. 32–72

RIXON, A. E. (1949) The use of acetic and formic acid in the preservation of fossil vertebrates. *Museums Journal,* **49,** 116–117

RIXON, A. E. (1955) The use of new materials as temporary supports in the development and examination of fossils. *Museums Journal,* **55,** 54–58

RIXON, A. E. (1976) *Fossil Animal Remains: Their Preparation and Conservation.* Athlone Press

RIXON, A. E. and MEADE, M. J. (1956) Casting technique. *Museums Journal,* **56,** 9–13

ROFF, W. J. and SCOTT, J. R. (1971) *Fibres, Films, Plastics and Rubbers.* Butterworths

ROSENQVIST, A. M. (1959) The stabilisation of wood found in the Viking ship of Oseberg – part II. *Studies in Conservation,* **4,** 62–72

ROSSI-MANARESI, R. (1976) Treatments for sandstone consolidation. In Rossi-Manaresi (ed.) (1976), pp. 547–571

ROSSI-MANARESI, R. (ed.) (1976) *The Conservation of Stone I. Proceedings of the International Symposium, Bologna, June 19–21, 1975.* Centro per la Conservazione della Sculture All'Aperto, Bologna

ROSSI-MANARESI, R. (1981) Effectiveness of conservation treatments for the sandstone of monuments in Bologna. In Rossi-Manaresi (ed.) (1981), pp. 665–688

ROSSI-MANARESI, R. (ed.) (1981) *The Conservation of Stone.* Centro per la Conservazione della Sculture All'Aperto, Bologna

ROSSI-MANARESI, R. and TORRACA, G. (eds) (1971) *Treatment of Stone.* Centro per la Conservazione della Sculture All'Aperto, Bologna

RUHEMANN, H. (1968) *The Cleaning of Paintings.* Faber & Faber

RUTENBERG, M. W. (1980) Starch and its modifications. In Davidson (ed.) (1980), chapter 19

SALVA, M. (1977) Epoxy resin adhesives. In Skeist (ed.) (1977), pp. 434–445

SALZBERG, H. K. (1977) Casein glues and adhesives. In Skeist (ed.) (1977), pp. 158–171

SALZER, T. (1887) Zur Conservierung von Eisen-Alterthümern. *Chemiker Zeitung,* **11,** 574

SANDS, R. E. and GLICKSMAN, M. (1973) Seaweed extracts of potential economic importance. In Whistler and BeMiller (eds) (1973), pp. 147–195

SANTUCCI, L. and PLOSSI, M. (1969) Resistance and stability of paper. Part 8. An investigation on sizing. *Bol. Istit. Pat. Libro,* **28,** 97–117

SATO, K. (1984) Physical significance of the pendulum hardness of coating films. *Journal of Coatings Technology,* **56,** no. 708, 47–57

SAUCOIS, C. (1981) La restauration des papiers calques aux archives nationales. In ICOM (1981) 81/14/16

SAVKO, M. (1971) The mural paintings in the church of St Huidrechts-Hern. Treatment and tentative identification. *Bulletin Institut Royale du Patrimonie Artistique,* **13,** 91–130

SAWADA, M. (1981a) A new technique for the removal of stratigraphical sections in archaeology. In ICOM (1981) 81/21/4

SAWADA, M. (1981b) Zur Konservierung eines bemalten japanischen Lackgefäkses. *Arbeitsblätter,* **1,** Gruppe **11,** Seite 31–34

SAX, N. I. (1984) *Dangerous Properties of Industrial Materials,* 6th edn. Van Nostrand Reinhold

SCHAFFER, E. (1978) Water soluble plastics in the preservation of artifacts made of cellulose materials. In ICOM (1978) 78/3/7

SCHMIDT, A. (1939) New transparent mounting medium. *Museums Journal,* **39,** 295–296, *Natur und volk,* Feb.

SCHOLLENBERGER, H. *et al.* (1969) Naturlatex und Poly-Urathan-Schäume als Absfomungsmaterialien. *Arbeitsblätter,* 1, Gruppe **18,** Seite 1–8

SCHURR, G. G. (1972) Flexibility. In Sward (ed.) (1972), pp. 333–338

SCOTT, A. (1923) *The Cleaning and Restoration of Museum Exhibits. 2nd Report.* HMSO, London

SCOTT, A. (1933) Deterioration and restoration, with especial reference to metallic exhibits. *Museums Journal,* **33,** 4–8

SEASE, C. (1981) The case against using soluble nylon in conservation work. *Studies in Conservation,* **26,** 102–110

SERCK-DEWAIDE, M. (1978) Disinfestation and consolidation of polychrome wood at the Institute Royal du Patrimonie Artistique, Brussels. In Brommelle *et al.* (eds) (1978), pp. 81–83

SHELL CHEMICALS LTD (1969) *Relative evaporation rates of solvents employing the Shell Liquid Film Evaporometer.* Technical Bulletin ICS/69/1

SHELL CHEMICALS LTD (1977a) *Evaporation of organic solvents from surface coatings.* Technical Bulletin ICS/77/4, 2nd edn

SHELL CHEMICALS LTD (1977b) *Predicting the flashpoint of solvent mixtures.* Technical Bulletin ICS/77/5

SHIELDS, J. (1984) *Adhesive Handbook,* 3rd edn. Newnes-Butterworths

SHORER, P. H. T. (1964) Soil section transfers: a method for the transfer of an archaeological soil section on to a flexible rubber backing. *Studies in Conservation,* **9,** 74–77

SHORER, P. H. T. (1969) The use of foamed polyurethane resins as mounts for antiquities in museum exhibition. *Studies in Conservation,* **14,** 174–176

SIEDERS, R., UYTEN BOGAART, J. W. H. and LEENE, J. E. (1956) The restoration and preservation of old fabrics. *Studies in Conservation,* **3,** 161–169

SMITH, A. W. and LAMB, M. H. (1981) Prevention of soil redeposition in the cleaning of historic textiles. In ICOM (1981) 81/9/4

SNETHLAGE, R. and KLEMM, P. D. (1978) Scanning electron microscope investigation on impregnated sandstones. *Preprint for the International Symposium: Deterioration and Protection of Stone Monuments (Paris) (1978),* Vol. 2, 5.7

SOLECHNIK, N. YA. (ed.) (1964) *New methods for the restoration and preservation of documents and books.* In *Restoration and Preservation of Library Resources, Documents and Books.* Israel Program for Scientific Translations

SPON, E. (1888) *Workshop Receipts.* Spon, London

SPURLOCK, D. (1978) The application of balsa wood blocks as a stabilizing auxiliary for panel paintings. In Brommelle *et al.* (eds) (1978), pp. 149–152

STANDAGE, H. C. (1931) *Cement Pastes, Glues and Gums.* Crosby Lockwood, London

STEEN, C. R. (1971) Some recent experiments in stabilizing adobe and stone. In Thomson (ed.) (1971a), pp. 59–63

STELZER, G. I. and KLUG, E. D. (1980) Carboxymethylcellulose. In Davidson (ed.) (1980), chapter 4

STEVENS, D. (1985) PEG instability? *Conservation News,* **27,** 16–17

STEVENS, W. C. and JOHNSON, D. D. (1950) *Tests to investigate the efficiency of various coatings and coverings applied to the backs of painted panels with a view to reducing distortions following changes in atmospheric conditions.* Forest Product Research Laboratory, London

STOIS, A. (1937) Steinschutz gegen Bautenverwitterung. *Technische Mitteilungen für Malerei,* **53,** 22–23

STOLOW, N. (1971) Solvent action. In Feller *et al.* (eds) (1971), pp. 45–116

STOUT, G. L. (1969) A Roman mosaic pavement rebuilt. *Studies in Conservation,* **14,** 165–169

STOUT, G. L. and CROSS, H. F. (1937) Properties of surface films. *Technical Studies in the Field of Fine Arts,* **5,** 241–249

STOUT, G. L. and GETTENS, R. J. (1932) Transport des fresques orientales sur de nouveaux supports. *Mouseion,* **17–18,** 107–112

STRAUB, R. E. (1962) Retouching with synthetic resin paint. *Museums Journal,* **62,** 113–119

STRONG, D. and CLARIDGE, A. (1976) Marble sculpture. In Strong, D. and Brown, D. (eds) *Roman Crafts.* Duckworth

SWARD, G. G. (ed.) (1972) *Paint Testing Manual.* American Society for Testing and Materials

SZWARC, M. S. (1976) Poly-para-xylylene. *Polymer Engineering and Science,* **16,** 473–479

TAKAKAGE, S. (1951) Application of synthetic resins to the preservation of antiques and art crafts. *Scientific Papers on Japanese Antiquities,* no. 1, 25–6

TAKAKAGE, H. S. and TOMOKICHI, I. (1952) Scientific treatments made on the Main Hall of the Horuyuji monastery after the fire of 1949. *Bijutsu Kenkyu,* no. 147, 99–107

TATE, J. O., TENNENT, N. H. and TOWNSEND, J. H. (eds) (1983) *Resins in Conservation.* Scottish Society for Conservation and Research

TENNENT, N. H. (1979) Clear and pigmented epoxy resins for stained glass conservation: light ageing studies. *Studies in Conservation,* **24,** 153–164

TENNENT, N. H. (1983) The selection of suitable ceramic retouching media. In Tate *et al.* (eds) (1983), chapter 9

TENNENT, N. H. and TOWNSEND, J. H. (1984a) The significance of the refractive index of adhesives for glass repair. In Brommelle *et al.* (eds) (1984), pp. 205–212

TENNENT, N. H. and TOWNSEND, J. H. (1984b) Factors affecting the refractive index of epoxy resins. In ICOM (1984) 84/20/26–28

TENNENT, N. H., TOWNSEND, J. H. and DAVIS, A. (1982) A simple integrating dosimeter for ultra violet light. In Brommelle *et al.* (eds) (1982), pp. 32–38

THIACOURT, P. (1868) *L'art de restaurer les faïences, porcelaines, etc.,* 2nd edn. August Aubry, Paris

THOMSEN, F. G. (1981) Repair of a Tlingit basket using molded cotton fibres. In ICOM (1981) 81/3/2

THOMSON, G. (1956) Test for cross-linking of linear polymers. *Nature,* **178,** 807

THOMSON, G. (1957) Some picture varnishes. *Studies in Conservation,* **3,** 64–79

THOMSON, G. (1963) New picture varnishes. In Thomson (ed.) (1963), pp. 176–184

THOMSON, G. (ed.) (1963) *Recent Advances in Conservation.* Butterworths

THOMSON, G. (ed.) (1971a) *Conservation of Stone.* IIC

THOMSON, G. (ed.) (1971b) *Conservation of Wood.* IIC

THOMSON, G. (1978) *The Museum Environment.* Butterworths

TOOMBS, H. A. (1948) The use of acetic acid in the development of vertebrate fossils. *Museums Journal,* **48,** 54–55

TORRACA, G. (1976) Treatment of stone in monuments. A review of principles and processes. In Rossi-Manaresi (ed.) (1976), pp. 297–315

TOYOSHIMA, K. (1973a) General properties of polyvinyl alcohol in relation to its applications. In Finch (ed.) (1973), pp. 17–66

TOYOSHIMA, K. (1973b) Properties of polyvinyl alcohol films. In Finch (ed.) (1973), pp. 339–389

TREOLAR, L. R. G. (1975) *The Physics of Rubber Elasticity*. Clarendon Press, Oxford

TROST, H. B. (1963) Soil redeposition. *Journal of the American Oil Chemists Society,* **40,** 669–674

TURWEN, P. A. (1983) The mending of stained glass; a technical instruction. In Tate *et al.* (eds) (1983), chapter 11

TUTTLE, P. H. (1983) The conservation of a 4th century Greek cuirass and helmet. In Tate *et al.* (eds) (1983), chapter 12

UEBERREITER, K. (1968) The solution process. In Crank, J. and Park, G. S. (eds) *Diffusion in Polymers,* pp. 219–257. Academic Press

UMBERGER, J. G. (1967) Solution and gelation of gelatin as related to solvent structure. *Photographic Sci. Eng.,* **11,** 385–391

UNESCO (1968) *The Conservation of Cultural Property.* UNESCO Press

UNWIN, M. (1950) New plastic for taking of impressions. *Museums Journal,* **50,** 155

UNWIN, M. (1951) A new method for the impregnation of wet objects in the field. *Museums Journal,* **50,** 237

VAN BAREN, J. H. V. and BOMER, W. (1979) *Procedures for the Collection and Preservation of Soil Profiles.* International Soil Reference and Information Centre

VAN KREVELEN, D. W. (1972, 1976) *Properties of Polymers,* 1st and 2nd edn. Elsevier

VAN SCHENDEL, A. (1958) Simon Eikelenberg's experiments on the preparation of varnishes. *Studies in Conservation,* **3,** 125–131

VAN STEENE, G. and MASSCHELEIN-KLEINER, L. (1980) Modified starch for conservation purposes. *Studies in Conservation,* **25,** 64–70

VASSALIO, J. C. and LEWIN, S. Z. (1981) Investigation of polymer impregnation of stone. I. *In situ* polymerisation of methyl methacrylate. In Rossi-Manaresi (ed.) (1981), pp. 587–603

VON KOCH, G. (1914) Experiments with Zellon in zoological and palaeontological preparations. *Museums Journal,* **14,** 259–263, *Museumkunde,* **9,** 216–219

VON REVENTLOW, V. (1978a) Use of B72 in the restoration of a marquetry surface – case history. In Brommelle *et al.* (eds) (1978), pp. 37–39

VON REVENTLOW, V. (1978b) Restoration and assembly of the Central Shrine of a late fifteenth century German altar from Cologne. In Brommelle *et al.* (eds) (1978), pp. 99–109

VOS-DAVIDSE, L. (1969) Note of the reversible glueing of broken glass objects. *Studies in Conservation,* **14,** 183

WAKE, W. C. (1978) Theories of adhesion and uses of adhesives: a review. *Polymer,* **19,** 291–308

WAKE, W. C. (1982) *Adhesion and the Formulation of Adhesives,* 2nd edn. Applied Science

WANG, P. (1977) Die Restaurierung geschnitzter Lackarbeiter. *Arbeitsblätter* Heft **1,** Gruppe **11,** Seite 14–16

WARD, A. G. and COURTS, A. (1977) *The Science and Technology of Gelatin,* 2nd edn. Academic Press

WARNES, A. R. (1926) *Building Stones.* Benn, London

WATERER, J. W. (1973) *A Guide to the Conservation and Restoration of Objects Made Wholly or Partly of Leather,* 2nd edn. Bell, London

WATERS, P. H. (1983) A review of the moulding and casting materials and techniques in use at the Palaeontology Laboratory, British Museum (Natural History). *The Conservator,* **7,** 37–43

WATKINSON, D. (1982) Making a large scale replica: the Pillar of Eliseg. *The Conservator,* **6,** 6–11

WEIDNER, M. K. (1967) Damage and deterioration of art on paper due to ignorance and the use of faulty materials. *Studies in Conservation,* **12,** 5–25

WELSH, E. C. (1980) A consolidation treatment for powdery matte paint. *American Institute for Conservation Preprints,* 141–150

WERNER, A. E. A. (1952) Plastics aid in conservation of old paintings. *British Plastics,* **25,** 363–366

WERNER, A. E. A. (1957) Synthetic waxes. *Museums Journal,* **57,** 3–5

WERNER, A. E. A. (1958) Technical notes on a new material for conservation. *Chronique d'Egypt,* **33,** 273–278

WERNER, A. E. A. (1962) Scientific methods in the conservation of antiquities. *Research Applied in Industry,* **15,** 353–359

WERNER, A. E. A. (1968a) The scientific conservation of antiquities. *Endeavour,* **27,** no. 100, 23–27

WERNER, A. E. A. (1968b) The conservation of leather, wood, bone and ivory and archival materials. In UNESCO (1968), pp. 265–290

WERNER, A. E. A. (1978) Consolidation of deteriorated wooden artifacts. *Conservation of Wood,* pp. 17–21. Organising Committee, Tokyo National Museum Research Institute of Cultural Properties

WESTERN, A. C. (1972) The conservation of excavated iron objects. *Studies in Conservation,* **17,** 83–87

WEXLER, H. (1964) Polymerisation of drying oils. *Chemical Review,* **64,** 591–611

WHEATLEY, M. D. (1941) Preservation of biological specimens with isobutyl methacrylate polymer. *Science,* **94,** 49–50

WHISTLER, R. L. and BeMILLER, J. N. (eds) (1973) *Industrial Gums.* Academic Press

WHITE, I. (1979) A drying and smoothing technique for three dimensional textiles. *The Conservator,* **3,** 14–15

WHITE, L. (1980) Chelsea C30. *Conservation News,* **12,** 10

WIHR, R. (1968) Possibilities of restoration and reproduction of ancient glass by the use of pourable synthetic resins. *Bulletin International Institute for Conservation – American Group,* **11,** 17–25, *Arbeitsblätter* Heft **2,** Gruppe 5, Seite 1–12

WIHR, R. (1976) Deep-impregnation for effective stone-protection. In Rossi-Manaresi (ed.) (1976), pp. 317–318

WIHR, R. (1977) *Restaurioren von Keramic und Glass.* Callwey

WIHR, R. (1979) The preservation of damaged stones by the so-called acrylic-total-impregnation-process. In *Deterioration and Preservation of Stones,* Proceedings of the 3rd International Congress, Venice

WILLIAMS, A. (1972) *Paint and Varnish Removers.* Noyes Data Corporation

WILLIAMS, N. (1983) *Porcelain, Repair and Restoration.* British Museum Publications

WILLISTON, S. S. (1982) Preliminary findings on the reactions of coatings and adhesives with metals. *Abstracts of Poster Sessions IIC Congress, Washington, September.* International Institute for Conservation

WILLS, P. (1984) The manufacture and use of Japanese wheat adhesives in the treatment of far eastern pictorial art. In Brommelle *et al.* (eds) (1984), pp. 123–126

WILSON, W. K. and FORSHEE, B. W. (1959) *Preservation of documents by lamination.* US Bureau of Standards, Monograph 5.

WINDING, G. C. and HIATT, G. D. (1961) *Polymeric Materials.* McGraw-Hill

WINTER, J. (1984) Natural adhesives in east Asian paintings. In Brommelle *et al.* (eds) (1984), pp. 117–120

WOODBURY, G. (1936) Note on the use of polymerised vinyl acetate and related compounds in the preservation and hardening of bone. *American Journal of Physical Anthropology,* **21,** 449–450

WRIGHT, J. A. and HANLAN, J. F. (1978) Poly(vinyl pyrrolidone) as an aid in removal of stains from textile and ceramic materials. *Journal of the International Institute for Conservation – Canadian Group,* **4,** no. 1, 32–36

YABROVA, R. R. (1953) The prevention of aging of books and newspapers. In Petrova (ed.) (1953), pp. 3–17

YUSUPOVA, M. V. (1979) Conservation and softening of leather in book bindings. *Restaurator,* **3,** 91–100

ZAPPALA, A. and LaMENDOLA, P. (1978) A method of preparing and using an acrylic resin coated paper. In ICOM (1978) 78/14/18

ZISMAN, W. A. (1977) Influences of constitution on adhesion. In Skeist (ed.) (1977), pp. 33–71

Subject index

The main source of information on each topic is given in **bold**. Manufacturers' names are given in *italics* and are listed in Appendix 5.

Author index